T0341902

SPiN

Teacher's Guide 2

with Resource CD-ROM

NATIONAL GEOGRAPHIC LEARNING | CENGAGE Learning

Australia • Brazil • Japan • Korea • Mexico • Singapore • Spain • United Kingdom • United States

Spin 2 Teacher's Guide with Resource CD-ROM

Publisher: Gavin McLean

Director of Content Development: Sarah Bideleux

Managing Editor: Angela Cussons

Art Director: Natasa Arsenidou

Cover Designer: Natasa Arsenidou

Text Designer / Compositor: InPraxis

National Geographic Liaison: Leila Hishmeh

Acknowledgements

Editorial and project management by hyphen

Recording and production at GFS-PRO Studio
by George Flamouridis

CD-ROM programmed at CONTEXT Publishing
Services by Paul Stafford: email: **info@context.gr**
web: **context.gr**

© 2013 National Geographic Learning, a part of Cengage Learning®

ALL RIGHTS RESERVED. No part of this work covered by the copyright
herein may be reproduced, transmitted, stored or used in any form
or by any means graphic, electronic, or mechanical, including but not
limited to photocopying, recording, scanning, digitialising, taping, Web
distribution, information networks, or information storage and retrieval
systems, except as permitted under Section 107 or 108 of the 1976
United States Copyright Act, or applicable copyright law of another
jurisdiction, without the prior written permission of the publisher.

For permission to use material from this text or product, submit all
requests online at **cengage.com/permissions**

Further permissions questions can be emailed to
permissionrequest@cengage.com.

ISBN: 978-1-4080-6111-4

National Geographic Learning
Cheriton House, North Way, Andover, Hampshire,
SP10 5BE United Kingdom

Cengage Learning is a leading provider of customised learning
solutions with office locations around the globe, including Singapore,
the United Kingdom, Australia, Mexico, Brazil and Japan.

Cengage Learning products are represented in Canada by
Nelson Education Ltd.

Visit National Geographic Learning online at **ngl.cengage.com**
Visit our corporate website at **www.cengage.com**

Photo credits

Cover image: Brian Skerry/National Geographic Image Collection. A school of juvenile marine catfish masses over the sandy bottom of Suruga Bay off Japan's Izu Peninsula.

All other images: Shutterstock

Printed in the United Kingdom by Ashford Colour Press Ltd.
Print Number: 05   Print Year: 2020

Contents

Contents of Student's Book	4
Introduction to Spin	6
Introduction	8
Unit 1	11
Unit 2	20
Review 1	28
Unit 3	31
Unit 4	39
Review 2	47
Unit 5	49
Unit 6	57
Review 3	65
Unit 7	67
Unit 8	75
Review 4	83
Unit 9	85
Unit 10	93
Review 5	101
Unit 11	103
Unit 12	111
Review 6	119
Notes on National Geographic DVD Worksheets	121
Recording Script	126
Key to Spin 2 Workbook	133

Contents

Unit	Reading	Vocabulary	Grammar	
Introduction p 4-7			Subject and object pronouns Be Possessive 's Question words	Prepositions of Place *There is/There Are* Possessive Adjectives *Have Got*
1 Relationships p 8-15	Families Bird Planet My Family	Family-related words Prepositions	Present Simple; Adverbs of Frequency Present Continuous Present Simple and Continuous; Stative verbs	
2 Homes p 16-23	The King's Palace The Golden City My Home	Furniture and appliances Parts of a house	Past Simple (regular verbs) Past Simple (irregular verbs)	
Review 1 p 24-25	Vocabulary & Grammar tasks / Project			
3 Free Time p 26-33	Let's go ice-skating! Snowshoeing Free Time	Phrasal verbs Adjectives with *-ed* and *-ing*	Past Continuous Past Simple and Past Continuous *Used to*	
4 Food and Drink p 34-41	Exotic Chicken I love chocolate! Daphne's World	Food and drink-related words Words used for preparing food	*Much, Many* *A lot of, Lots of, A few, A little* *Some, Any, Every, No; Some-, Any-, Every-* and *No-* with *-body, -thing* and *-where*	
Review 2 p 42-43	Vocabulary & Grammar tasks / Project			
5 Education p 44-51	A Night at the Museum A School for Champions Who's new at school?	Education-related words	Present Perfect Simple (aff); *For, Since, Already, Just, Never* Present Perfect Simple (neg, question); *Ever* and *Yet* Present Perfect and How long ...?	
6 The Body p 52-59	The African Tribe Body Painting How can I help you?	Body-related words Illnesses	Present Perfect and Past Simple Possessive Pronouns	
Review 3 p 60-61	Vocabulary & Grammar tasks / Project			
7 Nature p 62-69	We're in Australia! Frilled Lizards The Pet Rescue Centre	Nature-related words	*Be going to*; Future Simple Gerunds Question Tags	
8 The Environment p 70-77	Can I recycle your T-shirt? Solar Power Going Green in Greece!	Environment-related words Recycling-related words	First Conditional Second Conditional	
Review 4 p 78-79	Vocabulary & Grammar tasks / Project			
9 In Town p 80-87	I feel dizzy! A day in Tokyo City Guide	Directions Town-related words	*Have to; Must* *Can* and *Could* *Might; Should*	
10 New Technology p 88-95	The Video Game Tester Computer World My Favourite Video Game	Technology-related words	Present Simple Passive Past Simple Passive	
Review 5 p 96-97	Vocabulary & Grammar tasks / Project			
11 Transport p 98-105	I like travelling by globe! Travelling in Luxury Travel Guide	Means of transport Transport-related words	Comparatives and Superlatives *Both, Either* and *Neither* *Too* and *Enough*	
12 Jobs p 106-113	The Rescue The Conservationist Career Plans	Jobs Employment-related words	Adverbs of Manner Relative Clauses	
Review 6 p 114-115	Vocabulary & Grammar tasks / Project			

National Geographic DVD Worksheets   p 116-121
Speaking Skills   p 122-123
Writing Skills   p 124-125
Words to Learn   p 126-131
Irregular verbs   p 132-133

Listening	Speaking	Pronunciation	Functional Language	Writing
Introduction of characters				
Two-option lozenge True or false	Talk about how often you do things	Similar-sounding words	Emphasising	Time expressions and Adverbs of Frequency Description of a family
Number pictures Complete notes Change words in bold	Talk about when things happened Talk about a picture	ow sounds	Talking about homes	Connectors (and, but, because and so) Advert
True or false Label a picture	Talk about what you were doing in the past	Magic e	Talking about free time	Writing stories with the Past Simple and the Past Continuous Story
Complete a dialogue Number pictures Complete a table	Role-play shopping for food Talk about food	e, ee, ea and ey sounds	What's for dinner?	Letter and email language Email
Label a picture Two-option lozenge	Talk about things you've done at school this week	Aspirates	Talking about school	Paragraphs and topic sentences Email
True or false Tick correct pictures Complete a dialogue	Describe people in photos Find differences between pictures	s sounds	At the doctor's	Order of paragraphs Email
Change words in bold Complete sentences	Talk about going to the zoo	ough sounds	Talking about pets	Punctuation Postcard
Complete sentences Multiple choice Number pictures	Talk about recycling Talk about a picture	Stressing different parts of sentences	Talking about the environment	Giving advice with conditional sentences Poster
Label a picture Two-option lozenge	Give directions	Different pronunciation of the same letter combinations	Asking for and giving directions	Order of adjectives Description of a city or town
True or false Number sentences Number video games	Talk about a game Interview your partner about video games	Similar-sounding words	Expressing preferences	Spelling mistakes Review
Two-option lozenge True or false	Compare means of transport	th sounds	Talking about transport	Headings Report
Number pictures True of false Two-option lozenge	Talk about a job Talk about pictures of workers	t and d sounds	Talking about jobs	Making notes Article

Introduction to Spin

Welcome to *Spin*, an exciting new three-level course which takes students on an adventure in English language learning as they discover the sights and sounds of National Geographic. *Spin* has been designed to take students from beginner to pre-intermediate level.

Course Components

Spin 2 Student's Book

The student's book is divided into an Introduction, twelve topic-based units, each containing a unit opener and three two-page lessons, and six reviews. The Introduction revises basic vocabulary and grammar from *Spin 1* and reintroduces the main characters, Kristie, Mikey and Adam, who appear in the cartoon story in the units. Each lesson of the twelve units begins with a reading text that approaches the topic of the unit from a slightly different angle. In Lesson 1 students listen to and read an episode of the cartoon story involving Kristie, Mikey and Adam's adventures with the magic globe. Lesson 2 teaches students about the world we live in through a non-fiction reading passage inspired by National Geographic, and Lesson 3 links the theme of the unit to students' reality through a variety of text types such as emails, dialogues, articles and so on.

Each unit of *Spin 2 Student's Book* also contains:

- topic-related vocabulary tasks that practise and build on vocabulary in the reading texts.
- clear and concise grammar presentations followed by one or two tasks that practise form and usage.
- topic-related listening and speaking tasks that allow students to practise vocabulary and grammar presented in the lesson.
- a *Sounds of English* section that provides pronunciation practice.
- an *Express yourself!* section that focuses on functional English to aid communication.
- a strong writing sub-skill syllabus that enables students to write well from the start.

Spin 2 Student's Book contains six reviews, one after every two units, which consolidate vocabulary and grammar taught within those units and end with a theme-related project.

There is also a wealth of material at the back of the student's book: six DVD worksheets to accompany the National Geographic video clips included on *Spin 2 Interactive Whiteboard (IWB); Speaking Skills* and *Writing Skills* which provide an easy point of reference for students when communicating in English; *Words to Learn* lists with key vocabulary from each lesson and an irregular verbs list.

Spin 2 Workbook

The workbook accompanies *Spin 2 Student's Book*. Like the student's book, it is also divided into an Introduction, twelve units and six reviews. Lessons 1 and 2 of each unit consolidate vocabulary and grammar from the relevant lesson of the student's book. Lesson 3 also includes consolidation of the *Express yourself!* functional language and the writing sub skill found in the student's book lesson. In the reviews there is a non-fiction reading text inspired by National Geographic followed by vocabulary and grammar multiple-choice tasks. At the back of the workbook, there are six crosswords for further practice of key vocabulary.

Students will be motivated by the full-colour pages, lively illustrations and captivating National Geographic photographs. The workbook's clear and simple format means that it can be used at home as well as in class.

Spin 2 Grammar

The grammar progression in *Spin 2 Grammar* follows that in the student's book. Each lesson begins with a photograph and caption providing a light-hearted example of the grammar presented in that lesson. This is followed by grammar theory and example sentences. *Remember!* boxes appear often and serve to remind students of things they should be aware of. The lesson then continues with a selection of graded tasks before finishing with a speaking task, which allows students to practise the grammar they have learnt in realistic situations.

There is a review after every two units of *Spin 2 Grammar*. Each review contains a variety of tasks designed to consolidate the grammar covered in the preceding two units. The review ends with a non-fiction Writing Project featuring National Geographic photography. Students then have the opportunity to do their own Writing Project. At the back of the grammar book, there is an irregular verbs list and a word list of key vocabulary used in the grammar book.

Spin 2 Grammar Answer Key and Test Booklet contains the answer key to all tasks in *Spin 2 Grammar* as well as six photocopiable tests, one for use after each review, and the answer key to the tests.

Spin 2 Teacher's Guide with Resource CD-ROM

Spin 2 Teacher's Guide provides objective boxes, clear lesson plans with detailed instructions and the answer key to all tasks from *Spin 2 Student's Book*. The recording script with justification for the answers to listening tasks underlined and the answer key to *Spin 2 Workbook* are also included.

A wealth of photocopiable material can be found on *Spin 2 Resource CD-ROM* that accompanies *Spin 2 Teacher's Guide*. There are extra tasks for early finishers, extra writing tasks, cartoon DVD worksheets for use with the animated episodes of the Lesson 1 cartoon story found on *Spin 2 IWB* as well as lyrics for six optional songs also found on *Spin 2 IWB*. *Spin 2 Resource CD-ROM* also includes photocopiable tests for use with the student's book. There are 12 unit tests, 6 progress tests, a mid-year test and an end-of-year test as well as the answer key to all tests. Finally there is a photocopiable Student Progress Chart where students' marks in the tests and comments about their progress can be recorded.

Spin 2 Class Audio CDs

Spin 2 Class Audio CDs contain the recordings of the cartoon story, the narration of the reading texts in Lesson 2s and Lesson 3s, all listening tasks and all *Sounds of English* pronunciation sections. Six optional songs, lyrics for which can be found in the *Resource CD-ROM* that accompanies *Spin 2 Teacher's Guide*, are also included. Professional actors are used in all recordings to ensure clarity and accurate intonation and pronunciation.

Spin 2 Posters

There are two posters that are designed to be used as board games in class. Students can play in pairs or in two teams. They move around the board answering questions about things they have learnt or using functional language from the student's book. The first student or team to finish is the winner. The first poster is for use after Units 1–6 and the second poster is for use after Units 7–12. Interactive versions of both posters are included on *Spin 2 IWB*.

Spin 2 Interactive Whiteboard Software with Content Creation Tool

Spin 2 IWB contains the student's book and the workbook. The majority of tasks are interactive and all audio material, National Geographic DVDs as well as the animated episodes of the cartoon story found in Lesson 1 of the student's book units are included. The answer key to all tasks is available at the touch of a button. *Spin 2 IWB* has been developed to be easy to use by both students and teachers alike.

In addition to the student's book and the workbook, *Spin 2 IWB* also contains the following extra material to use in class:

- interactive versions of the *Spin 2 Posters* that can be played in class.
- interactive extra activities: a vocabulary task; a grammar task and a quiz for every two units of the student's book.
- six optional songs, theme-related to the units of the student's book.

Spin 2 IWB also provides a content creation tool, which allows teachers to create their own interactive tasks for use with students in class.

Spin 2 IWB is compatible with any interactive whiteboard hardware.

Spin 2 Student's e-Book

Spin 2 Student's e-Book contains an interactive version of the student's book complete with all audio, narration of the reading passages, National Geographic DVDs as well as the animated episodes of the cartoon story found in Lesson 1 of the student's book units. Students can be encouraged to re-visit tasks from the student's book and listen to the episodes and reading passages as a way of reinforcing the classroom experience. The answers are not included.

Introduction

Objectives

- Revising subject and object pronouns
- Revising the verb to be
- Revising possessive 's
- Revising question words
- Revising prepositions of place
- Revising there is / there are
- Revising possessive adjectives
- Revising the verb have got
- Meeting the characters in the cartoon story

Way in

- Greet students and welcome them to the new school year. Introduce yourself and go round the class asking each student to say his or her name and how old they are.
- Explain to students that the course book they will be using is *Spin 2*.
- Explain to students that the Introduction will revise basic English that they should already know from junior classes and from *Spin 1*, and that they will meet the main characters in the cartoon story in the book.

Did you know?

- Ask the class to look at the picture on page 4. Ask what animals are in the picture (*meerkats*). Ask students if they know anything about meerkats. Have they ever seen one at a zoo or animal park? Have they seen them on TV?
- Ask students to read the text about meerkats on page 4 and to tell you where they are from (*South America*).
- Read the information from the *Did you know?* feature to the class. Ask students if anyone can explain how the meerkats' 'sunglasses' work (*the dark skin around their eyes absorbs the sunlight, allowing them to see further in the bright sun*).
- Use the background information in the box below to give students further information about meerkats if they are interested. Check if they have any questions. If they ask for information you don't have, refer them to the website in the Background Information box and ask them to feed back to you at the next lesson.

Background Information

Meerkats are primarily insectivores, which means that they eat mostly insects, but they will also eat lizards, scorpions, snakes, plants and small mammals. When meerkats forage for food, one 'sentry' stands guard looking out for predators. The word 'meerkat' is Dutch for 'lake cat'. In captivity, meerkats can live for 12 to 14 years; in the wild they usually live for about 7 years. A group of meerkats is called a 'mob', a 'gang' or a 'clan'. There can be ➡

as many as 50 meerkats in one clan. For further information, go to www.nationalgeographic.com and search for 'meerkats'.

Extra Class Activity

Put students into pairs and ask them to think of different animals that live in large groups and to describe them to each other. Tell them to describe how big they are, what colour they are, what they eat and which part of the world they live in. Ask each pair to tell you which animals they talked about and to share their description with the class. If another pair has chosen the same animal, ask them if they have anything else to add.

Teaching Tip

Encourage students to speak in English as much as possible in the introductory lesson to revise the language they have learnt in previous years. This will help to rebuild their confidence as some months may have passed since their last English lesson, and they may not have spoken English since then.

Subject & Object Pronouns

1

- Ask students whether we put subject pronouns before a verb or after it (*before*). Ask them whether we put object pronouns before or after a verb (*after*).
- Ask students to complete the table individually, but check the answers as a class.
- Give students further example sentences using subject and object pronouns about people and objects in the classroom. For example, **She** *sits next to* **him**. **I** *am talking to* **you**, stressing the pronouns in each sentence.

Answers	
Subject Pronouns	**Object Pronouns**
I	**me**
you	**you**
he	him
she	**her**
it	it
we	**us**
you	**you**
they	them

2

- Remind students that we must always put a noun or a subject pronoun before a verb and point out that all these answers are after the verbs.
- Students can do the exercise individually, but check the answers as a class.

Answers

1	me	4	them
2	us	5	her
3	him		

Be

3

- Tell students that they are going to write the correct words on the lines. They can do the exercise in pairs. Check the answers as a class.

Answers

1	I'm	4	isn't
2	are	5	Is
3	Are the girls	6	Rome is

Possessive 's

4

- Ask students if they can remember why we sometimes use apostrophes (*in short forms to show there is a letter missing*). If they don't mention it, remind them that we also use apostrophes to show possession.
- Write *This is the teachers book.* on the board and ask students if they know where the missing apostrophe should go (*teacher's*). Invite a student to come to the board and add the apostrophe.
- Write some words on the board (eg *childrens, womens, Peters*) and ask students if they know where the apostrophe should go. Invite some of them to come to the board to add the apostrophe. Remind students to be careful with plurals.
- Tell students they have to add the apostrophe in the correct place in each sentence. Ask students to complete the exercise individually, but check the answers as a class.

Answers

1	men's	5	children's
2	John's	6	Helen's
3	boys'	7	dog's
4	women's	8	people's

Question Words

5

- Remind students that we use question words when we want more information in the answer than just *yes* or *no*. Ask students which question word we use to ask about people (*who*), things (*what*), time (*when*), places (*where*) and which word asks about who something belongs to (*whose*).
- Write *Whose pen is this?* and *Who's this girl?* on the board and remind students of the difference in meaning. Ask them which question *It's Sally's.* would answer and which one *It's Sally.* would answer. Explain that *Whose* can also go before a noun, for example, in question 2 we could also ask the question **Whose bag** *is this on the floor?*

- Tell students that they have to use the words from the wordbank to fill the gaps in the sentences. Ask students to complete the sentences individually, but check the answers as a class.

Answers

1	Who	5	When
2	Whose	6	Which
3	What	7	Why
4	Where	8	How

Let's Talk

Put students into pairs to talk about the picture at the bottom of page 5 of their books. They could take turns to ask their partner about the picture using the question words they have just revised. Tell them to use their imagination when answering!

Prepositions of Place

6

- Demonstrate the use of the prepositions *behind, between, in, in front of, near, next to, on* and *under* by pointing to objects in different positions and making sentences about them, using a different preposition for each object.
- Ask students to complete the sentences individually, but check the answers as a class.

Answers

1	between	6	near
2	next to	7	under
3	on	8	behind
4	in front of	9	next to
5	in		

Extra Class Activity

Put students into pairs and tell them to ask and answer questions about where different items are in the classroom. Tell them to choose objects in different positions so that they can use as many of the prepositions as they can from the exercise. Go round the class while they are doing the activity to check that they are forming questions and using the prepositions correctly.

There is/There are

7

- Point to objects that there are more than one of in the room and say, for example, *There are lots of desks in the classroom*. Place a book on a chair and say *There is a book on the chair*. Ask students questions about objects which are or aren't in the room, stressing the use of *any* in questions and negative answers.
- Remind students to use singular or uncountable nouns with *There is* and plural nouns with *There are*.
- Point out that there are question marks in 3 and 4 and ask students how we start questions from statements beginning with *There is* or *There are* (*Is there …? Are there …?*).

- Tell students to look at the prompts and explain that they have to rearrange them to make proper sentences. Ask students to complete the sentences individually, but check the answers as a class.

Answers
1 There aren't any children in the classroom.
2 There is a black cat in my room.
3 Are there any penguins in the zoo?
4 Is there a pencil on your desk?
5 There are lots of children at the beach.
6 There isn't a bag on the table.

Possessive Adjectives

8

- Demonstrate the use of possessive adjectives before you ask students to complete the exercise. Hold up your book and point to yourself, then say *It's **my** book.*, stressing the possessive adjective. Point to objects belonging to individual students and elicit sentences from the rest of the class, prompting the use of as many other possessive adjectives as possible.
- Explain that we put possessive adjectives before nouns to show who something belongs to.
- Students can do the task individually, but check the answers as a class.

Answers
1 Her
2 my
3 our
4 Its
5 their
6 his

Have Got

9

- Revise *have got* by going round the class asking *Have you got ...?* or *Has he / she got ...?* questions.
- Tell students they have to complete the sentences with the correct form of *have got*. Remind them about word order in questions.
- Ask students to complete the exercise individually, but check the answers as a class.

Answers
1 hasn't got
2 have got
3 Has, got
4 Have, got
5 haven't got
6 have got

Welcome back!

10

- Explain to students that, just as in *Spin 1*, the first lesson in every unit of *Spin 2* starts with an episode of the cartoon story.
- With books closed, ask students if they can remember the names of the characters from the cartoon story in *Spin 1* (*Kristie, Mikey* and *Adam)*. See what students can remember about the stories in *Spin 1*.

- Tell students to open their books at page 7 and ask them who they can see in the picture (*Kristie, Mikey* and *Adam*). Ask where the children are (*in a balloon flying over a village near some mountains and the sea)*. Ask what else is in the balloon (*the magic globe*).
- Explain that students are going to listen to and read the speech bubbles to find out what the children are saying.
- Play the recording. Ask students to follow the speech bubbles as they listen.
- Assign the roles of Kristie, Mikey and Adam to different students and ask them to read the speech bubbles out loud. Time permitting, repeat until all students have had a turn.
- As a class, ask students the questions below to check their understanding.
  1 Who is Kristie's brother? (*Mikey*)
  2 What sort of balloon are the children in? (*a hot air balloon)*
  3 What does Mikey love? (*adventures*)
  4 What does Adam want us to do? (*join the children on their travels around the world)*

Way in

- Ask students what animals they learned about in the Introduction (*meerkats*). See what they can remember about the dark marks round their eyes (*they act as sunglasses*).
- Write the subject pronouns in a list on the board and ask students to tell you the object pronoun for each one.
- Write *my book* on the board next to *I* and *me*. Then point to each of the object pronouns and ask students to say the possessive adjectives that match.
- Ask students to talk about themselves or their friend(s) using the verb *to be*.
- Ask students what words we use to start a question about people (*Who*), things (*What*), places (*Where*), time (*When*) and who something belongs to (*Whose*). Ask them what kind of word comes after the question word (*verb*).
- To check that students remember the prepositions of place, go round the class and pick up different objects and put them in different positions. Then ask students to say where they are, for example, *The bag is behind the chair*, etc.
- Ask students to write two questions, one beginning with *Is there?* and the other with *Are there?* Then tell each student in turn to ask a question and get different students to answer using *There is* or *There are*. Make sure they remember that we use singular or uncountable nouns with *There is* and plural nouns with *There are* and that we can use *any* in questions and negative forms.

Did you know?

- With books closed, put students into pairs and ask them to take turns thinking of animals or birds that are black and white (*cat, dog, zebra, penguin*, etc). Ask the pairs to report back to the class.
- Ask students to open their books at pages 8 and 9 and look at the picture. Ask if they know what the birds are (*puffins*). Explain that the reason the birds have got feet like ducks is because they live in the water a lot of the time; their feet help them to swim. Ask students what they think is the most unusual thing about puffins (they will probably refer to their colourful bills).
- Ask students to read the paragraph about puffins on page 9. Explain that puffins don't swim the whole time they are at sea; they often rest on the waves and can be seen bobbing up and down in the sea. Tell students that female puffins only lay one egg and that both parents take turns incubating it (keeping it warm until it hatches).
- Read the information from the *Did you know?* feature to the class. Ask students if they can guess how fast most small birds flap their wings (*about 250 times a minute*).

- Use the background information in the box below to give the students further information about puffins if they are interested. Check if they have any questions. If they ask for information you don't have, refer them to the website in the Background Information box and ask them to feed back to you at the next lesson.

Background Information

The picture shows a group of puffins. Note that one of them is tagged (it has metal clips around its legs), which might mean it is being observed as part of a wildlife study. The fact that puffins have got colourful bills has led to their nickname of 'sea parrot'. These colours fade in winter and are brighter in the summer. Puffins spend most of their time at sea and can dive to depths of more than 60 metres. They hunt small fish like herring. When flying, they can reach speeds of 88 kilometres an hour. They often nest on rocky cliff tops and puffin pairs usually meet up each year, often in the same place. Scientists are not sure how they navigate back to their nesting place every year but think they use reference points, sights and smells, and possibly also the stars! For further information, go to www.nationalgeographic.com and search for 'puffins'.

Let's Talk

Put students into pairs. Ask them to talk to their partner about other birds and to share information they know about them. Be available for questions and encourage students to go away and look up facts if there are things they want to find out more about.

Extra Class Activity

Ask students if they have ever seen baby birds, either on TV or in real life. Ask what they know about baby birds (*they can't fly, they are dependent on their parents for food, they usually live in a nest, sometimes they haven't got feathers, they can make a lot of noise*).

Lesson 1

Objectives

Reading	the cartoon story – circling the correct words
Vocabulary	text-related words; family-related words
Grammar	present simple; adverbs of frequency
Listening	circling the correct answers
Speaking	talking about how often people do things

The cartoon story

- Remind students that there is a cartoon story in Lesson 1 of every unit of *Spin 2* and that they are about to see or hear Episode 1.

- Ask students if they can remember the characters they met in *Spin 1* (and in the Introduction), and any information about them. Elicit the names of the main characters (*Mikey, Kristie, Adam*) and write them on the board. Ask which characters are brother and sister (*Kristie and Mikey*). Explain that the cartoon story in *Spin 2* will follow the children's new adventures.

1

- Ask students to look at the story pictures and make suggestions about what might be happening.
- Tell students they are going to listen to and read the story and say what the highlighted words mean.
- Play the audio recording of the whole episode without interruption and ask students to follow the dialogue in their books.
- Ask students to find the highlighted words and work through them as a class, one at a time. Then ask students to read out the sentence in the story containing the word. Ask students to say what the word means. If they don't know, encourage them to guess from the context.

Answers

That's right. – *That's correct.*
normal – *usual, common*
Sure. – *Of course*
favour – *an action done for someone else*
embarrassing – *causing you to feel silly or shy*
miss – *feel sad because someone isn't with you*

- Depending on whether you are using the DVD or the Audio CD, follow the relevant instructions.

For teachers using the DVD

- Make sure each student has a copy of Cartoon DVD Worksheet 1 that can be found on the *Resource CD-ROM*.

Before you watch

- Ask students to work in pairs and do the *Before you watch* task to encourage discussion.

Answers

1 Students should recognise: Mikey, Kristie and Adam. They should point and say, for example, *This is Kristie.*
2 Accept any logical answer. For example, a friend or a cousin.

- Play the whole episode without interruption before students do any more tasks on the worksheet. Ask students to watch the DVD carefully.

While you watch

- Ask students to look at the *While you watch* task so they can work out what information they need to find when they watch the episode for the second time. Play the whole episode without interruption and ask students to watch the DVD.

- Give the students a few minutes to complete the task and ask them to check their answers with a partner. If necessary, play the DVD again and ask students to fill in any missing information.

Answers
a3 b5 c2 d4 e6 f1

After you watch

- Ask students to read the story out loud. Assign the roles of the characters in the episode to different students and ask them to read the story out loud. Time permitting, repeat until all students have had a turn.
- Explain any vocabulary students don't know and correct their pronunciation where necessary.
- Ask students to answer the questions in the *After you watch* section of the worksheet individually, but check the answers as a class.

Answers

1	American	4	minutes
2	weather	5	favour
3	time	6	cat

For teachers using the Audio CD

- Ask students to look at page 10 in their student's book and to work in pairs. Ask them if there is anyone new in the story (*yes*). Ask them to guess who she might be but don't confirm any guesses yet; they will find out in the story.
- Tell students they are going to listen to and read the story. Ask them to look at the pictures and to follow the story as they listen.
- Play the recording once and ask students who Cuddles is (*Beth's cat*).
- Assign the roles of Kristie, Mikey, Adam and Beth to different students and ask them to read the story out loud. Time permitting, repeat until all students have had a turn.
- As a class, ask students the questions below to check their understanding of the episode.

1 Whose cousin is Beth? (*Kristie and Mikey's*)
2 Who does Beth live with? (*her family*)
3 Where does the globe take the children? (*anywhere it wants*)
4 Why does Beth want to go to Seattle? (*to see her cat*)
5 What does Kristie think of the cat? (*She thinks he's cute.*)

Comprehension

2

- Ask students to read sentences 1 to 5 so they know what information to look for when they read the cartoon story again. Ask them to circle the correct words in the sentences.
- Ask students to do the task individually, but check the answers as a class. Encourage students to explain their answer choices by giving evidence from the story.

Answers
1 Kristie's (*I'd like you to meet our favourite cousin, Beth.*)
2 Beth (*I live in Seattle ...*)
3 sometimes (*No, it sometimes rains.*)
4 magic (*It's magic!*)
5 Cuddles (*I wanted to see my cat, Cuddles. I really miss him!*)

Vocabulary

3

- Ask students to look at the words in the wordbank. Remind them that all the words are from the cartoon story on page 10 and point out that they already know the meaning of them. Check understanding of one or two of the words again if you think it's necessary.
- Ask students to do the task individually, but check the answers as a class. Correct their pronunciation where necessary.

Answers
1 favour
2 embarrassing
3 Sure
4 miss
5 normal

4

- Explain to students that they will learn some family words in this exercise. Elicit the words that students already know for family members and write them on the board. You can list them under the headings *men*, *women* and *both*. Check that students remember *brother*, *sister*, *mother*, *father*, *grandma* and *grandad*. Then elicit or explain the meaning of the new words in the exercise and add them to the lists on the board.
- Ask students if they can work out who Beth's parents are to Kristie and Mikey (*their aunt and uncle*).
- Ask students to do the task individually, but check the answers as a class.

Answers
1 grandchildren
2 wife
3 nephews
4 only
5 relatives
6 Aunt

Extra Class Activity

Get students to write six sentences using the words which were not the correct answers in the previous exercise.

Let's Talk

Put students into pairs and ask them to talk about their own family, using words from *Vocabulary 4*.

Teaching Tip

Before introducing new vocabulary, encourage students to remember as much vocabulary as they can related to the same topic. This helps because it is easier for students to relate new vocabulary to their existing knowledge.

Grammar

Present Simple

- Read the uses of the Present Simple in the grammar box and ask students to read the example sentences with you. Explain the grammar terms used if necessary.
- Ask students what they have to add to the verbs for *he*, *she* and *it* (*–es* or *–s*).
- Read the verb forms from the grammar box with the class. Ask them which word we put in front of the main verb in the negative (*don't / doesn't*). Then ask how we form questions (with *Do / Does* + subject + infinitive).
- Ask students a few questions using the Present Simple to elicit short answers (*Do you like basketball?*, *Do you play tennis?*, etc).
- Tell students that we often use time expressions with the Present Simple. Read the time expressions with them and explain any words they don't know.

5

- Ask students to read the sentences and to look at the verbs in the wordbank. Once they have done that, tell them to decide which verb fits the meaning of each sentence.
- Tell students to decide whether each sentence is affirmative, negative or a question, and remind them to add *–es* or *–s* for the third person singular affirmative.
- Ask students to do the task individually, but check the answers as a class.

Answers
1 travels
2 don't go
3 meet
4 gets up
5 doesn't teach

Extra Class Activity

Ask students to write three sentences like the ones in *Grammar 5*. Tell them to include one question, one affirmative and one negative sentence. Tell them to erase the verbs and to swap their books with a partner to complete them.

Adverbs of Frequency

- Read out the grammar box to the class and ask students to read the example sentences with you. Explain the grammar terms used if necessary.

6

- Tell students to look at each sentence and to decide which word is the subject and then to find the verb and the adverb.
- Tell students to decide whether the adverb comes before or after the verb, and tell them to make questions if a question mark is given.
- Tell students to look at the prompts and explain that they have to rearrange them to make proper sentences. Ask students to do the task individually, but check the answers as a class.

Answers
1 Are you usually late for school?
2 It sometimes rains in winter.
3 My sister never wears jeans.
4 I am always nice to my parents.
5 How often does Kristie visit her cousins?

Teaching Tip
Some students can remember grammar rules so well that they are able to form verb tenses without even knowing what the verbs mean. As a result, they appear to be learning well when they perform well in grammar tests, but this doesn't help them learn to use the language. It is essential to check that students understand the meaning of what they have written so that they will learn to apply the grammar rules to express themselves.

Listening

7

- Ask students to read through the sentences and the possible options.
- Explain to students that they are going to listen to Sally talking about four things she does, and that there is one question for each of the things.
- Play the recording and ask students to circle the correct answers.
- Give students a few minutes to compare their answers with a partner. Ask them to justify their answers if they are different.
- Play the recording again and ask students to check their answers and to fill in any missing information.
- Check the answers as a class and ask students to justify their answers.

Turn to page 126 of this Teacher's Guide for the recording script.

Answers
1 twice	3 never
2 always	4 Saturday

Speaking

8

- Explain that students are going to work in pairs to ask and answer questions about things they and their families do.

- Remind students of the adverbs of frequency they learnt, and tell them to use them to answer the questions.
- Read through the *Express yourself!* box with students. Explain that this box provides useful language that will help them complete the Speaking task. Give one or two example sentences, talking about yourself and your family. When students are confident with the language, they can do the task in their pairs.
- Go round the class monitoring students to make sure they are carrying out the task properly. Don't correct any mistakes at this stage, but make a note of any mistakes in structure and pronunciation.
- Ask each pair to say a sentence about how often they and their family do the things listed and repeat until each pair has had a turn.
- Write any structural mistakes that students made on the board, without saying who made them, and ask them to correct them. Deal with any problems in pronunciation.

Answers
Students' own answers

Extra Writing Task 1

- Make sure each student has a copy of Extra Writing Task 1 that can be found on the *Resource CD-ROM*.
- Explain to students that they are going to write six sentences about their routine – things they *usually, always, often, sometimes* or *never* do. Make sure they know that the adverbs of frequency go before the main verb in their sentences. Encourage them to write true sentences if they can and to use every adverb of frequency at least once.
- Ask students to write their sentences in their notebooks. You could set this task for homework if you are short of time.
- If time allows, ask each student to read one of their sentences to the class.

Extra Task (for early finishers)

See photocopiable material that can be found on the *Resource CD-ROM*.

Lesson 2

Objectives

Reading	factual article – true or false
Vocabulary	text-related words; prepositions
Grammar	present continuous
Listening	true or false

Way in

- Elicit as many words as students can remember for different family members, and then ask them to tell you about something one of their family members does.

- Ask and answer questions in the Present Simple like the ones below round the class. Students answer using the short answers. Try to make sure every student answers a question.
  - Do you have a brother?
  - Do you have a sister?
  - Do you visit your grandparents at the weekend?
  - Do you play football every day?

Reading

- Ask students to look at the picture on page 12 and ask them what they think these animals are (*albatrosses*). Ask them to read the title of the lesson (*Bird Planet*) and explain that it is the title of a TV wildlife series about birds and that they are going to read and hear a commentary from the TV show.

1

- Tell students they are going to listen to and read the commentary. Ask them to follow the commentary as they listen.
- Play the recording once. Ask students to tell you one fact they learned from the commentary that they didn't know before.
- Ask students to read the pre-reading question and to find the answer in the commentary.

Answer
Both parents feed the baby albatrosses.

2

- Explain that students are going to read the commentary again, this time to themselves. Ask them to focus on the meaning of the highlighted words or phrases. Check the meaning of those words or phrases as a class. If students don't know, encourage them to guess from the context. Encourage students to help each other work out the meaning of unknown words.

Answers
diary – *daily record of events*
safe – *free from harm*
taking care of – *protecting and keeping safe*
looking for – *searching for; trying to find*
distances – *length of space between places*
feed – *give food to*
turn – *time / opportunity to do something*
wings – *limbs birds have that enable them to fly*

Did you know?

- Ask students to read the information in the *Did you know?* feature and ask if they know how heavy human babies are when they are born (*usually between 3 and 4 kilos*).
- If students are interested, give them more information on albatrosses using the Background Information box below.

Background Information
Albatrosses can live to be as old as 50, though many of them die if they get caught in fishing lines. They can take years to find a new mate if their partner is killed; sometimes they never find one. They have the largest wingspan (the length from one wing tip across to the other when wings are outstretched) of all birds, at 3.5 metres, and can soar on wind currents for thousands of miles without flapping their wings. For further information, go to www.nationalgeographic.com and search for 'albatross'.

Comprehension
3

- Ask students to read sentences 1 to 5 so that they know what information to look for when they read the text for the second time.
- Ask students to read the text again to find out if the sentences are true or false and to write *T* or *F* in the boxes provided. Ask them to underline the information in the text that helps them to find the answers.
- Explain any vocabulary students don't know.

Answers
1 T (*The mother and father stay together for life ...*)
2 F (*... they both look after their babies.*)
3 F (*... they usually fly long distances ...*)
4 T (*When Fred comes back, it's Frieda's turn to go away.*)
5 T (*Some albatrosses can't fly until they are nine months old!*)

Vocabulary
4

- Explain that the words in the wordbank appear in the text on page 12. Ask students to find the words in the text and to underline them. Explain any words they don't understand.
- Ask students to do the task individually, but check the answers as a class. Correct their pronunciation where necessary.

Answers
1 feed
2 wings
3 turn
4 distance
5 safe

5

- Explain that each of the prepositions in this exercise makes a phrase with the words that come before or after it.
- Explain that most of the words appear in the commentary. Ask students to find the phrases with the prepositions that are in the commentary and to underline them. Explain any phrases they still don't understand.
- Ask students to do the task individually, but check the answers as a class. Correct their pronunciation where necessary.

Answers

1	for	4	after
2	at	5	on
3	of		

Extra Class Activity
Ask students to work in pairs to write sentences of their own using as many words as possible from *Vocabulary 4 and 5*. Ask them to read out their sentences to the class.

Grammar

Present Continuous

- Ask students the questions below about the *Reading* text.

  It's Monday 28th March – what are we watching?
  It's Sunday 9th April – what is Frieda doing?

- Write the answers on the board in full sentences (*We are watching a pair of albatrosses. She is taking care of the baby.*). Ask students what the main verbs are (*watch, take care of*) and tell them that they are in the Present Continuous tense. Underline *are* and *watching* in different colours and explain that in the Present Continuous, we have the verb *be* in the correct form and the main verb in the *–ing* form.
- Read the first part of the grammar box to the class and ask students to read the affirmative, negative and question forms with you. Then read through the short answers.
- Ask students to look back at the text on page 12 and to underline all the verbs in the Present Continuous (*are watching, is sitting, 's keeping, is taking care of, 's looking for, is moving, 's trying*).
- Ask students what spelling changes they remember for the *–ing* form. Elicit or explain that verbs with one syllable that end in a vowel and a consonant, like *run*, double the consonant in the *–ing* form and that verbs that end in *–e* drop the *–e* in the *–ing* form.
- Read the time expressions and explain that we normally put them at the end of the sentence. Refer students back to the second example sentence at the top of the grammar box.

6

- Ask students to read each sentence to find the subject in each one and to decide whether they need to use *am*, *are* or *is* to make the Present Continuous of the verb in brackets. Tell them to think about what other word they need to form the Present Continuous.
- Explain that the answers include affirmative, negative and question forms.
- Ask students to do the task individually, but check the answers as a class.

Answers

1	is / 's helping	4	are / 're visiting
2	are you cooking	5	is not / isn't wearing
3	am / 'm not going	6	Is Peter coming

7

- Ask students to look at the picture to see what each person is doing. Explain that the sentences below describe the picture. Tell students that they must choose a verb from the wordbank and use it in the Present Continuous tense to complete each sentence. Ask them to underline the subject in each sentence so that they know what form of *be* they need.
- Ask students to do the task individually, but check the answers as a class.

Answers

1 is / 's reading
2 are playing
3 is / 's talking
4 is / 's feeding
5 is / 's chasing

Listening

8

- Explain to students that they are going to listen to Dan and Helen talking about what they are doing tomorrow. Ask them to read sentences 1 to 5 quickly to find who is doing something in each one (1 to 3 *Dan*, 4 *Dan's grandma*, 5 *Helen*). Then ask them to underline what each person is doing (*going shopping, meeting Toby at three o'clock, going to a party, eating dinner at home, going out for dinner*). Explain that they need to pay attention to which person is talking and what they say they are doing as they listen.
- Make sure students understand that they have to write *T* if the sentence is correct or *F* if it is incorrect.
- Play the recording all the way to the end and ask students to write their answers. Ask them to discuss their answers with a partner and to justify any answers they have that are different. Play the recording again and ask students to check their answers or fill in any missing information.
- Check the answers as a class and make sure students can justify their answers.

Turn to page 126 of this Teacher's Guide for the recording script.

Answers

1 T (*We're going shopping …*)
2 T (*We're meeting at three o'clock.*)
3 F (*I'm going to a party tomorrow evening …*)
4 F (*… my family and I are taking Grandma out for dinner.*)
5 F (*OK, never mind. See you in the park at three o'clock tomorrow.*)

Let's Talk
Put students into small groups. Ask them to take turns to say sentences about what their family or friends are doing or not doing at the moment. Time permitting, extend this by asking them to take turns asking each other questions about what their friends or family are doing at the moment.

Extra Task (for early finishers)

See photocopiable material that can be found on the *Resource CD-ROM*.

Lesson 3

Objectives

Reading	family description – correcting information
Express yourself!	emphasising
Grammar	present simple and present continuous; stative verbs
Sounds of English	similar-sounding words
Writing	time expressions and adverbs of frequency; writing a description of your family

Way in

- Ask students to write the words *distance, feed, safe, wings* and *turn* in their notebooks and make sentences. Then ask them to work in pairs to check each other's spelling and meanings.
- Write the following words and phrases on the board:
  - look
  - the moment
  - take care
  - look
  - my own
- Ask students to tell you the preposition that comes before or after each word (*look for / after, at the moment, take care of, look after / for, on my own*) and to say the meaning of each phrase.
- Ask students which time expressions we use with the Present Continuous (*now, at the moment, today, this morning, tomorrow*). Then ask them to look at the photos next to the description on page 14 and elicit sentences using the Present Continuous about what the people are doing in each one.

Reading

1

- Explain to students that they are going to listen to and read a family description.
- Ask students to read the description to themselves and then to write the names under the photos.
- Tell students to compare their answers with a partner and ask them what information helped them to find the answers.

Answers
1 Brandon (*… he likes rollerblading.*)
2 Karen and Mabel (*In this photo, they're having a picnic in the park.*)
3 Alison (*Mum's a famous chef …*)
4 Jessica (*I like taking photos …*)

Comprehension

2

- Ask students to look at sentences 1 to 6 before they read the description for the second time so that they know what information they need to replace. Ask them to scan the description to find the answers and to underline the information that helps them to find the answer.
- Ask students to do the task individually, but check the answers as a class.

Answers
1 camera (*… I always carry my camera with me.*)
2 fashion photographer (*…, I want to be a fashion photographer.*)
3 cousin (*… he's visiting our cousin …*)
4 mum (*The chef in the photo is my mum, …*)
5 Canada (*… they live in Canada.*)
6 tennis (*The twins like playing tennis and they're very good at it, too.*)

Let's Talk
Put students into pairs. They take turns to ask each other questions about the information in the text.

Express yourself!

Emphasising

- Read the sentences in *Emphasising* to the class and ask students to repeat after you. Correct their intonation pattern and pronunciation if necessary. Draw their attention to the stress of *so* before the adjective and explain that we do this to emphasise the meaning of the adjective.

3

- Ask students to work in pairs to complete the dialogues. Remind them to practise the language shown.
- Ask each pair to role play one of the dialogues until all students have had the chance to speak.

Answers
1 It's so scary!
2 She's so clever!
3 You're so rude!

Grammar

Present Simple and Present Continuous

- Read the grammar box to the class and ask students to say the example sentences with you. Explain the grammar terms where necessary.
- Tell students to look back at the first main paragraph of the text on page 14 to find verbs in the Present Simple (*'m, go to, carry, like, grow up, want*) and in the Present Continuous (*'m taking*). Ask students to read the grammar rules again and to tell you why these verbs are in the different tenses.

- Elicit the time expressions and adverbs of frequency that we normally use with the Present Simple (*every day / night / week / month / year, at the weekends, always, usually, often, sometimes, never*) and the time expressions that we use with the Present Continuous (*now, at the moment, today, this morning, tomorrow*).

4

- Ask students to read each sentence to see what it is about and to find the subject in each one. Ask them which tense to use for general truths, things we do regularly and permanent states (*Present Simple*), and which we use to talk about things that are temporary or are happening now, for fixed plans or to say what is happening in a picture (*Present Continuous*). Remind them to think about which words they need to form the Present Continuous.
- Ask students to do the task individually, but check the answers as a class.

Answers
1 do not / don't go
2 am / 'm doing
3 are not / aren't listening
4 Do you meet
5 works
6 Is he having

Stative Verbs

- Read the grammar box to the class. Explain that these verbs are called stative verbs and that they are verbs of thought and feeling, not action.

5

- Ask students to read the sentences to decide which verb from the wordbank fits the meaning. Tell them that some of these are stative verbs and tell them to decide whether each sentence is affirmative, negative or a question (*1, 2, 4 and 6 – questions; 3 – negative, 5 – affirmative*).
- Ask students to do the task individually, but check the answers as a class.

Answers
1 do not / don't know
2 Is ... studying
3 does not / doesn't like
4 Are ... waiting
5 is / 's cooking
6 Does ... want

Sounds of English

6

- Explain to students that in English some words sound the same or very similar and that it's important to think of context when they hear words like that, so they can work out the meaning. Tell them that they are going to hear only one of the sentences in each pair on the recording and that they have to tick the sentence they hear. Before they listen, ask them to read the pairs of sentences to find words that have similar sounds (*eating / meeting, working / walking, talking / taking*).

- Play the recording once without stopping, then play again, stopping after each sentence. Ask students which sentence is being said. Write the correct sentence or ask a student to write the correct sentence on the board to avoid confusion.

Answers
1b 2a 3b

7

- Play the recording again and ask students to listen carefully. Put students into pairs to practise saying the sentences.

Extra Class Activity

Ask students to test each other in their pairs by saying one of the pair of sentences from *Sounds of English 6*; their partner guesses which sentence it was.

Teaching Tip

Tongue twisters can be used as a fun way to remember pronunciation. Make a list of your favourite tongue twisters and use them now and again to add to the lesson.

Writing

Time Expressions and Adverbs of Frequency

8

- Explain to students that they have to match the time expressions to the correct tense.
- Ask students to do the task individually, but check the answers as a class. Ask individual students to give one answer each and write the correct answers on the board so that students can check them.

Answers

1	PC	6	PS
2	PS	7	PS
3	PC	8	PC
4	PS	9	PS
5	PC	10	PC

9

- Ask students to read Mark's description and to choose the words that complete the sentences correctly. Ask them to do the task individually, but check the answers as a class. When you have checked the answers, ask students how their family is different to Mark's.

Answers
1 twice a week
2 in the summer
3 always
4 At the moment
5 always

Extra Class Activity

Ask students to think of sentences of their own using one of the time expressions from *Writing 9*. Go round the class eliciting their sentences.

Task

10

- Ask students to work in pairs to discuss what they are going to write and to say why.
- Make sure students understand the paragraph plan on page 15. Explain that each paragraph adds a different piece of information to the description to make it easy to follow.
- Ask students to use the plan to write a description like the one in *Writing 9*. Remind students that they should use the time expressions and adverbs of frequency from *Writing 8* with the correct verb tense. They can also draw a picture or stick on a photo of their family.
- Alternatively, you could assign this task as homework.

Example answer

Paragraph 1
I am eleven years old and I go to Kalamaki School. I am an only child. I have piano lessons once a week. I play volleyball on Tuesdays and Saturdays.

Paragraph 2
My cousins live in Athens. They usually come to Kalamaki in the summer, but this year they're visiting our aunt in Germany.

Paragraph 3
My mum loves playing tennis. She plays twice a week. Dad likes watching basketball on TV. His favourite team is Panathinaikos.

Paragraph 4
My best friend is Gina. She's an only child too. Sometimes she comes to my house after school. We play games and we always have a great time together.

11

- Ask students to read back through their descriptions to make sure that they have used time expressions and adverbs of frequency correctly. If you ask them to write the description for homework, then give them a few minutes to do this at the beginning of the next lesson.

Teaching Tip

Displaying students' writing in the classroom will give them a sense of pride in their achievements. Encourage them to decorate their work with drawings or photos to personalise it.

Extra Task (for early finishers)

See photocopiable material that can be found on the *Resource CD-ROM*.

Way in

- If you assigned Unit 1, Lesson 3 *Writing 10* for homework, then give students a few minutes to proofread their descriptions to check they've used the time expressions and adverbs of frequency correctly. Then ask them to read each other's paragraphs, or stick them on the wall so they can read them when they have time.
- Ask students which word we put before an adjective to emphasise the meaning (*so*) and ask them to say a sentence about somebody they know using *so* and an adjective (eg *He's so rude!*).
- Write the following sentences on the board and ask students to tell you the time expressions that we could use in each sentence.
  - I visit my grandparents. (*every day / week / month, never, once a week, sometimes, always*)
  - John is visiting his grandparents. (*at the moment, now, this week / summer / winter, today*)
- Ask students what kinds of verbs we don't use with continuous tenses and why (*stative verbs, they are verbs of thought or feeling*). Ask them what stative verbs they remember. Elicit *know, like, love, think, understand* and *want* and ask them to use the stative verbs to make sentences.

Did you know?

- With books closed, ask students to name (or describe, if they can't remember the word) as many different types of home as they can think of (*flat, house, houseboat, villa, castle*, etc). Write their suggestions on the board. Ask them to say which homes they would like to live in and which they wouldn't.
- Ask students to open their books at pages 16 and 17. Ask them to look at the picture and ask if they can guess whether the picture is of a hot country or a cold country (*a hot country – houses made of something like sand or mud; clothing cotton and light*). Ask them what they think is unusual about the houses (*no obvious windows, the whole house made of the same material*, etc).
- Ask students to read the paragraph about the mud huts in Syria on page 17. Explain that houses like the ones in the picture are called beehive houses and often families own several of them – one for the family, one for animals, one for cooking and so on.
- Read the information from the *Did you know?* feature to the class. Ask students if they can guess how old the oldest buildings in the world are (*the Megalithic Temples of Malta are thought to be about 5,500 years old*).

- Use the background information in the box below to give the students further information about mud huts if they are interested. Check if they have any questions. If they ask for information you don't have, refer them to the website in the Background Information box and ask them to feed back to you at the next lesson.

Background Information

The picture shows mud huts in Syria. There is usually one large entrance to the huts and no windows. The thick mud walls keep the houses warm in winter and cool in summer and repairs are easy – the family simply make more mud and plaster it onto the walls. Some people add leaves and sticks to the mixture they make their huts from. There are mud huts in other hot countries like India and Africa as well as Syria. Some of them have roofs made of tree branches or strong grasses. Farmers who look after animals and move from place to place often build new huts whenever they move. People often decorate the inside walls of their huts with tapestries to make them look attractive. For further information, go to www.nationalgeographic.com and search for 'mud huts'.

Let's Talk

Put students into pairs. Ask them to talk to their partner about what they think it would be like to live in a mud hut. Ask them to talk about the good and the bad things.

Lesson 1

Objectives

Reading	the cartoon story – completing sentences
Vocabulary	text-related words; furniture and appliances
Grammar	past simple (regular verbs)
Listening	numbering pictures
Speaking	talking about when things happened

Teaching Tip

Before introducing each episode of the cartoon story, quickly ask students to remember what happened in the previous episode and revise any new words they learnt there. For example, elicit who came to visit the children in Episode 1 (*Beth*), who she is (*Kristie and Mikey's cousin*), where she is from (*Seattle*) and who she missed (*Cuddles, her cat*).

The cartoon story

• Ask students if they can remember what happened in the previous episode of the cartoon story (*Kristie and Mikey's cousin, Beth, came from Seattle to visit. The children told her about the magic globe and she asked the globe to take her back to Seattle for a visit because she was missing her cat Cuddles.*).
• Ask students to look at the story pictures and suggest what might be happening.

1

• Please follow the procedure outlined in Unit 1, Lesson 1 on page 12 of this Teacher's Guide.

Answers
century – *a hundred years*
huge – *very big*
staff – *people who work for someone*
guest – *visitor*
furniture – *things like tables and chairs*
stairs – *the part of a building leading to the next floor*
shouted – *spoke in a loud, angry way*
swords – *long, thin, sharp metal weapons*

• Depending on whether you are using the DVD or the Audio CD, follow the relevant instructions.

For teachers using the DVD

• Make sure each child has a copy of Cartoon DVD Worksheet 2 that can be found on the *Resource CD-ROM*.
• Please follow the procedure outlined in Unit 1, Lesson 1 on page 12 of this Teacher's Guide for teachers using the DVD.

Before you watch

Answers
1 Adam
2 to the past, to a large house or palace

While you watch

Answers
1 history   4 kitchens
2 king   5 furniture
3 London   6 men

After you watch

Answers
1 awful   4 guest
2 16th century   5 bedroom
3 people   6 stairs

For teachers using the Audio CD

• Ask students to look at page 18 of their student's book and to work in pairs. Ask if they can guess who travelled with the magic globe in this episode (*Mikey*).

• Tell students they are going to listen to and read the story. Ask them to look at the pictures and to follow the story as they listen.
• Play the recording once and ask students how many men chase Mikey (*four*).
• Put students into pairs and assign the roles of Kristie and Mikey within the pairs. Ask the pairs to read the story out loud.
• As a class, ask students the questions below to check their understanding of the episode.
  1 What project has Mikey got? (*a history project*)
  2 Whose palace was Hampton Court? (*the king's palace*)
  3 What did the kitchen staff do all day? (*cooked*)
  4 Where was the king's bedroom? (*up the stairs*)
  5 Where was the king? (*in his bed*)

Comprehension

2

• Ask students to read sentences 1 to 5 so they know what information to look for when they read the cartoon story again. Ask them to complete the sentences with words from the story.
• Ask students to do the task individually, but check the answers as a class. Encourage students to explain their answer choices by giving evidence from the story.

Answers
1 project (*I've got a history project …*)
2 palace (*… the king's palace in London.*)
3 kitchens (*… the kitchens. They were huge and full of people.*)
4 bedroom (*I wanted to see his bedroom.*)
5 opened (*He shouted at me when I opened the door.*)

Vocabulary

3

• Ask students to look at the words in the wordbank. Remind them that all the words are from the cartoon story on page 18 and point out that they already know the meaning of them. Check understanding of one or two of the words again if you think it's necessary.
• Ask students to do the task individually, but check the answers as a class.

Answers
1 sword   4 huge
2 staff   5 guest
3 century   6 furniture

Grammar

Past Simple (regular verbs)

• Read the uses of the Past Simple in the grammar box with the class and ask students to read the example sentences with you. Explain the grammar terms used, if necessary. Draw students' attention to the fact that the Past Simple forms are the same for all subjects (*I / you / he / she / it / we / you / they*).

- Write the following verbs on the board: *live, follow, visit* and ask students to tell you the Past Simple (*lived, followed, visited*). Write the answers on the board as students say them. Correct their pronunciation where necessary.
- Ask students what changes we make to regular verbs in the affirmative of the Past Simple (we add *–ed* for most regular verbs and *–d* for verbs ending in *–e*). Explain that for verbs ending in *–y*, we change the spelling by taking off the *–y* and adding *–ied*. Tell them that we don't make any spelling change to verbs that have a vowel before the *–y*, like *play*.
- Read the verb forms from the grammar box with the class. Ask students which word we put in front of the main verb in the negative (*didn't*). Then ask how we form questions (*Did* + subject + infinitive). Stress that we don't put *–ed* on the main verb in the negative or the question form.
- Explain that we often use time expressions with the Past Simple. Read the time expressions and explain that *ago* means *before now*, and then explain any other words students don't know.

4
- Explain that students will find verbs in the cartoon episode in both the affirmative and the negative of the Past Simple.
- Ask students to do the task individually, but check the answers as a class.

Answers
Sixteen: happened, wanted, lived, asked, didn't, did, Did you travel, visited, walked, were, cooked, didn't stop, was, climbed, Did it look like, shouted, opened, chased

5
- Explain to students that they should read the sentences and complete each gap with the correct form of the Past Simple. Explain that the answers include the affirmative, negative and question forms. Remind them to use *didn't* to form the negative and *Did* to form questions.
- Ask students to do the task individually, but check the answers as a class.

Answers
1	shouted	4	Did Mikey visit
2	Did Kristie like	5	did your mum cook
3	did not / didn't tidy	6	stayed

Vocabulary

6
- Explain to students that they have to match words 1 to 10 with objects a to j in the picture. Explain any vocabulary that students don't know.
- Ask students to work in pairs to do the task, but check the answers as a class and correct pronunciation where necessary.

Answers
1g 2f 3j 4h 5c 6i 7e 8d 9a 10b

Extra Class Activity

Ask students to work in pairs. Tell them to talk about the kinds of things they think people had in their houses one hundred years ago. Tell them that it might be a good idea to think about what they have in their homes now and to think whether they existed one hundred years ago. Ask them to write three sentences together and then get each pair to read out one of their sentences.

Let's Talk

Put students into small groups to talk about which of the items from *Vocabulary 6* they have in their own houses. Time permitting, they can also take turns to describe one of the items; the other students in the group guess the item.

Listening

7
- Ask students to look at pictures a to e and tell you what they show (*fridge, oven, sofa, coffee table, bed*).
- Explain to students that they are going to hear Jemma talking to Carl about moving into her new flat and that they are going to note down the order in which they hear about each object. Tell students that they have to listen for the words that describe the things in the photos and they also have to listen for words that tell them when each thing was moved.
- Play the first two exchanges and ask students to number the first picture.
- Play the recording to the end and ask students to put the pictures in the correct order. Then play the recording again and ask students to check their answers and to fill in any missing information.

Turn to page 126 of this Teacher's Guide for the recording script.

Answers
a 4 (*… at two o'clock, some men arrived with our new fridge.*)
b 5 (*Did a new oven arrive too? … No, the oven didn't arrive yesterday.*)
c 2 (*Then …. I helped Dad with the chairs and the sofa.*)
d 3 (*At the table. Dad carried that in.*)
e 1 (*First we moved the beds in. My bed is next to the wardrobe.*)

Speaking

8
- Explain that students are going to work in pairs to talk about when they did different things.
- Remind students of the time expressions that they learnt in *Grammar*, and tell them to use them with the Past Simple (*I went shopping last week.*, etc).

- Read through the *Express yourself!* box with students. Explain that this box provides useful language that will help them complete the Speaking task. Give one or two example sentences, talking about when you did the things in the list. When students are confident with the language, they can do the task in their pairs.
- Go round the class monitoring students and make sure they are carrying out the task properly. Don't correct any mistakes in structure and pronunciation at this stage, but make a note of them.
- Ask each pair to talk about when they did things and repeat until each pair has had a turn.
- On the board, write some of the mistakes in structure that you heard while students were doing the task, without saying who made them, and ask students to correct them. Deal with any problems in pronunciation.

Answers
Students' own answers

Extra Writing Task 2

- Make sure each student has a copy of Extra Writing Task 2 that can be found on the *Resource CD-ROM*.
- Explain to students that they are going to write six sentences about things they did last weekend. Before they write, put students into pairs to tell each other about what they did last weekend. Encourage them to use the words from Lesson 1 if possible and help them with any new words that they want to use but don't know.
- Ask students to write their sentences in their notebooks. You could set this task for homework if you are short of time.
- If time allows, ask each student to read one of their sentences to the class.

Extra Task (for early finishers)

See photocopiable material that can be found on the *Resource CD-ROM*.

Lesson 2

Objectives

Reading	article – open-ended questions
Vocabulary	text-related words; parts of a house and appliances
Grammar	past simple (irregular verbs)
Listening	completing notes
Sounds of English	*ow* sounds

Way in

- Write the words *century, furniture, guest, huge, staff* and *sword* on the board. Tell students to write sentences in their notebooks using each of the words. Then ask students at random to read out one of their sentences.
- Ask students to see how many words they can remember from Unit 2, Lesson 1 for furniture and appliances.

- Write the words *want, arrive, move, tidy* and *stay* on the board and ask students to come up and write the Past Simple form of the words (*wanted, arrived, moved, tidied, stayed*).
- Ask students which words are needed to make the negative (*didn't* + infinitive) and ask how we change the word order of questions (*Did* before the subject + infinitive).
- Tell students that they are going to learn more words about homes in this lesson.

Reading

1

- Tell students they are going to listen to and read the article. Ask them to follow the article as they listen.
- Play the recording once. Ask students to tell you one fact they learned from the article that they didn't know before.
- Ask students to read the pre-reading question and to find the answer in the article.

Answers
Inside the walls of the city there were palaces, temples and some amazing houses.

2

- Please follow the procedure outlined in Unit 1, Lesson 2 on page 15 of this Teacher's Guide.

Answers
temples – *large churches*
floors – *storeys, levels in a house*
stone – *rock*
balcony – *extra area of a house, outside a window or door*
wooden – *made of wood*
rugs – *small carpets*
roof – *the top covering of a building*
buckets – *large containers to carry water or other things*

Did you know?

- Ask students to read the information in the *Did you know?* feature and ask if they know which is the largest desert in the world (*the continent of Antarctica*).
- If students are interested, give them more information on Jaisalmer using the Background Information box below.

Background Information
Jaisalmer is in Rajasthan, India and is surrounded by the Thar Desert. In the past, rich Indian Maharajas lived there and their palaces and homes are still there today, which is what makes the place so amazing. Temperatures there can go up to 47 degrees Celcius in the summer, making it extremely hot. For further information, go to www.nationalgeographic.com and search for 'Jaisalmer'.

Comprehension

3

- Ask students to read questions 1 to 5 before they read the text again so that they know what information to look for.
- Ask students to do the task individually, but check the answers as a class. Ask students to underline where they get the answer from in the text so they can justify their answers.
- Explain any vocabulary students don't know and correct their pronunciation if necessary.

Answers
1. Jaisalmer
2. three
3. wooden furniture and rugs on the floors
4. samosas
5. Chandra

Vocabulary

4

- Explain that the words in the wordbank appear in the article on page 20. Ask students to find the words in the text and underline them. Explain any words they don't understand.
- Ask students to do the task individually, but check the answers as a class.

Answers
1 floor	4 bucket
2 temple	5 wooden
3 balcony	

5

- Ask students to look at the words in the wordbank and to tell you which three things they read about in the article on page 20 (*balcony, rug, roof*).
- Explain to students that they have to label pictures 1 to 9 with the words in the wordbank.
- Ask students to do the task individually, but check the answers as a class.

Answers
1 curtains	6 bookcase
2 vacuum cleaner	7 fireplace
3 roof	8 balcony
4 washing machine	9 mirror
5 rug	

Extra Class Activity

Divide the class into two teams. Give each team five sheets of paper and ask them to write a different word related to homes on each sheet. Tell them not to let the other team see what they are writing. Each team should then take turns at describing one of the words they have written, without using the word itself. The other team should try to guess the word. Give each team a point for every word they guess correctly. The team with the most correct guesses is the winner.

Grammar

Past Simple (irregular verbs)

- Read the grammar box to students and ask them to read the example sentences with you.
- Draw students' attention to the list of irregular verbs on pages 132 and 133. Explain that these are all irregular verbs and that the second column shows the Past Simple in the affirmative. Write the following verbs on the board: *meet, go, have, spend, drink, eat*. Ask students to look back at the article on page 20 in their student's book and to tell you the Past Simple affirmative (*met, went, had, spent, drank, ate*). Write the answers on the board as students say them. Correct their pronunciation where necessary.
- Ask students to find a Past Simple verb in the negative form in the story (*didn't have*). Remind them that we make the Past Simple negative of irregular verbs with *didn't* + infinitive and we make questions with *Did* + subject + infinitive.
- Tell students that the short answers to Past Simple questions with irregular verbs are the same as short answers for regular verbs. Write this question on the board *Did the house have running water?* and elicit the short answer *No, it didn't*.
- Ask students to find the negative forms of *be* from the list on page 132 and explain that this is the only irregular verb that is different for different subjects. Write *I* and *he / she / it* on the board. Write *was* next to them, in a different colour if possible, and then write *you, we* and *they* with *were* next to them. Explain that the negative of *was* and *were* is *wasn't* (*was not*) and *weren't* (*were not*).
- Ask students to recall how we make questions with *is* and *are* (we put *Is* or *Are* before the subject pronoun of singular or plural nouns). Explain that we make the Past Simple questions of *be* in the same way by putting *Was* before *I / he / she / it* or a singular noun, and we put *Were* before *you / we / they* or a plural noun.
- Write the short answers for questions with *Was* and *Were* on the board.
  - Yes, I / he / she / it was.
  - No, I /he / she / it wasn't.
  - Yes, we / you / they were.
  - No, we / you / they weren't.

6

- Ask students to find and underline the Past Simple verbs in the article.

Answers

There are 11 verbs in the Past Simple; 9 of them are irregular: met, went, lived, was / were, had, took, spent, slept, carried, drank, ate.

7

- Explain that students are going to complete the paragraph using the Past Simple of the verbs in brackets.

- Explain to students that all the verbs in brackets in the paragraph are irregular. Tell students to look at the list of irregular verbs on pages 132 and 133 to help them find the Past Simple form of these verbs.
- Ask students to do the task individually, but check the answers as a class. Write the answers on the board as students say them to make sure they have spelt them correctly.

Answers

1	sold	5	came
2	bought	6	gave
3	found	7	became
4	was	8	took

Listening

8

- Explain to students that they are going to listen to Lara talking to Neil about Lara's holiday home and that they are going to complete the notes. Explain that in some gaps they will write words and in others they will write numbers and words. Give students a few minutes to read the notes and then ask them what kind of information is missing from each one (1 *length of time*, 2 *a meal*, 3 *a place*, 4 *a place*, 5 *length of time*).
- Play the recording to the end and ask students to fill in their answers. Ask students to discuss their answers with a partner and to justify any answers they have that are different.
- Play the recording again and ask students to check their answers and to fill in any missing information.

Turn to page 126 of this Teacher's Guide for the recording script.

Answers

1	3 months	4	Italy
2	breakfast	5	2 weeks
3	floor		

- Once you have finished the exercise, ask students whether they would like to have a holiday home like Lara's.

Sounds of English

9

- Ask students to work in pairs to say the words to each other. Explain that the *ow* in *yellow* has a short sound as in *hello* and that *ow* in *shower* is a longer sound that sounds like *ah* and *oh* together.

10

- Ask students to work in pairs to say the words to each other so that they can work out which words in *Sounds of English 9* go in which column together.
- Play the recording and ask students to check their answers.
- Check the answers as a class.

Answers

below		town	
1	yellow	5	shower
2	know	6	now
3	snow	7	how
4	show	8	brown

Let's Talk

Put students into pairs. They take turns to say sentences to each other using words from *Sounds of English 9*. Walk round while they are working and gently correct any pronunciation errors.

Teaching Tip

Maybe once a term, you could bring in an English DVD related to the subject of the lesson for students to watch and discuss afterwards. For example, for this subject, students may enjoy watching a cartoon in English on the *rags to riches* theme. Remember, if a film is too long, you can always show it in two parts.

Extra Task (for early finishers)

See photocopiable material that can be found on the *Resource CD-ROM*.

Lesson 3

Objectives

Reading	descriptions – multiple matching
Express yourself!	talking about homes
Listening	changing words in bold
Speaking	talking about a picture
Writing	connectors (*and, but, because* and *so*); writing an advert for your home

Way in

- Ask students to tell you what household appliances they have at home.
- Write *balcony, bucket, floor, temple* and *wooden* on the board. Tell students to come up with sentences using each of the words. Then ask each student to read out one of their sentences to the class.
- Write the words *buy, come, find, give, sell* and *take* on the board and ask different students to come up and write the Past Simple of each one. Ask students what other irregular verbs they can recall from Lesson 2.
- Explain that students are now going to read about four different homes. Ask them to look at the photos next to the text and to tell you where they think these homes are (*on a river, in a hot country, in the country, in the city*).

Reading

1

- Ask students to look at the pictures and ask them which type of home they like best.
- Tell students to read the descriptions on their own and then to write the names under each of the pictures.
- Ask students to work with a partner to compare their answers and then ask students what helped them to find the answers.

Answers
1	Michael	3	Jason
2	Trina	4	Ashley

Comprehension

2

- Ask students to read questions 1 to 5 before they read the text again so that they know what information to look for on their second read through.
- Ask students to do the task individually, but check the answers as a class. Ask students to underline parts of the text that justify their answers.

Answers
1 A (*It's got a balcony and a great view of a park.*)
2 M (*It's really cool to live on a river!*)
3 T (*It hasn't got a kitchen ...*)
4 J (*It's got two floors ...*)
5 A (*... in the city centre.*)

Express yourself!

Talking about homes

- Explain to students that they are now going to learn some phrases we use in English when talking about homes.
- Read the sentences in *Talking about homes* with the class. Correct their pronunciation and intonation patterns if necessary.

3

- Tell students that they are now going to look at the dialogue and complete it using some of the phrases they have just learnt. After they have done that tell them to change the words in red to make the dialogue true for them.
- Once students have completed the dialogue give them a few minutes to role play it. Ask each pair to read out their dialogue in front of the class. Repeat until all students have had a turn. If there is an odd number of students, you could role play with one of the students.
- Correct students' pronunciation and intonation patterns where necessary.

Answers
1	Where do	3	I moved into
2	I live	4	is modern

Extra Class Activity

Write the following headings on the board:
- Places
- Kinds of homes
- Rooms
- Furniture
- Appliances
- Adjectives about homes

Ask students to work in teams to write down the headings on a piece of paper and then to write as many words as they can remember under each heading. Give them 5 minutes to write the words, then ask one member from each team to give you their list. Put the lists on the wall for students to compare. The team with the most words is the winner.

Listening

4

- Explain to students that they are going to listen to Paula talking to Billy about her cousin's new home. Ask students to read sentences 1 to 6 and to pay attention to the words in bold so that they know what information to listen for. Tell them that the words in bold are different to what Paula says and that they have to write the correct word on each line.
- Play the recording once and then ask students to compare their answers with a partner. Ask them to justify any answers that are different. Play the recording a second time and ask them to check their answers or fill in any missing information.
- Check the answers as a class and make sure students can justify their answers.

Turn to page 126 of this Teacher's Guide for the recording script.

Answers
1 cottage
2 awful
3 dirty
4 small
5 old
6 rubbish

Speaking

5

- Explain that students are going to work in pairs to talk about the flat in the picture. Remind students to use the vocabulary they learnt for rooms, furniture and appliances.
- Go round the class monitoring students to make sure they are carrying out the task properly. Don't correct any mistakes at this stage, but make a note of any mistakes in structure and pronunciation.
- Ask each pair to describe the picture and if time allows repeat until each pair has had a turn.
- Write any structural mistakes that students made on the board, without saying who made them, and ask them to correct them. Deal with any problems in pronunciation.

Suggested answers
- The flat has got a big sitting room and a kitchen.
- There is a large window with a blue curtain.
- In the kitchen, there is a sink, a cooker, a fridge and cupboards.
- In front of the fridge, there is a table with four chairs.
- In the sitting room, there is a red sofa, an armchair and a coffee table on a blue and yellow rug.

Writing

Connectors

6

- Read the rules about connectors to the class. Explain the meaning of *reason* and *result* and any other new vocabulary where necessary.
- Explain that the words before and after *and* and *but* must be the same kind of words. For example, they can both be adjectives, like the ones in the example sentences, nouns, adverbs or they can be two sentences joined by *and* or *but*.
- Tell students that we use *because* or *so* to join two complete sentences.

7

- Ask students to read through the sentences and possible options.
- For sentences 2 and 3, tell them to work out whether the words after the connector (*and* or *but*) add something else to the sentence or show that something is different to the first part of the sentence.
- For sentences 1, 4 and 5, tell students to work out whether the words after the connector are a reason or a result of the first part of the sentence.
- Ask students to do the task individually, but check the answers as a class.

Answers
1	because	4	but
2	but	5	so
3	and		

8

- Ask students to read the advert to themselves so they understand its meaning before they complete it. Then tell them to read it again carefully to decide whether the words after each gap add something else to the meaning or show something different, or whether they are a reason or a result of the part of the sentence before the gap.
- Ask students to do the task individually, but check the answers as a class.

Answers
1	because	3	but
2	and	4	so

Task

9

- Ask students to work in pairs to ask and answer the questions about their homes on page 23.
- Ask students to use their answers to write an advert like the one in *Writing 8*. Remind students that they should use the linking words from *Writing 6* in their adverts. They can also draw a picture or stick on a photo of their home.
- Alternatively, you could assign this task as homework.

Example answer
Flat For Sale!
This beautiful flat with a balcony is in the city centre. It is great for small families because it has got three bedrooms, two bathrooms and a sitting room. It has also got a small kitchen with a great view of the river. The flat is modern but all the furniture is old. There is a shopping centre in the same street, so you can walk to the shops in five minutes.
Come and see this great flat soon!

10

- Ask students to read back through their adverts to make sure that they have used linking words correctly. If you ask them to write the advert for homework, then give them a few minutes to do this at the beginning of the next lesson.

Extra Task (for early finishers)

See photocopiable material that can be found on the *Resource CD-ROM*.

Review 1

Objectives

- To revise vocabulary and grammar from Units 1 and 2
- Project – my home

Preparing for the review

- Explain to students that there will be a review after every two units in *Spin 2*. Tell them that the tasks in *Review 1* revise the material they learnt in Units 1 and 2.
- Explain to students that they can ask you for help with the exercises or look back at the units if they're not sure about an answer, as the review is not a test.
- Decide how you will carry out the review. You could ask students to do one task at a time and then correct it immediately, or ask students to do all the tasks and then correct them together at the end. If you do all the tasks together, let students know every now and again how much time they have got left to finish the tasks.
- Ask students not to leave any answers blank and to try to find any answers they aren't sure about in the units.
- Revise the vocabulary and grammar as a class before students do the review.

Vocabulary Revision

- Ask students to tell you the words they remember connected with families (*grandparents, grandchildren, sister, wife, nephews, nieces, only child, relatives, aunt, cousin*). Ask students to make sentences using these words.
- Ask students to tell you the preposition phrases they learned in Lesson 2 (*look for, at the moment, take care of, look after, on my own*). Ask them to talk about their friends and families using these phrases.
- Check that students remember the words related to homes. Make three columns on the board with the titles *part of a home, furniture* and *appliances* and ask students to put the words related to homes into the correct column.

Grammar Revision

- Write *I, you, he / she / it* and *we / you / they* one below the other on the board and ask a student to come and write the Present Simple affirmative forms of *go* beside the subject pronouns. Ask the other students to help the student who's writing. Then ask individual students at random round the class to tell you the negative forms. Do the same for the question forms and short answers. Then ask students which time expressions we often use with the Present Simple.
- Write *I laugh at Grandma's jokes.* and *Mum is late.* on the board and the adverb of frequency *usually* next to them. Then ask students to put the adverb in the correct position in each sentence.

- Write *I, you, he / she / it* and *we / you / they* one below the other on the board and ask a student to come and write the Present Continuous affirmative forms of *play* beside the subject pronouns. Ask the other students to help the student who's writing. Then ask individual students at random round the class to tell you the negative forms. Do the same for the question forms and short answers. Then ask students which time expressions we often use with the Present Continuous.
- Ask students to tell you some verbs that we don't use with continuous tenses.
- Write *I / you / he / she / it / we / you / they* together on the board and ask students to tell you the Past Simple affirmative of *walk*. Write the answer on the board and then ask a student to come up and write the negative and question forms. Elicit the short answers and time expressions we use with the Past Simple.
- Write *be, become, buy, come, find, give, get, sell* and *take* on the board and ask students to come up and write the Past Simple affirmative forms.

Vocabulary

1

- Ask students to say each of the words as a class and then individually. Correct their pronunciation if necessary.
- Ask students to go to the first page of stickers at the back of the book and find the stickers for *Review 1*. Tell them to decide which thing each sticker shows and to stick it in the correct box.
- Check that students have put the correct stickers above each word.

2

- Explain to students that they should only write one or two words in each sentence to replace the word in bold.
- Tell students to look for clues in the sentences to find the meaning of the correct word.

Suggested answers			
1	washing machine	4	rug
2	distance	5	century
3	uncle	6	staff

3

- Explain to students that they should read the whole paragraph so that they understand the context for each of the missing words.
- Tell students that all the words in the wordbank have appeared in the previous two units, so they should know the meaning of all of them.

Answers

1	sitting room	4	coffee table
2	furniture	5	huge
3	wooden	6	oven

4

- Tell students to read the sentences and both the answer options and to concentrate on the prepositions.

Answers

1	for	4	on
2	do	5	into
3	care	6	for

Grammar

5

- Explain to students that they should rewrite each sentence with the adverb of frequency in the correct place.
- Tell students to look back at the Unit 1, Lesson 1 grammar box for a reminder if they need to.

Answers

1 We don't always visit our grandparents on Sundays.
2 They are never at work in the evening.
3 My best friend often sleeps at my house.
4 Is your maths teacher always nice to his students?
5 Do your brothers sometimes argue? / Do your brothers argue sometimes?
6 Are Kristie and Mikey usually late for school?

6

- Ask students to read each sentence and to find the subject of each missing verb. Remind them that the subjects will help them decide on the correct form of the Present Simple or the Present Continuous each time. Remind students to pay attention to the spelling rules for the –ing forms when completing the sentences.
- Tell students to look back at the Unit 1, Lesson 1 grammar box for a reminder if they need to.

Answers

1 is moving
2 do you meet
3 are / 're flying
4 does not / doesn't think
5 Is your brother talking
6 does not / doesn't want

7

- Explain to students that they should write the Past Simple form of each verb on the line. Tell them to decide whether each verb is regular or irregular.
- Tell students to look back at the Unit 2, Lessons 1 and 2 grammar boxes and to look at the list of irregular verbs on pages 132 and 133 for a reminder if they need to.

Answers

1	studied	7	lived
2	ran	8	sold
3	was	9	bought
4	enjoyed	10	had
5	came	11	spent
6	stopped	12	ate

8

- Explain to students that they should read the paragraph before trying to write the answers to decide whether to use the Present Simple, Present Continuous or the Past Simple. Tell them to look for time expressions and to find the subject of each sentence to help them decide on the correct form of the verb in brackets.
- Remind students to use the list of irregular verbs on pages 132 and 133 and tell them to look back at the grammar boxes in Unit 1, Lessons 1 and 2, and Unit 2, Lesson 1 for a reminder if they need to.

Answers

1 cleaned
2 tidied
3 cooked
4 made
5 loves
6 bought
7 collects
8 is / 's taking

9

- Explain to students that they have to write the short answer for each question. Tell them to look at each question to see if the verb is affirmative or negative and which tense it is.
- Tell students to look back at the grammar boxes in Unit 1, Lessons 1 and 2, and Unit 2, Lesson 1 for a reminder if they need to.

Answers

1 I'm not
2 I do
3 we are
4 they didn't
5 she did
6 he / she isn't

Project 1

1

- Explain to the students that they are going to do a project about their home. Ask them to say what type of house they live in. If they prefer, they can do their project about an imaginary house.
- Point out that students should find a photo of their house or that they can draw and colour a picture of it.
- Ask students to read the bullet points and explain that the paragraph they write must address these points.
- Read through the example paragraph about a flat with the class.

- Ask students to complete their projects. They can do this in the lesson or for homework.
- When the projects are complete, stick them on the classroom wall.

2

- Invite students to tell the class about their home.

> **Teaching Tip**
> When checking students' answers to the review tasks, make a note of any problem areas in vocabulary and grammar that they still have. Try to do extra work on these areas so that your students progress well.

3 Free Time

Way in

- If you assigned Unit 2, Lesson 3 *Writing 9* for homework, then give students a few minutes to proofread their adverts to check they've used linking words correctly. Then ask them to read each other's adverts, or stick them on the wall so they can read them when they have time.
- Write *and*, *but*, *because* and *so* on the board and ask students to write four sentences, one with each of these words. Ask them to read out their sentences to the class.
- Write *bedroom*, *kitchen*, *sitting room* and *bathroom* on the board. Ask students to tell you as many things they can think of that you might find in each room. You can either write the things under the correct headings or let students write them on the board.

Did you know?

- With books closed, ask students what water sports they know. If there are some they know of but they don't know the name, ask them to describe the sport and give them the word(s) for the sport.
- Ask students to open their books at pages 26 and 27. Ask them to look at the picture and see if they know the name of the sport (*kite surfing*). Ask if any of them have ever seen people kite surfing.
- Ask students to read the paragraph about kite surfing on page 27. Explain that although all sports use quite a lot of energy, some sports are much more energetic than others. Sports that use different parts of our bodies are the most energetic.
- Read the information from the *Did you know?* feature to the class. Ask students how they think Phillip McCoy Midler felt at the end of his journey.
- Use the background information in the box below to give the students further information about kite surfing if they are interested. Check if they have any questions. If they ask for information you don't have, refer them to the website in the Background Information box and ask them to feed back to you at the next lesson.

Background Information

The picture shows some people kite surfing. Kite surfing as a sport started on the east coast of the USA in the late 1990s. However, the idea dates back to 13th century China, when people used kites to help them get around more quickly. Since then it has become one of the most popular extreme sports. With strong winds, kite surfers can move at more than 60 kilometres an hour. They can also jump up to 10 metres in the air. Kite surfers need two pieces of equipment – a kite and a board. The kite is similar to the chute paragliders use and has a control bar for steering. There is also a safety control that kite ➡

surfers attach to their wrist so if their kite goes out of control or is going too fast, they can let go. For further information, go to www.nationalgeographic.com and search for 'kite surfing'.

Let's Talk

Put students into pairs. Ask them to talk about dangerous sports like kite surfing. Ask them to talk about why the sports are dangerous and whether or not they would like to try them.

Lesson 1

Objectives

Reading	the cartoon story – circling the correct words
Vocabulary	text-related adjectives; phrasal verbs
Grammar	past continuous
Listening	true or false
Speaking	asking and answering questions about actions in progress in the past

The cartoon story

- Ask students if they can remember what happened in the previous episode of the cartoon story (*Mikey had a history project and asked the magic globe to take him to a palace. The globe took Mikey back in time and he visited Hampton Court. He looked round the palace, then went into the bedroom, where the king was in bed. The king shouted at Mikey and men with swords chased him away.*).
- Ask students to look at the story pictures and suggest what might be happening.

1

- Please follow the procedure outlined in Unit 1, Lesson 1 on page 12 of this Teacher's Guide.

Answers
brilliant – *very good, amazing, fantastic*
skater – *person who skates*
by the way – *an idiom used when adding information*
give up – *stop trying*
take up – *start*
practise – *do something again to try to learn it*
fault – *the cause of a problem*

- Depending on whether you are using the DVD or the Audio CD, follow the relevant instructions.

For teachers using the DVD

- Make sure each child has a copy of Cartoon DVD Worksheet 3 that can be found on the *Resource CD-ROM*.

- Please follow the procedure outlined in Unit 1, Lesson 1 on page 12 of this Teacher's Guide for teachers using the DVD.

Before you watch

Answers
1 ice-skating
2 a girl

While you watch

Answers
1	Mikey	4	Mikey
2	Adam	5	Kristie
3	Kristie	6	Adam

After you watch

Answers
1F 2T 3F 4T 5F 6T

For teachers using the Audio CD

- Ask students to look at page 28 of their student's book and to work in pairs. Ask them to say where the children are (*at the ice rink*).
- Tell students they are going to listen to and read the story. Ask them to look at the pictures and to follow the story as they listen.
- Play the recording once and ask students what time the magic globe took the children home (*4 o'clock*).
- Assign the roles of Kristie, Mikey, Adam and Diana to different students and ask them to read the story out loud. Time permitting, repeat until all students have had a turn.
- As a class, ask students the questions below to check their understanding of the episode.
  1 Where did Mikey meet Diana before? (*at Sonia's party*)
  2 What was Mikey wearing at the party? (*a black T-shirt with a skateboard on it*)
  3 Who needs to take up a new hobby? (*Adam*)
  4 What does Kristie suggest she and Adam should do? (*practise a bit more*)
  5 What's on TV? (*an ice-skating competition*)

> **Teaching Tip**
> When students read the cartoon episodes out loud, ask them to listen to how each person speaks in the recording and to copy it the best they can. This will improve their intonation and help them remember useful chunks of language that they can reproduce later.

Comprehension

2
- Ask students to read sentences 1 to 5 so they know what information to look for when they read the cartoon story again. Ask them to choose the correct words to complete the sentences.

- Ask students to do the task individually, but check the answers as a class. Encourage students to explain their answer choices by giving evidence from the story.

Answers
1 party ('*Did we meet at Sonia's party last Saturday?' 'I think so.'*)
2 Ian (*You were dancing with Ian.*)
3 bad at (*I give up. I need to take up a new hobby!*)
4 Adam (*I asked the globe to bring us back at four o'clock.*)
5 skating (*It's better to skate than watch other people do it!*)

Vocabulary

3
- Ask students to look at the words in the wordbank. Remind them that all the words are from the cartoon story on page 28 and point out that they already know the meaning of them. Check understanding of one or two of the words again if you think it's necessary.
- Ask students to do the task individually, but check the answers as a class. Correct their pronunciation where necessary.

Answers
1	practise	4	brilliant
2	way	5	fault
3	competition	6	skater

4
- Tell students to read the words in the wordbank and the gapped sentences. Explain that the words in the wordbank are all phrasal verbs (verbs made up of a verb and a preposition).
- Ask them to complete the exercise individually but check the answers as a class.

Answers
1	give up	4	Keep on
2	take up	5	go off
3	try out		

Grammar

Past Continuous

- Read the uses of the Past Continuous in the grammar box and ask students to read the example sentences with you. Explain the grammar terms used if necessary.
- Remind students of the spelling changes we make for the –*ing* form. Elicit or explain that verbs with one syllable that end in a vowel and a consonant, like *run*, double the consonant in the –*ing* form (*running*), that verbs that end in –*e*, like *take*, drop the –*e* in the –*ing* form (*taking*).
- Ask students to look back at the cartoon to find examples of the Past Continuous and to underline them (*were dancing, were you wearing, wasn't looking, were practising, were skating, were having, wasn't thinking*).

- Read through the time expressions and explain that we can put them at the beginning or end of the sentence. Refer students back to the first and second example sentences at the top of the grammar box.

5

- Ask students to read each sentence and to find the subject of each missing verb. Remind them that the subjects will help them decide on the correct form of the Past Continuous each time. Remind students to pay attention to the spelling rules for the *–ing* forms when completing the sentences.
- Ask students to do the task individually, but check the answers as a class.

Answers
1 were not / weren't surfing
2 was studying
3 was wearing
4 was raining
5 were not / weren't having

6

- Ask students to look at the picture to see what the people were doing. Ask them to read the prompts in question 1 and to tell you whether the subjects are singular or plural (*singular*) and which word the verb is (*read*). Ask them to tell you the question and then ask whether the short answer will begin with *Yes* or *No* (*Yes*).
- Ask a student to come up and write the first question and short answer on the board, then ask the class whether the example on the board is correct or not. Make any corrections necessary on the board.
- Ask students to do the rest of the task individually and then to swap books with a partner to check each other's answers. Check the answers as a class, correcting intonation patterns where necessary.

Answers
1 Was the boy reading a book? Yes, he was.
2 Were the girls playing tennis? No, they weren't.
3 Was Mum listening to the radio? No, she wasn't.
4 Was Dad drinking juice? No, he wasn't.

Listening

7

- Explain to students that they are going to listen to two friends talking about what they were doing yesterday evening. Ask students to read sentences 1 to 5 quickly to find out which people are mentioned in each one (*Annabel, Annabel / her dad, Sandy, Annabel / her family, Larry*). Ask them to underline the verbs and any time expressions in the sentences. Explain that they need to pay attention to which person is speaking and whether they are talking about what they were doing or what another person was doing as they listen.
- Ask students to read through all of the sentences again and remind them that they have to write *T* if the sentence is correct and *F* if it is incorrect.

- Play the recording to the end and ask students to compare their answers with a partner. Ask them to justify any answers that are different. Play the recording a second time and ask them to check their answers or fill in any missing information.
- Check the answers as a class and make sure students can justify their answers.

Turn to page 127 of the Teacher's Guide for the recording script.

Answers
1 T (*I had a great evening yesterday.*)
2 F (*... from six o'clock till seven I was listening to my favourite show, Hot Hits, on the radio ... At the same time I was helping Dad with dinner.*)
3 F (*... but I wasn't listening to the radio last night. I was out with my mum ...*)
4 T (*At seven I had dinner with my parents and my brother Toby.*)
5 F (*... my cousin Larry arrived. We were trying out my new computer game ...*)

Speaking

8

- Explain that students are going to work in pairs to ask and answer questions about things people were doing at different times in the past.
- Remind students that we use the Past Continuous to talk about things that were happening at a particular time in the past, and tell them to use this tense to answer the questions.
- Read through the *Express yourself!* box with students. Explain that this box provides useful language that will help them complete the Speaking task. Give one or two example sentences, talking about when you did the things in the list. When students are confident with the language, they can do the task in their pairs.
- Go round the class monitoring students to make sure they are carrying out the task properly. Don't correct any mistakes at this stage, but make a note of any mistakes in structure and pronunciation.
- Ask each pair to ask and answer one of the questions and repeat until each pair has had a turn.
- Write any structural mistakes that students made on the board, without saying who made them, and ask them to correct them. Deal with any problems in pronunciation.

Answers
Students' own answers

Extra Class Activity

Encourage every student to speak in class by playing a quick game. Hold up an object from your desk, for example, a ruler or a rolled up piece of paper. Look at one student and ask *What were you doing at 7 o'clock last night?* and hand the object to the student. Explain that the student with the object should answer the question and then give the object to somebody else while asking a question with a different time expression. Each student in turn has ➥

to answer the question and pass on the object to the next person, asking *What were you doing on / at …?* with a different time expression until every student has had a chance to ask and answer.

Extra Writing Task 3

- Make sure each student has a copy of Extra Writing Task 3 that can be found on the *Resource CD-ROM*.
- Explain to students that they are going to write six sentences about what they were doing at specific times yesterday. Write these times on the board (if students are doing the task for homework, ask them to make a note of these times): *seven o'clock in the morning; nine o'clock in the morning; twelve o'clock; three o'clock in the afternoon; seven o'clock in the evening; eleven o'clock at night.*
- Ask students to write their sentences in their notebooks, using the past continuous. If they can't remember what they were doing, encourage them to use their imagination. You could set this task for homework if you are short of time.
- If time allows, ask each student to read one of their sentences to the class.

Extra Task (for early finishers)

See photocopiable material that can be found on the *Resource CD-ROM*.

Lesson 2

Objectives

Reading	information leaflet – missing sentences
Vocabulary	text-related words; adjectives with –ed or –ing
Grammar	past simple and past continuous
Listening	labelling a picture
Sounds of English	pronunciation of e

Way in

- Check students' spelling of the words they learnt in Lesson 1 by asking them to come and write the following words on the board: *brilliant, competition, fault, practise, skater.*
- Ask students which words we use to make the Past Continuous affirmative (*was / were + –ing* form of main verb). Ask them which time expressions we use with Past Continuous (*all day yesterday, all morning, at 3 o'clock, last Thursday, last year, this morning, at this time last week / year, from three o'clock till four*) and then ask them to give one example of the affirmative, negative and question forms, using different time expressions. Make sure they remember that the short answers end with *was / were* or *wasn't / weren't* without the main verb.

- Ask students to work in pairs to make sentences with the phrasal verbs *go off, give up, try out, keep on* and *take up.* Ask each pair to read one of their sentences to the rest of the class until each pair has had the chance to speak and they have used all the phrasal verbs. Correct their answers where necessary.

Reading

1

- Tell students they are going to listen to and read the information leaflet. Ask them to follow the text as they listen.
- Play the recording once. Ask students to tell you one fact they learned from the information leaflet that they didn't know before.
- Ask students to read the pre-reading question and to find the answer in the article.

Answer
a pair of snowshoes

2

- Please follow the procedure outlined in Unit 1, Lesson 2 on page 15 of this Teacher's Guide.

Answers
snowshoeing – *a sport involving walking on snow wearing snowshoes*
activity – *an action, often energetic*
entertaining – *having the ability to entertain*
nervous – *scared*
putting on – *getting dressed with*
sliding – *moving on a slippery surface*
hill – *small mountain*
stepping – *putting a foot onto*

Did you know?

- Ask students to read the information in the *Did you know?* feature and ask if they can think of other animals that can move easily on snow or ice (*polar bears, penguins*, etc).
- If students are interested, give them more information on snowshoeing using the Background Information box below.

Background Information
Snowshoeing is a very safe form of exercise. About 12% of people who snowshoe are children aged 7–17. The sport uses every muscle group in our bodies, so although it's safe, it also burns a lot of calories and helps us to get fit. Although snowshoeing is a new sport, snowshoes have been in use for 6,000 years and were one of the first forms of transport. For further information, go to www.nationalgeographic.com and search for 'snowshoeing'.

Comprehension

3

- Ask students to read the sentences and to complete the leaflet. Once they have finished, tell them to read back through the text to make sure that they have chosen the correct sentences.
- Ask students to do the task individually, but check the answers as a class.
- Explain any vocabulary students don't know and correct their pronunciation where necessary.

Answer
1d 2c 3b 4a

> **Teaching Tip**
> When students are doing missing-sentence tasks, remind them to look for clues that will help them place the sentences correctly. For example, they should look for patterns in structure or meaning. In this task, the sentence before gaps 1 and 2 are both questions, so they should look at the sentence options to find suitable answers. Another kind of clue is subject pronouns. In this task, sentence b is in the first person (*I*) and so are the sentences before and after gap 3.

Vocabulary

4

- Ask students to read through the sentences and explain that they are definitions and that students have to write the missing letters to complete the word for the meaning each time. Point out that the first letter is given.
- Explain that the words in the exercise appear in the information leaflet.
- Ask students to do the task individually, but check the answers as a class.

Answer
1 snowshoeing   4 entertaining
2 hill   5 activity
3 nervous

5

- Ask students to look at the information leaflet on page 30 and to find the words *exciting* and *entertaining*. Write them on the board and next to them write *entertained* and *excited*. Ask them which adjectives tells us how somebody feels (*excited, entertained*) and which are about something that causes somebody to feel a particular way (*exciting, entertaining*).
- Explain to students that adjectives ending in *–ed* are used to describe how someone feels and that adjectives ending in *–ing* are used to describe something that makes someone feel a particular way. Ask students to complete the first pair of sentences and check that they understand the difference in meaning between.
- Ask students to do the rest of the task individually, but check the answers as a class.

Answer
1 bored   4 excited
2 relaxed   5 interesting
3 tiring

Grammar

Past Simple and Past Continuous

- Read the rules in the grammar box for using the Past Simple and the Past Continuous and ask students to read the example sentences with you. Explain all the grammar terms used if necessary.
- Explain that we often use *when* before the Past Simple because this talks about a specific time. Then explain that we often use *while* before the Past Continuous because this talks about a period of time when an action was still in progress.

6

- Ask students to read sentences 1 to 5 to see what it is about and to find the subject in each one. Explain that each sentence should have one verb in the Past Simple and one verb in the Past Continuous. Ask them to decide whether the verb in brackets is an action which interrupted another action or if it is an action that was happening before and up to a particular time in the past. Remind them to think about what words they need to form the Past Continuous and to look at the list of irregular verbs on pages 132 and 133 to find the Past Simple forms if necessary.
- Explain that the answers include affirmative, negative and question forms.
- Ask students to do the task individually, but check the answers as a class.

Answer
1 were you doing, called
2 was sliding, saw
3 got, was swimming
4 was walking, started
5 rang, was writing

Listening

7

- Before listening to the recording, ask students to work in pairs. Assign each pair to one of the people in the picture and ask them to describe what they were doing using words they have learnt so far.
- Give each pair a few minutes on their own to talk about their person and then ask them to tell the class. Don't correct any mistakes they make, but make a note of them to pick up on after they listen to the recording.
- Explain to students that they are going to listen to a child talking about things that some family members and friends were doing in the park on a rainy day. Ask students to look at the list of names above the picture and to tell you which are boys' names and which are girls' names. Ask them to listen to the recording and write the names in the correct boxes.

- Play the recording all the way through again asking students to check their answers and to complete any missing information.

Turn to page 127 of this Teacher's Guide for the recording script.

Answers

(Names on the picture from the top down)

Lucy	(... *Mark, was sliding down a hill with his friend Lucy.*)
Adam	(*My cousin Adam was showing off and he fell in the water.*)
Mark	(... *Mark, was sliding down a hill with his friend Lucy.*)
Daisy	(... *Daisy was riding her bike.*)
Tommy	(*There he is, under the tree.*)

Sounds of English

8

- Ask students to work in pairs to say the words to each other and to note the difference in the sound of the vowel when the –e comes at the end of the word. Explain the meaning of any new vocabulary where necessary.
- Read out each pair of words to the class stressing the sounds of letters in red and ask students if they were right. Then read the words once more and ask students to say them with you.

Answers

The *i* in *Tim* is pronounced /ɪ/, but in *time* it's pronounced /aɪ/.
The *u* in *tub* is pronounced /ʌ/, but in *tube* it's pronounced /uː/.
The *a* in *hat* is pronounced /æ/, but in *hate* it's pronounced /eɪ/.

9

- Ask students to work in pairs to say the words to each other.
- Ask students to listen to the recording to see if their pronunciation was right. Play the recording again, stopping after each pair of words for students to check their answers. Explain the meaning of any new vocabulary where necessary.
- Play the recording once more without stopping and ask students to repeat the words as a class.

Extra Class Activity

To help students with pronunciation, write a limerick with students using words with the different sounds from the *Sounds of English* tasks. Write on the board: *There was a young boy called Tim.* and *There was a young girl called Kate.* Tell students to choose one of the sentences to begin their limerick. Help them write four more lines to complete the limerick. Then them that the second and fifth line should end with a word that rhymes with *Tim* or *Kate* and that the last word in the third and fourth lines must rhyme with each other.

Extra Task (for early finishers)

See photocopiable material that can be found on the *Resource CD-ROM*.

Lesson 3

Objectives

Reading	interview – multiple choice
Express yourself!	talking about free time
Grammar	used to
Writing	writing stories with the Past Simple and Past Continuous; writing a story about something that happened in your free time

Way in

- Write on the board:
  - Kate is *exciting* today.
  - Mark's going to watch an *excited* film.

  Ask students what is wrong with each sentence and ask one to come up and make the corrections on the board. Then read out the other adjectives ending in –ing and –ed from Lesson 2 and ask students to tell you which ones describe how people feel and which ones describe something that causes them to feel a certain way.

- Ask students what connecting words we often use before the Past Simple (*when*) and before the Past Continuous (*while*). Make sure they remember which tense to use for each action when they talk about one action interrupted by another or tell a story.

- Write *fin – fine, hat – hate, tub – tube* on the board and ask students at random to say each pair. Correct pronunciation if necessary.

Reading

1

- Ask students to look at the picture of the girl on page 32 and the title of the interview and to tell you what they think it might be about.

- Tell students that they are going to listen to and read an interview with a teenage girl called Anna. Then ask students to read the interview on their own to find out how old Anna was when she took up tennis (*nine*).

- Play the recording and ask students to listen and follow in their books.

Comprehension

2

- Ask students to read questions 1 to 4 before they read the interview again so that they know what information to look for. Ask them to scan the text to find the answers and to underline the information in the interview that helps them find the answers.

- Ask students to do the task individually, but check the answers as a class.

- Explain any vocabulary that students don't know.

Answers

1 a (*Now that I'm fourteen, ...*)
2 b (*... I was really sad when I gave it up.*)
3 a (*I used to listen to music for about two hours every day.*)
4 c (*I still have dance lessons twice a week.*)

Extra Class Activity

Ask the following extra questions to check students' understanding of the dialogue.

1 Where did Anna train for tennis? (*at the local sports centre*)
2 What does Anna have less of now? (*free time*)
3 When does she listen to music now? (*when she is on the school bus*)
4 How old was Anna when she started dance classes? (*eight*)

Express yourself!

Talking about free time

- Read the structures in *Talking about free time* to the class and ask students to read the example sentences with you. Correct their intonation pattern if necessary. Draw their attention to the use of the gerund after the verbs *like, love, hate, can't stand, start* and *stop*.

3

- Ask students to work in pairs to ask and answer questions about their free time activities. Explain that the activities in the box are examples and that they can talk about these and any other activities that they do. Remind students to practise the language shown.
- To finish ask each pair to tell the class about what they do in their free time.

Answers

Students' own answers

Let's Talk

Invite individual students to come to the front of the class to answer questions about what they do in their free time; the rest of the students ask questions. Time permitting, allow as many students as possible to have a turn at answering.

Grammar

Used to

- Read the uses of *used to* in the grammar box and ask students to read the example sentences with you. Explain the grammar terms used if necessary. Draw students' attention to the fact that the forms of *used to* are the same for all subjects.
- Write the following words on the board:
  - go swimming
  - play chess

Ask students how to make affirmative and negative sentences with *used to*. Write the answers as students say them.

- Draw students' attention to the fact that we take off the *–d* from *used to* to make the negative and question forms.

Teaching Tip

Hold students' attention when you are explaining grammar rules by giving examples from real-life situations. Tell them about funny situations that you have experienced in the past or strange things that somebody you know used to do.

4

- Ask students to look at the first picture and to read the first prompt. Explain that they have to write a sentence about Dan and whether he used to be good at maths or not. Ask a student to tell you the answer and to write it on the board.
- Ask students to do the rest of the task individually and then to swap books with a partner to check each other's answers. Check the answers as a class correcting pronunciation and stress where necessary.

Answers

1 Dan didn't use to be good at maths.
2 Dan used to collect insects.
3 Dan used to read comics.
4 Dan didn't use to have his own bedroom.

Writing

Writing Stories

5

- Tell students to close their books, and then ask them which tense we use after *when* (*Past Simple*) and *while* (*Past Continuous*). Then ask them which word we use to link two halves of a sentence to talk about two actions that were happening at the same time (*and*).

6

- Ask students to read through the sentences and decide which tenses are correct in each gap. Remind them to use the examples in *Writing 5* to help them.
- Ask students to do the task individually, but check the answers as a class.

Answers

1 fell
2 was reading
3 were skating

7

- Ask students to read through the story and decide which words complete it correctly. Explain any words students don't understand.
- Ask students to do the task individually, but check the answers as a class.

Answers

1	while	4	When
2	and	5	When
3	While	6	and

Task

8

- Ask students to work in pairs to discuss ideas about something that happened in their free time which they can write about. Point out that this is a story so they can use their imagination and write about something that didn't really happen if they like.
- Make sure students understand the paragraph plan on page 33. Remind them that each paragraph adds a different piece of information to the description to make it easy to follow.
- Ask students to use the plan to write a story like the one in *Writing 7*. Remind students that they should use *and, when* and *while* with the correct verb tenses.
- Alternatively, you could assign this task as homework.

Example answer

Last month, I was riding my bike in the park when I saw a lot of people. They were watching a funny game of chess.

The chess pieces in the game were people. They were wearing special clothes while they were moving around like chess pieces on a huge chess board. Suddenly, the game finished when the black team caught the white team's king.

While the players were walking off the board, they were asking children to come and play chess. I used to play chess, but I didn't want to wear silly clothes! One hour later, I was wearing the king's clothes when my team won the game. It was really exciting and I had a great time.

9

- Ask students to read back through their stories to make sure that they have used *and, when* and *while* correctly. If you ask them to write the story for homework, then give them a few minutes to do this at the beginning of the next lesson.

Extra Task (for early finishers)

See photocopiable material that can be found on the *Resource CD-ROM*.

Food and Drink

Way in

- If you assigned Unit 3, Lesson 3 *Writing 8* for homework, then give students a few minutes to proofread their stories to check they've used *and*, *when* and *while* correctly with the Past Simple and Past Continuous. Then ask them to read each other's stories, or stick them on the wall so they can read them when they have time.
- Ask students to tell you about something they *used to* do and something they *didn't use to* do. Get different students to write the affirmative and negative answers on the board and ask the rest of the class whether they are correct. If necessary, correct students' examples.
- Tell students that this unit is about food and drink. Elicit the words for meals which they have learnt already (*breakfast*, *lunch*, *dinner*). Briefly ask some students what their favourite food is and what they like to drink.

Did you know?

- With books closed, ask students to brainstorm different fruits. Write their suggestions on the board. Have a quick class survey to find the most popular three fruits.
- Ask students to open their books at pages 34 and 35. Ask them to look at the picture and see if they know the names of any of the fruits in the picture. They may only recognise the baby tomatoes – explain that there are hundreds of different varieties of fruit and that each country only grows a small selection.
- Ask students to read the paragraph about different fruits on page 35. Explain that different fruits grow in different countries, according to the climate. Citrus fruits like oranges and lemons, for example, grow in hot countries.
- Read the information from the *Did you know?* feature to the class. Ask students if they knew tomatoes were a fruit.
- Use the background information in the box below to give the students further information about unusual fruits if they are interested. Check if they have any questions. If they ask for information you don't have, refer them to the website in the Background Information box and ask them to feed back to you at the next lesson.

Background Information
The picture shows a variety of exotic fruits. Here are some fun facts about fruit: strawberries are the only fruit to have their seeds on the outside; banana plants can grow an inch or more while you are sleeping at night; the juiciest, tastiest oranges in the world are grown in Florida; there are 7,000 different types of apple in the world; dried fruits are just as good for you as fresh fruits; you should try to eat five portions ➡

of fruit or vegetables every day; fruit with lots of vitamin C, like oranges, will help cuts to heal faster. For further information, go to www.nationalgeographic.com and search for 'fruit'.

Let's Talk
Put students into small groups. Ask them to talk about their favourite fruit. They should start by describing the fruit; the others in the group try to guess what it is.

Lesson 1

Objectives

Reading	the cartoon story – true or false
Vocabulary	text-related phrases; matching statements about food & drink
Grammar	much, many; a lot of, lots of, a few, a little
Listening	completing a dialogue
Speaking	practising a dialogue; role-playing going shopping for food

- Ask students if they can remember what happened in the previous episode of the cartoon story (*The children were at the ice rink, where Mikey was talking to Diana. Mikey had met Diana at Sonia's party the Saturday before and he liked her. But the magic globe took the children away from the ice rink and back home because Adam wanted to watch a skating competition on TV.*).
- Ask students to look at the story pictures and suggest what might be happening.

The cartoon story
1
- Explain that students are going to listen to the words in the wordbank. Play the recording and ask them to point to each word as they hear it.
- Play the recording again and encourage students to repeat as a class. You could ask individual students to repeat on their own if you feel they are confident enough.
- Put the students in pairs and ask them to find the words in the story and underline them. When they have all found the words, work through them one at a time as a class, asking students to read out the sentences in the story containing the word. Ask students to say what the word means. If they don't know, encourage them to guess from the context.

2
- Depending on whether you are using the DVD or the Audio CD, follow the relevant instructions.

For teachers using the DVD

- Make sure each child has a copy of Cartoon DVD Worksheet 4 that can be found on the *Resource CD-ROM*.
- Please follow the procedure outlined in Unit 1, Lesson 1 on page 12 of this Teacher's Guide for teachers using the DVD.

Before you watch

Answers
1 a laptop
2 Accept any logical answers based on what students see in the pictures.

While you watch

Answers
a1 b2 c3

After you watch

Answers
1 a recipe
2 exotic (chicken)
3 lemon juice / a bottle of lemon juice
4 China
5 Mikey
6 exotic chicken and kumquat marmalade

For teachers using the Audio CD

- Tell students to look at page 36 of their student's book and to work in pairs. Ask students to say who falls out of a tree (*Mikey*).
- Tell students they are going to listen to and read the story. Ask them to look at the pictures and to follow the story as they listen.
- Play the recording once and ask students which country the children went to (*China*).
- Assign the roles of Mikey, Adam and Kristie to different students and ask them to read the story out loud. Time permitting, repeat until all students have had a turn.
- As a class, ask students the questions below to check their understanding of the episode.
  1 Who wants to cook a surprise dinner? (*Kristie*)
  2 What recipe does Adam suggest? (*prawn noodles*)
  3 How many chicken legs do they need? (*six*)
  4 Have they got much lemon juice? (*No, they haven't.*)
  5 What does Mum love? (*marmalade / exotic food*)

Comprehension

3

- Ask students to read sentences 1 to 6 so they know what information to look for when they read the cartoon story again. Ask them to choose the correct words to complete the sentences.

- Ask students to do the task individually, but check the answers as a class. Encourage students to explain their answer choices by giving evidence from the story.

Answers
1 T (*I want to cook a surprise birthday dinner for Mum today.*)
2 T (*We need six chicken legs ...*)
3 T (*Let's use oranges, then.*)
4 F (*What are kumquats?*)
5 T (*They look like mini oranges ...*)
6 F (*We only need a few, Mikey.*)

Vocabulary

4

- Explain that all the words the students have to find appear in the cartoon episode. Point out that the first letter of each word is given.
- Ask students to do the task individually, but check the answers as a class.

Answers
1 onion   4 prawn
2 marmalade   5 exotic
3 recipe

5

- Explain that sentences a to e are all things we say in relation to food and drink. Explain any words students don't understand.
- Ask them to read sentences 1 to 5 and to match them with sentences a to e.
- Ask students to do the task in pairs to encourage discussion, but check the answers as a class.

Answers
1c 2e 3a 4d 5b

Grammar

Much, Many

- Read the grammar box to the class and ask students to read the example sentences with you. Write *much apples* and *How many money?* on the board, and ask students why *much* and *many* in these examples are wrong (*apples* is a countable noun and *money* is an uncountable noun).
- Draw students' attention to the use of *How much ...?* to ask about prices.

6

- Ask students to read the sentences and to find and underline the noun that the answer describes or asks about in each sentence. Tell them to see whether each noun is countable or uncountable to help them decide which word is correct.
- Ask students to do the task individually, but check the answers as a class.

Answers

1	many	4	many
2	much	5	much
3	much	6	many

A lot of, Lots of, A few, A little

- Read the grammar box to the class and ask students to read the example sentences with you. Explain that *a lot of* and *lots of* mean a large number or amount of something, and that *a few* means *some* and *a little* means a small amount.

7

- Ask students to read the sentences to decide which words fit the meaning of each sentence. Tell them to see whether the words after each gap are countable or uncountable and to decide whether the meaning is affirmative or negative.
- Ask students to do the task individually, but check the answers as a class.

Answers

1	a lot of	4	a lot of
2	a few	5	a little
3	a little		

Let's Talk

Put students into pairs. They take turns to say sentences to each other about things in their kitchen, using the words from *Grammar 6* and *7*.

Listening

8

- Explain to students that they are going to listen to a shopkeeper talking to a woman who is shopping. Explain that they will write words they learnt in the grammar tasks to complete the dialogue. Give students a few minutes to read the dialogue and then ask them what kinds of nouns come after each gap from 1 to 5 (1 *plural countable*, 2 *uncountable*, 3 *uncountable*, 4 *plural countable*, 5 *plural countable*). Then ask them what kind of information question 6 is about (*price*).
- Play the recording to the end and ask students to fill in their answers. Ask them to work with a partner to check their answers and to justify any answers they have that are different.
- Play the recording again and ask students to check their answers and to fill in any missing information.

Turn to page 127 for the recording script.

Answers

1 a few
2 a lot of
3 a little
4 a few
5 How many
6 How much

Speaking

9

- Explain that students are going to work in pairs to practise the dialogue from the *Listening* task, and then to make their own similar dialogue using the words given.
- Remind students of the words that they learnt to describe or ask questions about quantities and tell them to use them when answering the questions.
- Read through the *Express yourself!* box with students. Explain that this box provides useful language that will help them complete the Speaking task. Give one or two example sentences, talking about when you did the things in the list. When students are confident with the language, they can do the task in their pairs.
- Go round the class monitoring students to make sure they are carrying out the task properly. Don't correct any mistakes at this stage, but make a note of any mistakes in structure and pronunciation.
- As a class, ask each pair to say their dialogue until each pair has had a turn.
- Write any mistakes that you heard on the board, without saying who made them, and ask students to correct them. Deal with any problems in pronunciation.

Answers

Students' own answers

Teaching Tip

Always keep a low profile as you go around the room and don't stand close to any one pair longer than others. Students may feel self-conscious and embarrassed about speaking together in English if they notice you monitoring them.

Extra Writing Task 4

- Make sure each student has a copy of Extra Writing Task 4 that can be found on the *Resource CD-ROM*.
- Explain to students that they are going to write a short dialogue about shopping. Ask students to look back at the dialogue in the previous speaking exercise. Encourage them to use the phrases from the *Express yourself!* box in their dialogues. Remind them to use phrases like *How much* and *How many* as well as words like *few, little* and *lot*.
- Ask students to write their dialogues in their notebooks. You could set this task for homework if you are short of time.
- If time allows, invite some students to choose a partner and to read out their dialogues to the class.

Extra Task (for early finishers)

See photocopiable material that can be found on the *Resource CD-ROM*.

Lesson 2

Objectives

Reading	article – completing sentences
Vocabulary	text-related words; cooking-related verbs
Grammar	some, any, every, no; some–, any–, every– and no– with –body, –thing, –where
Listening	numbering pictures

Way in

- Read out the sentences from *Vocabulary 5* in Lesson 1 and elicit the correct responses from students.
- Write *much, many, a few, a lot of, lots of, a little* on the board and ask students to make a sentence for each. You can then invite students at random to come and write one of their sentences on the board.

Reading

1

- Explain that students are going to listen to the words in the wordbank. Play the recording and ask them to point to each word as they hear it.
- Play the recording again and encourage students to repeat as a class. You could ask individual students to repeat on their own if you feel they are confident enough.
- Put the students in pairs and ask them to find the words in the article. When they have all found the words, work through them one at a time as a class, asking students to read out the sentences in the article containing the word. Ask students to say what the word means. If they don't know, encourage them to guess from the context.

2

- Tell students they are going to listen to and read the article. Ask them to follow the article as they listen.
- Play the recording once. Ask students to tell you one fact they learned from the article that they didn't know before.
- Ask students to read the pre-reading question and to find the answer in the article.

> **Answer**
> Because he believed it could bring power to anyone drinking it.

Did you know?

- Ask students to read the information in the *Did you know?* feature and ask them to share their opinions about chocolate.
- If students are interested, give them more information about chocolate using the Background Information box below.

> **Background Information**
> Here are some fun facts about chocolate: a single chocolate chip provides enough energy for an adult to walk about 50 metres; there are ingredients in chocolate that increase brain power and function; the biggest thing ever made from chocolate was an Easter egg weighing almost 2,000 kilograms and it was more than 2 metres tall – it was made in Melbourne, Australia. For further information, go to www.nationalgeographic.com and search for 'chocolate'.

> **Let's Talk**
> Put students into small groups. Ask them to talk about foods they think are good for you and foods they think are bad for you.

Comprehension

3

- Ask students to read sentences 1 to 5 so that they know what information to look for when reading the text again.
- Ask students to read the text again to find the words to complete the sentences.
- Explain any vocabulary students don't know and correct their pronunciation if necessary.

> **Answers**
> 1 bitter
> 2 cocoa beans
> 3 emperor
> 4 Europe
> 5 relaxed, calm and happy

Vocabulary

4

- Explain that the words in the wordbank appear in the article. Ask students to find the words in the text and to underline them. Explain any words again if necessary.
- Ask students to do the task individually, but check the answers as a class.

> **Answers**
> | | | | |
> |---|---|---|---|
> | 1 | emperor | 4 | add |
> | 2 | bitter | 5 | bar |
> | 3 | luxury | | |

5

- Ask students to work in pairs to look at pictures 1 to 6 and explain that each picture shows the meaning of the sentence with the same number. Ask them to read the sentences and decide which words fit the meaning. Explain that they should use the verbs in the same form as shown in the wordbank.
- Check the answers as a class and explain the meanings of any verbs which students have not already been taught.

Answers

1	Chop	4	Add
2	Fry	5	Mix
3	Boil	6	Slice

Let's Talk

Put students into pairs. Ask them to talk about recipes, using the words from the exercise.

Grammar

Some, Any, Every, No

- Read the uses of *some*, *any*, *every* and *no* in the grammar box and ask students to read the example sentences with you. Explain all the grammar terms used, if necessary.

6

- Ask students to read the sentences to decide which words fit the meaning. Tell them to see whether the meaning is affirmative, negative or a question.
- Explain that students must use *some*, *any*, *every* and *no* at least once. Remind them that *no* has a negative meaning but is used with the affirmative verb form.
- Ask students to do the task individually, but check the answers as a class.

Answers

1	no	4	no
2	every	5	any
3	some		

Some–, Any–, Every–, and No– with –body, –thing and –where

- Read the rules in the grammar box and ask students to read the example sentences with you. Explain that when we use *nobody*, *nothing* or *nowhere* we use an affirmative verb but the meaning of the sentence is negative.

7

- Explain that 1 to 5 are the first halves of sentences and that students have to match them with the second halves a to e to make complete sentences. Point out that a to e begins with a word from the grammar box. Tell them to see whether the first half of the sentence is affirmative or negative as this may help them to find the correct answers.
- Ask students to do the task individually, but check the answers as a class.

Answers

1e 2d 3a 4c 5b

Extra Class Activity

Ask students to work in pairs to write four sentences like the ones in *Grammar 7*. Tell them to include words beginning with *some–*, *any–*, *every–* and *no–* in the middle of their sentences. Then give each pair ➡

a sheet of paper and tell them to write the first halves of their sentences on the left and number them 1 to 4, and to mix up the order of the second halves and label them a to d to make a matching task. Tell students to swap their sentences with another pair and then see if they can find the answers.

Listening

8

- Ask students to look at pictures a to f and decide what they show and which words from *Vocabulary 5* they think will describe the pictures.
- Explain to students that they are going to hear a recipe and that they are going to note down the order in which they hear each instruction. Tell students that they have to listen for the words that talk about the things in the pictures and they also have to listen for words that tell them what to do with each thing.
- Ask students to listen to the recording and to number the pictures. Remind students to number each picture as they hear about them rather than trying to find the answers from a to f respectively.
- Play the recording again and ask students to check their answers and to complete any missing information.
- Check the answers as a class and make sure students can justify their answers.

Turn to page 127 of this Teacher's Guide for the recording script.

Answers

a 4 (*… add a tin of tomatoes to the onions …*)
b 5 (*… add the spaghetti to the sauce and mix together.*)
c 3 (*… chop an onion …*)
d 6 (*Add lots of cheese …*)
e 1 (*First, boil some water in a pan.*)
f 2 (*… add a packet of spaghetti and boil …*)

Extra Task (for early finishers)

See photocopiable material that can be found on the *Resource CD-ROM*.

Lesson 3

Objectives

Reading	webpage – circling the correct words
Express yourself!	making suggestions for dinner; agreeing or disagreeing
Listening	completing a table
Speaking	describing what people think of food
Sounds of English	pronunciation of /ɪː/
Writing	letters and emails; opening and closing phrases; writing an email with a recipe

Way in

- Ask students to tell you the verbs they learnt that explain how to make food in Lesson 2, *Vocabulary 5*. Ask different students at random to come up and write a word on the board and then ask the rest of the class if the spelling is correct.
- Ask students if they use computers and, if so, what they use them for. Ask them if they know what a webpage is (*a page of information which is part of a website*) and what kind of webpages they are interested in.

Reading

1

- Tell students that they are going to listen to and read a webpage that contains a strange recipe. Ask students to read the webpage on their own to find out where you can buy snake meat (*Minnesota*).
- Play the recording and ask students to listen and follow in their books.

Comprehension

2

- Ask students to read through sentences 1 to 5 and the options before they read the text again so that they know what information to look for.
- Explain that both options in questions 1 to 5 appear in the webpage, for example in question 1, the names *Daphne* and *Abbie* are on the webpage, but students have to find out which one sent the recipe. Ask students to underline where they get the answer from in the text so they can justify their answers. Explain any words they don't understand.
- Ask students to do the task individually, but check the answers as a class.

Answers
1 Abbie
2 400g
3 boil
4 mix
5 snake meat

Teaching Tip

Help students develop their reading comprehension skills by drawing their attention to the parts of the text where they found the answers to this task. Point out that in question 1, the clue in the sentences they underlined was a subject pronoun that referred to the correct option. That is, they had to find out that *She* referred to *Abbie* in the previous sentence.

Express yourself!

What's for dinner?

- Read the structures in *What's for dinner?* to the class and ask students to say the example sentences with you. Correct their intonation pattern if necessary. Draw their attention to the use of the gerund after *How about / What about*. Explain that we often begin suggestions with *Would you like…?* because this sounds more polite than *Do you want…?*

3

- Ask students to work in pairs to make two suggestions and to use the model answers to agree or disagree with each other. Remind students to practise the language shown in the box.
- Give students time to practice their suggestions and responses and then ask each pair to make one suggestion and to agree or disagree, until all students have a chance to speak.

Answer
Students' own answers

Listening

4

- Explain to students that they are going to hear a man called Tom talking about what people in his family like and dislike eating. Ask them to look at the table to work out what information they need to listen out for.
- Tell students that they will hear Tom speaking about the people in the order their names appear on the table.
- Play the recording and ask students to write in their answers. Ask them to discuss their answers with a partner and to justify any answers they have that are different.
- Play the recording again and ask students to check their answers and to fill in any missing information.

Turn to page 127 for the recording script.

Answers
Anna   cheese (*… but she hates cheese!*)
Jimmy   honey (*… Jimmy likes honey.*)
Susie   raw carrots (*… Susie, likes raw carrots.*)
Tom   spaghetti (*… I love spaghetti …*)

Speaking

5

- Explain that students are going to work in pairs to talk about what the people in Tom's family think about the food in the *Listening* task.
- Explain the meanings of the adjectives, if necessary, and tell students to use them in their answers where they can.
- Read through the *Express yourself!* box with students. Explain that this box provides useful language that will help them complete the Speaking task. Give one or two example sentences, talking about when you did the things in the list. When students are confident with the language, they can do the task in their pairs.

- Go round the class monitoring students to make sure they are carrying out the task properly. Don't correct any mistakes at this stage, but make a note of any mistakes in structure and pronunciation.
- Ask each pair to ask and answer one of the questions and repeat until each pair has had a turn.
- Write any structural mistakes that students made on the board, without saying who made them, and ask them to correct them. Deal with any problems in pronunciation.

Answers
Students' own answers

Extra Class Activity

Have a class discussion about exotic food. Ask students what exotic food they have eaten. If they have never eaten any, ask them to say what exotic food they have heard of. Ask if there are any foods students would refuse to eat. Are there any exotic foods they would like to try?

Sounds of English

6

- Tell students they are going to listen to several words being spoken. Play the recording once without stopping and ask students what sound the letters in red make. Explain the meaning of any new vocabulary where necessary.
- Play the recording once more without stopping and ask students to repeat the words as a class.

Answer
They all make the sound /iː/.

7

- Tell students they are going to listen to a rhyme.
- Play the recording, stopping after each line so that students can repeat it.
- Play the recording again without stopping and ask students to repeat the rhyme as a class. Then ask students at random to say the rhyme to the rest of the class.

Writing

Letters and Emails

8

- Tell students to look at the phrases and read them through together. Emphasise the fact that we use these phrases when we are writing to somebody we know very well, like friends or family. Explain the meaning of any new vocabulary where necessary.
- Ask students to decide which two phrases we use at or near the beginning of a letter (*Dear ..., How are you?*) and which two we use at or near the end (*Bye for now! Love from ...*).

9

- Ask students to read through the email before they fill in any of the answers. Tell them to use each of the phrases once to complete the email. When they have finished, ask them to read the email again to check it makes sense.
- Ask students to do the task individually, but check the answers as a class.

Answers
1	Dear	3	Bye for now!
2	How are you?	4	Love from

Task

10

- Ask students to work in pairs to discuss ideas for recipes which they can write an email about.
- Make sure students understand the plan on page 41. Explain that they have to answer the questions and use their answers to write an email like the one in *Writing 9*. Remind students that they should use *First, Then, After that* and *Last of all* to show the correct order for the instructions. They should also make sure they use all the useful phrases from *Writing 8*.
- Alternatively, you could assign this task as homework.

Example answer
Dear Daphne,

Hi! How are you? I'm great! I'm sending you a recipe for Fresh Fruit Salad for your website. I hope you like it!

You need:
one apple
one orange
one banana
strawberries
yoghurt

First, chop the apple and banana and put them in a bowl. Then slice up the orange and add it to the apple and banana. After that, wash the strawberries and add them. Last of all, mix the fruit together and put the yoghurt on the top. Enjoy your dessert!

Bye for now!

Love from Ken

11

- Ask students to read back through their emails to make sure that they have used *First, Then, After that* and *Last of all* correctly. They should also have used the phrases from *Writing 8*. If you ask them to write the email for homework, then give them a few minutes to do this at the beginning of the next lesson.

Teaching Tip

Ask students to try out their recipes at home (with appropriate permission and adult supervision, of course) and to bring some of the food they make to the next lesson so they can have a class picnic.

Extra Task (for early finishers)

See photocopiable material that can be found on the *Resource CD-ROM*.

Review 2

Objectives

- To revise vocabulary and grammar from Units 3 and 4
- Project – choosing a menu

Preparing for the review

- Explain to students that the tasks in *Review 2* revise the material they learnt in Units 3 and 4.
- Remind students that they can ask you for help with the exercises or look back at the units if they're not sure about an answer, as the review is not a test.
- Decide how you will carry out the review. You could ask students to do one task at a time and then correct it immediately, or ask students to do all the tasks and then correct them together at the end. If you do all the tasks together, let students know every now and again how much time they have got left to finish the tasks.
- Remind students not to leave any answers blank and to try to find any answers they aren't sure about in the units.
- Revise the vocabulary and grammar as a class before students do the review.

Vocabulary Revision

- Check that students remember the adjectives from Unit 3, Lesson 1 by reading the gapped sentences from *Vocabulary 3* on page 29 and asking students to call out the missing words.
- Ask students what phrasal verbs they remember. Make sure they revise *give up, go off, keep on, take up* and *try out*. Tell them to think of a sentence for each one and write them down in their notebooks.
- Check that students know the difference in meaning between *–ing* and *–ed*. Make sure they know that when we use *–ed* it tells how someone feels and when we use *–ing* it is about something that causes someone to feel a particular way.
- Write the following words on the board:
  - disgusting
  - full
  - thirsty
  - starving
  - delicious

  Ask students to work in pairs to make sentences using the words. Ask students at random to read out one of their sentences. Correct their pronunciation if necessary.
- Write the words *exotic, kumquat, marmalade, recipe* and *shopping list* on the board and ask students to tell you what they mean.
- Write c_ _ _, a _ _, f _ _, b _ _ _, m _ _ and s _ _ _ _ on the board and ask students to complete the words with verbs related to recipes from *Vocabulary 5* on page 39.

Grammar Revision

- Write *I, you, he / she / it* and *we / you / they* one below the other on the board and ask a student to come and write the Past Continuous affirmative forms of *walk* beside the subject pronouns. Ask the other students to help the student who's writing. Then ask individual students at random round the class to tell you the negative forms. Do the same for the question forms and short answers. Then ask students which time expressions we often use with the Past Continuous.
- Write *I was dancing. Mum came home.* on the board and write *when / while* next to them. Ask students which word we can use to join the two sentences. Then ask them to make another sentence using *while* with the Past Continuous and Past Simple.
- Write *I used to play football.* on the board and ask students to tell you the negative and question forms and the short answers.
- Write *much* and *many* on the board and ask students when we use these (*to describe quantities*). Then ask students which of the words we use with countable nouns, such as bananas (*many*) and which we use with uncountable nouns, such as orange juice (*much*). Then write *apples, coffee, doughnuts, eggs, lemonade, milk, money, potatoes, sandwiches* and *tomatoes* on the board and ask students if they should use *many* or *much* before each of the words.
- Write *a lot of / lots of, a few* and *a little* on the board and ask students which words we can use with countable nouns like *apples* (*a lot of / lots of, a few*) and which words we can use with uncountable nouns like *milk* (*a lot of / lots of, a little*).
- Write *some, any, every* and *no* on the board and ask students to come up and write sentences or questions using these words. Make sure they remember which words we can use with affirmative or negative verb forms and in questions. Then ask students what words we can make from *some–, any–, every–* and *no–* to talk about people, things or places.

Vocabulary

1

- Ask students to say each of the words as a class and then individually. Correct their pronunciation if necessary.
- Ask students to go to the first page of stickers at the back of the book and find the stickers for *Review 2*. Tell them to decide which thing each sticker shows and to stick it in the correct box.
- Check that students have put the correct stickers above each word.

2

- Explain to students that they should replace the words in bold with a word that means the same from the wordbank.

Answer
1 brilliant
2 entertaining
3 starving
4 boring
5 awful
6 bitter

3

- Ask students to read the whole sentence and the possible options before choosing the correct answer. After they have completed the exercise tell them to read the sentences again to make sure their answers make sense.

Answers
1a 2b 3c 4b 5b 6c

Grammar

4

- Explain to students that they should read the whole paragraph before trying to write the answers to decide whether to use the Past Simple or the Past Continuous form. Tell them to look for time expressions and to find the subject of each sentence to help them choose the correct form of the verb in brackets.
- Remind students to use the list of irregular verbs on pages 132 and 133 and tell them to look back at the grammar boxes in Unit 3, Lessons 1 and 2 for a reminder if they need to.

Answers

1	was snowing	5	fell
2	went	6	was skating
3	took up	7	were laughing
4	was putting on	8	did

5

- Tell students to look at the nouns in each sentence and to see if the verb is in the affirmative, negative or question form before they circle the answer.
- Tell students to look back at the Unit 4, Lesson 1 grammar boxes for a reminder if they need to.

Answers

1	a few	5	anywhere
2	anything	6	a lot of
3	much	7	somewhere
4	is	8	much

6

- Tell students to look at the verb in each sentence and to check that the verb is formed correctly.
- Tell students to look back at the Unit 3, Lesson 2 grammar box and Unit 3, Lesson 3 *Writing 5* for a reminder if they need to.

Answers
1 X Where were you **going** when you met Charles?
2 X I was getting ready for school **when** the phone rang.
3 X We fell asleep **while** we were waiting for you.
4 ✓
5 X **When** he was sliding down the hill, someone shouted his name.
6 X David was cooking and I **was making** the salad.

7

- Tell students to decide whether the meaning is affirmative, negative or a question or whether the word in bold is about a person, a thing or a place. Point out that sometimes the correct word will begin with a capital letter.
- Tell students to look back at the grammar boxes in Unit 3, Lesson 3 and Unit 4, Lesson 2 for a reminder if they need to.

Answers

1	used	5	anywhere
2	use	6	some
3	Nobody	7	started
4	use to be	8	someone

Project 2

1

- Explain to the students that they are going to do a project about choosing menus for a restaurant. Ask them to say what type of restaurant they are going to write about.
- Point out that students should find photos of the food they are going to have in their restaurant or that they can draw and colour pictures of it.
- Ask students to read the instructions and explain that the menu they write must address these points.
- Read through the example menu with the class.
- Ask students to complete their projects. They can do this in the lesson or for homework.
- When the projects are complete, stick them on the classroom wall.

2

- Invite students to tell the class about their menus.

> **Teaching Tip**
> When checking students' answers to the review tasks, make a note of any problem areas in vocabulary and grammar that they still have. Try to do extra work on these areas so that your students progress well.

Education

Way in

- If you assigned Unit 4, Lesson 3 *Writing 10* for homework, then give students a few minutes to proofread their recipes to check they've ordered the instructions correctly. Then ask them to read each other's recipes, or stick them on the wall so they can read them when they have time.
- If students have brought samples of the food they made using their recipes, as suggested in Unit 4, Lesson 3, ask them to share them with the class. Tell them to go around the class and offer their food to other students saying: *Would you like to try …?* with *some*, *a little* or *a few*. Make sure food is divided into small portions so that there will be enough to go round. Ask them what they think of each other's food and which recipes they would like to try out.
- Tell students that this unit is about education. You can explain that this means helping people to learn, not only by reading books and writing things that the teacher says in school, but also by doing or making things themselves, just as students did when they learnt to make food by following a recipe.

Did you know?

- With books closed, ask students to brainstorm different ways they learn things. They might say things like *at school, from the TV, online, by reading books, from their parents,* etc. Accept all reasonable suggestions and encourage students to say more about their ideas if they can.
- Ask students to open their books at pages 44 and 45. Ask them to look at the picture and see if they can guess what's happening (*the children are spending the night at the museum*). Ask students if they would like to do this. If so, how do they think it would feel to be in a dark museum at night. Encourage them to speculate. Ask them if they would like to stay in the museum in the picture (*the Field Museum of Natural History in Chicago*).
- Ask students to read the paragraph about the museum on page 44. Explain that in some countries, including England, young people are allowed to spend the night in a museum as part of an educational project. Ask students why they think this might help young people learn.
- Read the information from the *Did you know?* feature to the class. Ask students if they can guess how big the biggest dinosaur ever discovered was (*the Argentinosaurus, which is thought to have been 30–35 metres long*).
- Use the background information in the box below to give the students further information about museums in London if they are interested. Check if they have any questions. If they ask for information you don't have, refer them to the website in the Background Information box and ask them to feed back to you at the next lesson.

Background Information

London has 22 national museums and about 200 other museums. The Natural History Museum in London also has a model of a dinosaur, like the museum in Chicago. In London there are more than 70 million other exhibits, collected over 400 years, so it has one of the largest collections in the world. The Science Museum in London has more than 300,000 objects and there are lots of interactive displays to help people understand how science works. The other huge museum in London is the British Museum. There are 70 million objects in this museum and they cover the whole history of human culture. All the museums in London are free. For further information, go to www.nationalgeographic.com and search for 'museums'.

Let's Talk

Put students into small groups. Ask them to talk about why it's important to have places like museums where lots of old objects are kept.

Extra Class Activity

Ask students if they have ever been to a museum. If so, which one and what did they see there? Invite them to share their experiences with the class.

Lesson 1

Objectives

Reading	the cartoon story – open-ended questions
Vocabulary	text-related words; education-related words
Grammar	present perfect simple (affirmative); for, since, already, just, never
Listening	labelling a picture
Speaking	completing sentences about what you have / haven't done; talking about things your partner has / hasn't done

The cartoon story

- Ask students if they can remember what happened in the previous episode of the cartoon story (*Kristie wanted to cook a surprise dinner for her mum so Adam was looking for recipes on the Internet. They chose an exotic recipe and needed kumquats, but the shops didn't have them. So the magic globe took the children to China to get kumquats.*).
- Ask students to look at the story pictures and suggest what might be happening.

1

- Please follow the procedure outlined in Unit 1, Lesson 1 on page 12 of this Teacher's Guide.

Answers
flashing – *a light going on and off*
show – *display or demonstrate something*
real dinosaur – *a dinosaur that's living*
term – *part of the school year*
head teacher – *teacher in charge of the school*
died out – *stopped living*
gigantic – *extremely big*

- Depending on whether you are using the DVD or the Audio CD, follow the relevant instructions.

For teachers using the DVD

- Make sure each child has a copy of Cartoon DVD Worksheet 5 that can be found on the *Resource CD-ROM*.
- Please follow the procedure outlined in Unit 1, Lesson 1 on page 12 of this Teacher's Guide for teachers using the DVD.

Before you watch

Answers
1 in a museum
2 night

While you watch

Answers
1 flashing
2 slept
3 third
4 tyrannosaurus
5 gigantic
6 sharp

After you watch

Answers
1 the globe
2 bad
3 excited about
4 spring
5 the globe
6 friends

For teachers using the Audio CD

- Tell students to look at page 46 of their student's book and to work in pairs. Ask them to look at the pictures and say who is chased by a dinosaur (*Mikey*).
- Tell students they are going to listen to and read the story. Ask them to look at the pictures and to follow the story as they listen.
- Play the recording once and ask students when the tyrannosaurus died out (*65 million years ago*).

- Put students into small groups of three and ask them to assign the roles of Kristie, Adam and Mikey within their groups. Ask them to read the story out loud in their groups.
- As a class, ask students the questions below to check their understanding of the episode.
  1 What is flashing and where is it? (*the magic globe; in Mikey's rucksack*)
  2 Who is excited about sleeping in the museum and who isn't excited? (*Adam is excited; Kristie isn't excited*)
  3 When was Kristie at the museum before? (*at the end of the spring term*)
  4 Whose idea was it to see a real dinosaur? (*Mikey's*)
  5 What has the dinosaur got? (*very sharp teeth*)

Comprehension

2

- Ask students to read sentences 1 to 5 so they know what information to look for when they read the cartoon story again. Ask them to answer the questions using information from the story.
- Ask students to do the task individually, but check the answers as a class. Encourage students to explain their answer choices by giving evidence from the story.

Answers
1 the magic globe (*I've brought the globe with me.*)
2 Mikey (*Maybe it can show us a real dinosaur.*)
3 Kristie (*... it's the third time I've slept in this museum.*)
4 Kristie's head teacher (*The head teacher is mad about dinosaurs!*)
5 tyrannosaurus (*That dinosaur is a tyrannosaurus ...*)

Let's Talk

Put students into small groups. Tell them to imagine the magic globe could take them back in history to see something or someone special. Ask them where they would like to go with the globe. You could do this as a class discussion if you think that will work better with your student group.

Vocabulary

3

- Ask students to look at the words in the wordbank. Remind them that all the words are from the cartoon story on page 46 and point out that they already know the meaning of them. Check understanding of one or two of the words again if you think it's necessary.
- Ask students to do the task individually, but check the answers as a class.

Answers
1 flash
2 die out
3 show
4 real
5 gigantic

4

- Explain that phrases 1 to 6 are the first halves of sentences and that students have to match them with the second halves, a to f, to make complete sentences. Tell them to find the meaning of the first half of each sentence and to decide which phrases fit this meaning.
- Ask students to do the task in pairs to help each other work out the meanings, but check the answers as a class.

Answers
1b 2e 3a 4f 5d 6c

Grammar

Present Perfect Simple (affirmative)

- Read the uses of the Present Perfect Simple in the grammar box with the class and ask students to read the example sentences with you. Write the example *I've just finished my homework.* on the board. Explain that we begin the Present Perfect Simple with *have* when the subject is *I, you, we, they* or a plural noun and with *has* when the subject is *he, she, it* or a singular or uncountable noun. Then explain that we need two words to make the Present Perfect Simple and that the second word is called a *past participle*. Tell students that the past participle in the example is *finished* and explain that for regular verbs, we make the past participle by adding –*ed* to the verb. Ask students to turn to pages 132 and 133 to look at the list of irregular verbs. Explain that they will find the past participles in the third column.
- Ask students to look at the example sentences a, c and d in the grammar box and to tell you the past participles (*gone, been, broken*), then ask students to look at the list again to find the infinitive forms of these verbs (*go, be, break*). Draw students' attention to the difference between *have been* and *have gone*.

5

- Ask students to read each sentence to decide whether the verb in brackets is regular or irregular. Tell them to find out whether the subject is singular or plural to see whether to use *has* or *have*. Tell them to use the list of irregular verbs on pages 132 and 133 to find the past participles of the irregular verbs.
- Ask students to do the task individually, but check the answers as a class.

Answers
1 has finished
2 have learnt
3 have had
4 have done
5 has been

For, Since, Already, Just, Never

- Read the rules in the grammar box and ask students to read the example sentences with you. Explain the meanings where necessary.
- Ask students to look at the example sentences and to tell you which words we can put after *have* and before the past participle (*already, just, never*), which word comes before a period of time (*for*) and which word comes before a particular time in the past (*since*).

6

- Ask students to read through the sentences and options. Tell them to see if the words after the options are past participles, a period of time or a particular time and to compare these with the examples in the grammar box.
- Give students a few minutes to compare their answers with a partner. Ask them to justify their answers if they are different.
- Check the answers as a class and ask students to justify the answers they give.

Answers
1 already
2 for
3 since
4 just
5 never

Extra Class Activity

Ask students to find the irregular verbs from the two grammar boxes and the tasks they have just done. List the verbs on the board as students give their answers.

break	*know*
do	*learn*
go	*meet*
have	*teach*

Ask students to come up and write the past participle form of these verbs on the board. Correct their spelling where necessary. Then ask students to learn these Present Perfect forms for the next lesson.

Listening

7

- Before listening to the recording, ask students to work in pairs. Assign each pair one of the people in the picture and ask them to describe what that person is doing.

- Give each pair a few minutes on their own to talk about their person and then ask students to tell the class what the person is doing. Don't correct any mistakes they make, but make a note of them to pick up on after they listen to the recording.
- Explain to students that they are going to listen to Lucy talking to her teacher about things that the students have done to get ready for the school dance. Ask students to look at the list of names above the picture and to tell you which are boys' names and which are girls' names.
- Play the recording all the way to the end and ask students to write the names in the correct boxes. Play the recording again. Ask students to check their answers and to complete any missing information.

Turn to page 127 of this Teacher's Guide for the recording script.

Answers
Girl left: Lucy (*I watched the other kids ...*)
Girl centre: Ada (*Ada took the chairs away.*)
Girl right: Jane (*Jane brought the balloons in ...*)
Boy left: Bill (*Bill moved the desks ...*)
Boy right: Andrew (*... Andrew cleaned the floor.*)

Extra Class Activity

Write the sentences on the board which justified the answers in *Listening 7*, describing what each student did. Then ask students to change the verbs in these sentences to the Present Perfect Simple. Write their answers on the board as they say them, and then ask students to correct them. Correct pronunciation and intonation where necessary.

Speaking

8

- Explain that students are going to work in pairs to talk about things they have or haven't done at school.
- Remind students of the words they need to form the Present Perfect Simple that they learnt (*has / have +* past participle), and tell them to use them to complete the sentences. Tell them to use the list of irregular past participles on page 132 and 133 if they need a reminder.
- Read through the *Express yourself!* box with students. Explain that this box provides useful language that will help them complete the Speaking task. Give one or two example sentences, talking about when you did the things in the list. When students are confident with the language, they can do the task in their pairs.
- Go round the class monitoring students to make sure they are carrying out the task properly. Don't correct any mistakes at this stage, but make a note of any mistakes in structure and pronunciation.
- Ask each student to tell the class one thing that they have or haven't done at school.
- Write any structural mistakes that students make on the board, without saying who made them, and ask them to correct them. Deal with any problems in pronunciation.

Answers
Students' own answers

Extra Writing Task 5

- Make sure each student has a copy of Extra Writing Task 5 that can be found on the *Resource CD-ROM*.
- Explain to students that they are going to write a short paragraph about things they have and have not done in their lives. Ask them to look back at the *Grammar* section in Lesson 1 and to say how we form the Present Perfect Simple (*with the verb have and the past participle of the main verb*).
- Ask them to write their paragraphs in their notebooks. You could set this task for homework if you are short of time.
- If time allows, put students in pairs and encourage them to ask each other questions about the things they have written about, using the Present Perfect Simple.

Extra Task (for early finishers)

See photocopiable material that can be found on the *Resource CD-ROM*.

Lesson 2

Objectives

Reading	article – true or false
Vocabulary	text-related words; education-related words
Grammar	present perfect simple (negative, questions, short answers); ever and yet
Listening	circling the correct answers
Sounds of English	aspirates

Way in

- Ask students how we form the Present Perfect Simple of regular verbs, elicit that we use *has / have* and we add *–ed* to the main verb. Then tell them to write down the verbs *break, do, go, have, know, learn, meet* and *teach*, and to write the Present Perfect Simple forms they learnt in Lesson 1. Ask students to swap books with a partner to check each other's work. Then tell one student from each pair to come up and write one of the answers on the board.
- Ask students which words we often use with the Present Perfect Simple (*for, since, already, just, never*) and ask them to give you example sentences using each one.
- Ask students to look at the picture on page 48 and to tell you what they think the building is (*a school*). Ask whether they have seen school buildings like this in their own country.

Reading

1

- Tell students they are going to listen to and read the article. Ask them to follow the article as they listen.
- Play the recording once. Ask students to tell you one fact they learned from the article that they didn't know before.
- Ask students what *SMS* stands for (*Stratton Mountain School*).
- Ask students to read the pre-reading question and to find the answer in the article.

Answer

Students train in sports at the school.

2

- Please follow the procedure outlined in Unit 1, Lesson 2 on page 15 of this Teacher's Guide.

Answers

champion – *person who beat everyone else in a sport*
labs – *abbreviation for laboratories*
professional coaches – *trained experts who teach other people sport*
successful – *doing well*
medals – *prizes for winning, usually on a ribbon and worn round the neck*
university – *form of further education college*

Did you know?

- Ask students to read the information in the *Did you know?* feature and ask if they know how many pupils there are in their school.
- If students are interested, give them more information on sports schools using the Background Information box below.

Background Information

In many countries, including England, there are specialist sports colleges, where young people can learn various sports and they can also learn about the science of sport. Also, in England there is an organisation called Youth Sport Trust, which works with schools all over the country to make School Sport Partnerships, so young people everywhere get the chance to try out different sports. For further information, go to www.nationalgeographic.com and search for 'sports schools'.

Comprehension

3

- Ask students to read sentences 1 to 5 before they read the article again so that they know what information to look for. Ask them to scan the text to find the answers and to underline the information in the description that helps them find the answer.
- Ask students to do the task individually, but check the answers as a class.
- Explain any vocabulary that students don't know and correct pronunciation where necessary.

Answers

1. F (*Apart from winter sports, there's also football, running ...*)
2. T (*... go to normal classes in the afternoon.*)
3. T (*Its indoor sports centre has a skate park and a gym.*)
4. F (*Students train with their coaches six days a week.*)
5. F (*... four have won medals.*)

Vocabulary

4

- Tell students that they have to use the words in the wordbank to complete the sentences. Explain that the words all appear in the article.
- Ask students to do the task individually, but check the answers as a class.

Answers

1	indoor	4	medals
2	lab	5	university
3	champion		

5

- Explain that students will learn more words to do with education in this exercise. Ask students to work in pairs to read the paragraph and to decide which word fits the meaning for each gap.
- Check the answers as a class. Correct their pronunciation where necessary.

Answers

1	education	4	marks
2	experience	5	reports
3	library	6	exams

Extra Class Activity

When you get the chance, play a miming game. Divide students into two teams and ask each team to write down words they can explain without speaking. Then ask different students from each team to mime a word for the other team to guess. The team which guesses the most words correctly is the winner.

Grammar

Present Perfect Simple (negative, questions, short answers)

- Read the rules in the grammar box and ask students to read the example sentences with you. Explain the meanings where necessary. Point out that we put *not* between *has / have* and the past participle to make the negative form and that we use *has / hasn't* or *have / haven't* without the past participle in short answers.

Ever and Yet

- Read the rules in the grammar box and draw students' attention to the position of *ever* and *yet* in the example sentences. Explain the meanings if necessary.

6

- Ask students to read each sentence to decide whether they need to use the negative or the question form of the Present Perfect Simple of the verb in brackets. Tell them to see if the verb in brackets is regular or irregular. Tell them to pay attention to the position of *not* in negative sentences and the word order in the questions. Remind students to use the list of irregular verbs on pages 132 and 133 to find the past participles of the irregular verbs.
- Ask students to do the task individually, but check the answers as a class.

Answers
1 Have you finished
2 has not / hasn't passed
3 have not / haven't studied
4 Has she had
5 have not / haven't been

7

- Ask students to read questions 1 to 5 and to choose the correct word for each sentence, remembering what they have just learned about using *ever* and *yet*.
- Ask students to do the task individually, but check the answers as a class.

Answers
1 ever	4 ever
2 yet	5 yet
3 yet	

Listening

8

- Ask students to read through the sentences and possible options.
- Explain to students that they are going to listen to a new teacher talking to some pupils about what the class has done.
- Play the recording to the end and ask students to circle the correct answers. Ask students to discuss their answers with a partner and to justify and answers they have if they are different. Play the recording again and ask students to check their answers and to circle any missing answers.

Turn to page 127 of this Teacher's Guide for the recording script.

Answers
1 Mr Rogers (*… because Mr Rogers is away.*)
2 fifty (*… has the class done exercise five on page fifty yet? Yes, Miss Andrews.*)
3 has not (*What about the text on the next page? … No, we haven't read that yet.*)
4 elephants (*That's right, it's about elephants.*)
5 Henry (*Well, Henry, you read it, then.*)

Let's Talk
Put students into pairs. Ask them to take turns to say as many sentences as they can to their partner within a time limit of two minutes. Their sentences must contain *ever* or *yet*. The pair with the most sentences wins.

Sounds of English

9

- Explain to students that they are going to hear four pairs of words. Ask them to pay attention to the sound of the letter *h* at the start of the words on the left. Explain the meaning of any new vocabulary where necessary.
- Read out each pair of words to the class stressing the sound of *h* in the words in the left column. Then read the words once more and ask students to say them with you.

10

- Ask students to work in pairs to say the sentence to each other.
- Ask students to listen to the recording to see if they pronounced it correctly. Explain the meaning of any new vocabulary where necessary.
- Play the recording once more without stopping and ask students to repeat the sentence as a class.

Teaching Tip
Tongue twisters are a useful tool to help students remember sounds. Make up your own tongue twisters using the sounds you want to teach and ask students to try and say them as quickly as possible.

Extra Class Activity
Write the name *Henry* on the board and say it clearly stressing the sound of *h*. Then say *Henry says ha ha ha* and ask the class to say it with you. Ask students to repeat it and correct their pronunciation of the aspirate sound where necessary. Then ask students to think of other names that begin with *H* and to repeat the sentence using these names (eg *Helen, Harry, Hannah*).

Extra Task (for early finishers)
See photocopiable material that can be found on the *Resource CD-ROM*.

Lesson 3

Objectives

Reading	interview – open-ended questions
Express yourself!	talking about school
Grammar	present perfect simple and How long
Writing	paragraphs; topic sentences; writing an email about what you are doing in school

Way in

- Write *experience, marks, exams, library, report* and *education* on the board. Ask students to use the words to make sentences and to write them in their notebooks. If time allows, ask students to come up and write one of their sentences on the board.
- Write the following on the board: *eaten / I / not / yet / have* and ask students to put the words in the correct order (*I have not eaten yet.*). Then ask them how we form questions using the Present Perfect Simple and how we form short answers.

Reading

1

- Tell students that they are going to listen to and read an interview with a new teacher. Then ask them to read the interview on their own to find how Mrs Green found out about the job (*she saw an advert on the Internet*).
- Play the recording and ask students to follow the interview in their books.

Comprehension

2

- Ask students to read questions 1 to 5 before they read the text again so that they know what information to look for.
- Ask students to do the task individually, but check the answers as a class. Ask students to underline where they find the answers in the text so they can justify their answers.
- Explain any vocabulary students don't know and correct their pronunciation if necessary.

Answers

1 in Bristol (*... I was working in Bristol ...*)
2 three months (*I've been here for three months.*)
3 yes (*... I worked in a school in Finchley ...*)
4 six (*Hampstead School is my sixth.*)
5 They're great. (*The teaching staff is great ...*)

Express yourself!

3

Talking about school

- Ask students to work in pairs to ask and answer the questions about school. Explain that they will take turns to ask each other the questions and that they must reply with their own answers.

- As a class, ask each pair to ask and answer one of the questions until all students have had the chance to speak. Correct their pronunciation and intonation patterns if necessary.

Answers
Students' own answers

Grammar

Present Perfect Simple and How long

- Read the grammar box to students and ask them to read the examples with you. Remind them of the word order for questions with the Present Perfect Simple.

4

- Ask students to read the prompts for question 1 and to tell you whether the subject is singular or plural (*singular*), which word the verb is (*work*) and whether the verb is regular or irregular (*regular*). Ask them to tell you the Present Perfect Simple of *work* (*has worked*).
- Ask a student to come up and write the first question on the board, then ask the class whether this is correct or not. Make any corrections necessary on the board.
- Tell students to do the rest of the task individually. Remind them to use the list of irregular verbs on pages 132 and 133 to help them find the past participles where necessary.
- Encourage students to swap books with a partner to check each other's questions. Check the answers as a class.

Answers

1 How long has Mrs Green worked at Hampstead School?
2 How long has James had this car?
3 How long have Ann and Tina lived in Canada?
4 How long have you known Diana?
5 How long have they been students at this school?
6 How long has Kim had French lessons?
7 How long has Paul been ill?
8 How long has Mr Jones taught science?

Let's Talk

Put students into pairs. They take turns to ask and answer questions or to make sentences about the picture in *Grammar 4*. Encourage them to use the present perfect. Walk round while they're talking and gently correct any errors of pronunciation.

Writing

Paragraphs

5

- Read the rules about paragraphs and topic sentences to the class. Explain the meaning of any new vocabulary where necessary.

Teaching Tip

Explain to students that we write in paragraphs to make our writing easier to read and to make the meaning clear. Each paragraph should have a topic sentence that tells us what we are writing about and the other sentences in the same paragraph will tell us more about this topic.

6

- Tell students to read the email and look for the sentence that explains what each paragraph is about.
- Ask students to do the task individually, but check the answers as a class.

Extra Class Activity

To give students more practice in identifying topic sentences, ask them to read a page from a graded reading book and to underline the topic sentences on the page. Alternatively, choose a page from a story they might find interesting, give students photocopies of the page and ask them to find the topic sentences.

Answers

Students should underline the following:

Paragraph 1
I'm writing because I've got a long break and I can tell you about school this week.

Paragraph 2
We've already had two tests in English and we're having a maths test this afternoon.

Paragraph 3
Why don't you come over this weekend?

Task

7

- Ask students to work in pairs to discuss ideas about what they are doing in school this week.
- Make sure students understand the paragraph plan on page 51. Remind them that each paragraph adds a different piece of information to the email to make it easy to follow.
- Ask students to use the plan to write an email like the one in *Writing 6*. Remind students that paragraphs 1, 2 and 3 must have topic sentences.
- Alternatively, you could assign this task as homework.

Example answer

Hi Jenny!

How are you? I'm writing because it's lunchtime I have free time to tell you about school this week.

We've just had a sports lesson in the playground. I'm really tired. We played basketball. My team won! We've got an exam in English this afternoon and we've already had two this week! I've never done three English exams in one week before. I have studied a lot!

Why don't you come over to my house this weekend? You haven't seen my new pet dog yet. She's brilliant! You can have lunch with us.

Let me know about the weekend! Bye for now!
Jane

8

- Ask students to read back through their emails to make sure that each paragraph contains a topic sentence. If you ask them to write the email for homework, then give them a few minutes to do this at the beginning of the next lesson.

Extra Task (for early finishers)

See photocopiable material that can be found on the *Resource CD-ROM*.

Way in

- If you assigned Unit 5, Lesson 3 *Writing* 7 for homework, then give students a few minutes to proofread their emails to check that each paragraph has a topic sentence. Then ask them to read each other's emails, or stick them on the wall so they can read them when they have time.
- Tell students to ask a partner two questions beginning with *How long*, and to answer their partners' questions. Then ask each pair to ask and answer two questions in front of the class. Correct their pronunciation where necessary.
- Tell students that this unit is about the body. Ask students to call out any words they already know connected with the body.

Did you know?

- With books closed, ask students if they have ever had their face painted or used face paints at home. If so, encourage them to share the experience with the class. What were they painted as? Was it fun?
- Ask students to open their books at pages 52 and 53. Ask them to look at the picture and see if they can guess why the people are painted (*they are preparing for their annual sing-sing*).
- Ask students to read the paragraph about the Huli wigmen dancers on page 52. Explain that in some countries, people wear brightly coloured clothes or costumes when they go to special celebrations but in other countries, like Papua New Guinea, people paint their bodies instead.
- Ask students what they think of the people in the picture. Do they think they look attractive, scary or silly?
- Read the information from the *Did you know?* feature to the class. Ask students if they can guess how many people go to the world's largest body painting festival each year (*over 24,000*).
  Use the background information in the box below to give the students further information about body painting if they are interested. Check if they have any questions. If they ask for information you don't have, refer them to the website in the Background Information box below and ask them to feed back to you at the next lesson.

Background Information
Body painting using clay and other natural colours has existed for thousands of years and is still common in countries like Africa, Australia, New Zealand and the Pacific Islands. In India, many people have patterns painted on their bodies using a dye called henna. These body pictures or temporary tattoos last longer than the normal body paints – up to two or even three weeks. As well as being used for decoration, body painting can be used to show how important people are or what religion they belong to. Often, in tribes ➡

like the Huli wigmen, the designs and colours that can be used are strictly controlled. For further information, go to www.nationalgeographic.com and search for 'body painting'.

Let's Talk
Put students into small groups. They take turns to talk about the people in the picture, describing them and saying what they think about them.

Lesson 1

Objectives

Reading	the cartoon story – true or false
Vocabulary	text-related words; body-related words
Grammar	present perfect simple and past simple
Listening	true or false
Speaking	describing people in photos

The cartoon story

- Ask students if they can remember what happened in the previous episode of the cartoon story (*The children spent the night in a museum. Mikey took the magic globe. He asked the globe to show them a real dinosaur so the globe took the children back in time to 65 million years ago and they saw a real dinosaur. Kristie and Adam were scared but Mikey thought it was exciting.*).
- Ask students to look at the story pictures and suggest what might be happening.

1
- Please follow the procedure outlined in Unit 1, Lesson 1 on page 12 of this Teacher's Guide.

Answers
abroad – *in another country*
landed – *reached the ground*
documentary – *informative TV programme*
tribe – *group of people who share the same beliefs*
painted – *covered in paint*
colourful necklaces – *necklaces with different colours*
handsome – *good looking / attractive*

- Depending on whether you are using the DVD or the Audio CD, follow the relevant instructions.

For teachers using the DVD
- Make sure each child has a copy of Cartoon DVD Worksheet 6 that can be found on the *Resource CD-ROM*.
- Please follow the procedure outlined in Unit 1, Lesson 1 on page 12 of this Teacher's Guide for teachers using the DVD.

Before you watch

Answers
1 Beth (Kristie and Mikey's cousin)
2 in the sitting room
3 Accept any logical answer based on what students see in the pictures.

While you watch

Answers
a3 b1 c4 d5 e2

After you watch

Answers
1 Africa
2 a documentary
3 They've painted them.
4 She likes their colourful necklaces and the way they're dancing.
5 half an hour ago
6 handsome

For teachers using the Audio CD

- Tell students to look at page 54 of their student's book and to work in pairs. Ask them to look at the pictures and say who the girl is with Kristie, Mikey and Adam (*Beth, Kristie and Mikey's cousin, who first appeared in Episode 1 of the cartoon story.*)
- Tell students they are going to listen to and read the story. Ask them to look at the pictures and to follow the story as they listen.
- Play the recording once and ask students what Kristie likes about the African people (*their colourful necklaces and the way they're dancing*).
- Put students into small groups of four and ask them to assign the roles of Kristie, Adam, Beth and Mikey within their groups. Ask them to read the story out loud in their groups.
- As a class, ask students the questions below to check their understanding of the episode.
  1 Where did Kristie land the last time she went to Africa? (*on a tree*)
  2 What did Beth see a documentary about? (*an African tribe*)
  3 What have the African people painted? (*their bodies and their faces*)
  4 When did Adam come to the house? (*half an hour ago*)
  5 How did Mikey look in his costume? (*handsome*)

Comprehension

2

- Ask students to read sentences 1 to 5 so they know what information to look for when they read the cartoon story again. Ask them to decide if the sentences are true or false, using information from the story.

- Ask students to do the task individually, but check the answers as a class. Encourage students to explain their answer choices by giving evidence from the story.

Answers
1 F (*The globe took us there a month ago ...*)
2 F (*... I watched a documentary about an African tribe ...*)
3 T (*They've also painted their faces!*)
4 F (Kristie: *I like ... the way they're dancing!*)
5 T (*I came here half an hour ago ...*)

Let's Talk

Put students into small groups and ask them to take turns asking the other members of their group a question about the cartoon story. They can ask about this episode or any episode that they have read so far.

Vocabulary

3

- Ask students to look at the words in the wordbank. Remind them that all the words are from the cartoon story on page 54 and point out that they already know the meaning of them. Check understanding of one or two of the words again if you think it's necessary.
- Ask students to do the task individually, but check the answers as a class. Correct their pronunciation where necessary.

Answers

1 tribe	4 paint
2 abroad	5 colourful
3 documentary	

4

- Tell students to look at the pictures and then to match letters a to h with words 1 to 8. Explain any vocabulary that students have not been taught yet.
- Ask students to work in pairs to do the task, but check the answers as a class. Correct pronunciation where necessary.

Answers
1e 2d 3b 4c 5f 6g 7h 8a

Extra Class Activity

Play a game to practise the body-related vocabulary. Start the game by pointing at a part of a student's body and ask *Is this your ...?* using a word for a different body part. The student must answer *No, it's my ... .* using the correct word, then it's their turn to ask the next student a question, and so on until everyone has had a turn to ask and answer. Tell students they can use the words from *Vocabulary 4* and any other body-related words they have already learnt.

Grammar

Present Perfect Simple and Past Simple

- Read the rules in the grammar box and ask students to read the example sentences with you. Remind students that we form the Present Perfect Simple with *have / has* + the past participle of the main verb, and that we make the Past Simple of regular verbs by adding –*ed* to the main verb.
- Draw students' attention to the time expressions we use with the Past Simple and those we use with the Present Perfect Simple. Remind them that *ago* means *before now*, then explain that *ever* means *at any time* and *never* means *not at any time*.

5

- Ask students to read the sentences and options and to find any time expressions which match the Past Simple or the Present Perfect Simple. Tell them to compare each sentence with the examples in the grammar box to see which grammar rule it matches.
- Give students a few minutes to compare their answers with a partner. Ask them to justify their answers if they are different.
- Check the answers as a class and ask students to justify the answers they give.

Answers
1 have broken
2 Have
3 fell down
4 haven't eaten
5 have seen, saw

6

- Ask students to read each sentence to decide whether they need to use the Past Simple or the Present Perfect Simple of the verb in brackets and whether the sentence is affirmative, negative or a question. Tell them to see if the verb in brackets is regular or irregular.
- Explain that the answers include negative and question forms and remind students to use the list of irregular verbs on pages 132 to 133 to find the Past Simple and past participles of irregular verbs.
- Ask students to do the task individually, but check the answers as a class.

Answers
1 Did she stay
2 Have ... travelled
3 hurt
4 have not / haven't seen
5 Has ... sent

Listening

7

- Explain to students that they are going to listen to Polly talking to her mum about making an elephant. Ask students to read sentences 1 to 5 quickly to find out what Polly has or hasn't done. Then ask them to underline the verbs in the sentences (*made*, *has seen*, *hasn't made*, *has fallen off*, *has finished*). Explain that they need to pay attention to whether the verb forms are affirmative or negative as they listen.
- Remind students that they have to write *T* if the sentence is true or *F* if a sentence is false.
- Play the recording once and then ask students to compare their answers with a partner. Ask them to justify any answers that are different. Play the recording a second time and ask them to check their answers or fill in any missing information.
- Check the answers as a class and make sure students can justify their answers.

Turn to page 128 of this Teacher's Guide for the recording script.

Answers
1 T *(I've made an elephant.)*
2 F *(I didn't have a good picture and I haven't seen a real elephant.)*
3 F *(I put the tail on an hour ago …)*
4 T *(… but it's already fallen off.)*
5 F *(I haven't finished the legs yet.)*

Speaking

8

- Explain that students are going to work in pairs to describe what the people in the photos are doing.
- Remind students of the body-related words that they learnt and tell them to use them in the descriptions.
- Read through the *Express yourself!* box with students. Explain that this box provides useful language that will help them complete the Speaking task. Give one or two example sentences, talking about when you did the things in the list. When students are confident with the language, they can do the task in their pairs.
- Go round the class monitoring students to make sure they are carrying out the task properly. Don't correct any mistakes at this stage, but make a note of any mistakes in structure and pronunciation.
- Tell each pair to ask and answer one of the questions and repeat until each pair has had a turn.
- Write any structural mistakes that students made on the board, without saying who made them, and ask them to correct them. Deal with any problems in pronunciation.

Answers
Students' own answers

Extra Writing Task 6

- Make sure each student has a copy of Extra Writing Task 6 that can be found on the *Resource CD-ROM*.
- Explain to students that they are going to write six sentences about things that happened or didn't happen, or that have or have not happened in the last 24 hours. Tell students you want them to use a mixture of the past simple and the present perfect tenses in their sentences. If they can use both tenses in the same sentence, that's even better.
- Ask students to write sentences in their notebooks. You could set this task for homework if you are short of time.
- If time allows, ask each student to read one of their sentences to the class.

Extra Task (for early finishers)

See photocopiable material that can be found on the *Resource CD-ROM*.

Lesson 2

Objectives

Reading	article – circling the correct words
Vocabulary	text-related words; illnesses
Grammar	possessive pronouns
Listening	ticking the correct pictures
Sounds of English	pronunciation of *s* sounds

Way in

- Write *abroad, landed, documentary, painted, colourful* and *handsome* on the board and ask students to write one sentence for each word in their notebooks. Ask them to swap books with a partner to compare sentences and check spelling. Ask students at random to read one of their sentences to the class.
- Draw a monster similar to the ones on page 55 on the board. Point to different parts of its body and ask students to tell you what they are.
- Ask students which time expressions we use with the Past Simple (*yesterday, last night / week year*, etc, *three days / months / years ago, in January, in 2009*). Ask which time expressions we use with the Present Perfect Simple (*ever, never, already, just, for, since, yet*).

Reading

1

- Explain that students are going to listen to the words in the wordbank. Play the recording and ask them to point to each word as they hear it.
- Play the recording again and encourage students to repeat as a class. You could ask individual students to repeat on their own if you feel they are confident enough.

- Put the students into pairs and ask them to find the words in the article. When they have all found the words, work through them as a class one at a time, asking students to read out the sentences in the article containing the word. Ask students to say what the word means. If they don't know, encourage them to guess from the context.

2

- Tell students they are going to listen to and read the article. Ask them to follow the article as they listen.
- Play the recording once. Ask students to tell you one fact they learned from the article that they didn't know before.
- Ask students what colour paint African tribes wear when they go to war (*red*).
- Ask students to read the pre-reading question and to find the answer in the article.

Answer
so that people could see them

Did you know?

- Ask students to read the information in the *Did you know?* feature and ask if they are surprised by how long ago people painted their bodies.
- If students are interested, give them more information on ancient Greek theatre using the Background Information box below.

Background Information
In the old days, almost every Greek city had a theatre. They were used for celebrations as well as for religious festivals. The theatres were built on hillsides in the open air and could often hold up to 18,000 people! At one time, the actors painted their faces and later they wore masks – usually either a sad or a happy face. For further information, go to www.nationalgeographic.com and search for 'ancient Greek theatre'.

Comprehension

3

- Ask students to read through the sentences and options before they read the text again so that they know what information to look for.
- Ask students to underline where they get the answer from in the text so they can justify their answers. Explain any words they don't understand.
- Ask students to do the task individually, but check the answers as a class.

Answers
1 different reasons (*People have painted their skin for different reasons.*)
2 Greece (*In ancient Greek theatre, actors painted their faces white ...*)
3 Red (*They use the colour red when they go to war ...*)
4 enemies (*... to scare their enemies.*)
5 on special days (*In India women paint their bodies at festivals and weddings.*)

Vocabulary

4
- Tell students that they have to use the words in the wordbank to complete the sentences. Explain that all the words appear in the article.
- Ask students to do the task individually, but check the answers as a class. Correct their pronunciation if necessary.

Answer
1 scare	4 hunt	
2 wedding	5 war	
3 make-up		

5
- Ask students to work in pairs to read the sentences and options and decide which option fits each sentence. As most of the vocabulary is new, encourage students to use dictionaries if they have them as well as looking for clues in the rest of the sentence.
- Check the answers as a class and explain the meanings of words where necessary.

Teaching Tip
Make sure students know how to look up words in a dictionary as this is a valuable learning aid.

Answers
1 toothache
2 temperature
3 sore
4 skin
5 cough

Grammar

Possessive Pronouns

- Write the following sentence from the article on page 56 on the board: *From pictures, we can see that the famous Queen Cleopatra painted hers often.* Underline the word *hers* and ask students what it means (*the Queen's face*). Explain that *hers* is a possessive pronoun and that we use possessive pronouns instead of a possessive adjective and a noun when we are talking about something that we have mentioned before.

- Ask students to look at the grammar box and read the first sentence and the example. Ask students what *mine* means in this example (*my necklace*). Explain that we only use possessive pronouns when we have already mentioned the person and the object that belongs to them.
- Read through the other rules and examples, then read the list of possessive adjectives and possessive pronouns and ask students to repeat them after you. If necessary remind students that possessive adjectives appear before nouns and tell us who something belongs to.
- Ask students to read through the article on page 56 again to find any other possessive pronouns and to underline them (*theirs* in paragraph 2, *theirs* in paragraph 3).

6
- Ask students to read the sentences and options and to check whether the option comes before a noun or whether it is on its own, replacing a possessive adjective and a noun. Tell them to compare each sentence with the examples in the grammar box to see which example it matches.
- Give students a few minutes to compare their answers with a partner. Ask them to justify their answers if they are different.
- Check the answers as a class and ask students to justify the answers they give.

Answers
1 yours
2 my
3 hers
4 her
5 ours

7
- Ask students to read through the sentences and to see if the words in bold are about something that belongs to a man or a woman, or whether there is a possessive adjective which tells us who something belongs to. Tell them to use the list of possessive pronouns and possessive adjectives in the grammar box to help them find the correct answers.
- Ask students to do the task individually, but check the answers as a class.

Answers
1 ours	4 theirs	
2 his	5 mine	
3 hers		

Listening

8
- Ask students to read through the questions and to find the differences between the two pictures below each question.
- Explain to students that they are going to listen to a woman talking to a doctor about illnesses that people in her family have got.

- Play the recording and ask students to tick the correct pictures.
- Give students a few minutes to compare their answers with a partner. Ask them to justify their answers if they are different.
- Play the recording again and ask students to check their answers and to fill in any missing information.
- Check the answers as a class and ask students to justify their answers.

Turn to page 128 of this Teacher's Guide for the recording script.

Answers

1 a (*Good morning, Doctor Kipling here.*)
2 b (*The twins have got a temperature …*)
3 b (*… Grandad's in bed with a really bad cough.*)
4 a (*Yes, Doctor, I've got a very bad headache.*)

Extra Class Activity

Ask students to describe what they can see in the pictures that showed the wrong options in *Listening 8*.

Answers

1 b This shows a dentist.
2 a The twins are coughing.
3 a Grandad is sitting in a chair in the garden.
4 b Mrs Myers has got sunburn.

Sounds of English

9

- Play the recording once and ask students to note the sound that the letters in red make. Explain the meaning of any new vocabulary where necessary.
- Play the recording once more without stopping and ask students to repeat the words as a class.

Answers

1 sound like *z*
2 sound like *s*

10

- Play the recording, stopping after each line for students to repeat.
- Play the recording once more without stopping and ask students to repeat the rhyme as a class. Then ask some students to say the rhyme to the rest of the class.

Extra Task (for early finishers)

See photocopiable material that can be found on the *Resource CD-ROM*.

Lesson 3

Objectives

Reading	letters from a magazine – missing sentences
Express yourself!	at the doctor's
Listening	completing a dialogue
Speaking	talking about the differences between two pictures
Writing	order of paragraphs; emailing a friend about when you were sick

Way in

- Ask students to write the words they can remember from Lesson 2 describing illness in their notebooks. Ask students at random to read out one of their words. Alternatively they can come and write one of their words on the board. They should remember *headache, toothache, temperature, burn, sick, sore throat, skin, pain, cough* and *sneeze*. Ask them to swap books with a partner to check their spelling.
- Point to something belonging to a student (eg *a book*) and say *This is (Mary's) book.* and say *It's ….* to elicit the possessive pronoun *hers*. Continue talking about other objects until students have used all the possessive pronouns correctly.

Reading

1

- Tell students that they are going to listen to and read a letter about a problem that Robert sent to a magazine and the reply that Dr Murray sent back to him. Play the recording and ask students to follow in their books. Then ask them to read the letters again on their own and note down what Dr Murray tells Robert he must do (*spend less time in front of the computer, not stay up late if he has school the next morning, not look at the screen for too long, not sit on a chair for too long, take anything out of his rucksack that he doesn't need*).
  Tell them they don't need to complete the gaps in the letters yet.
- Explain any vocabulary students don't know and correct their pronunciation if necessary.

Comprehension

2

- Ask students to read through the letters again in order to find clues about what information is missing.
- Ask students to read the sentences and to complete the letters. Tell them to read back through the letters once they have finished, making sure that they have chosen the correct sentences. Explain any vocabulary students don't know.
- Ask students to do the task individually, but check the answers as a class.

Answers

1d 2c 3a 4b 5e

Express yourself!

At the doctor's

3

- Ask students to work in pairs to read the sentences and to complete the dialogues. Then tell them to practise the dialogue and to take turns at being the doctor and the patient. Correct their pronunciation and intonation pattern if necessary.
- If time allows, ask pairs of students at random to say their dialogue to the rest of the class until all students have the chance to speak.

Answers

1 What's the matter?
2 I've got a bad cough.
3 Open your mouth.
4 Is it serious?
5 Take this medicine.

Extra Class Activity

Ask students to work in pairs to make new dialogues like the one in *Express yourself!* to talk about different illnesses. Ask each pair to say their dialogue in front of the class.

Listening

4

- Explain to students that they are going to listen to Lizzie talking to her grandma who is feeling ill. Explain that they will write words they learnt in Lessons 1 and 2 to complete the dialogue. Give students a few minutes to read the dialogue and then ask them whether they think the answers in each gap from 1 to 5 will be a body part, a sign of illness or something the doctor gives you (1 & 2 *body part*, 3 *sign of illness*, 4 *something the doctor gives you*, 5 *sign of illness*).
- Play the recording to the end and ask students to fill in their answers. Ask them to work with a partner to check their answers and to justify any answers they have that are different.
- Play the recording again and ask students to check their answers and to fill in any missing information.

Turn to page 128 of this Teacher's Guide for the recording script.

Answers

1 finger (*... I've got a pain in my finger.*)
2 leg (*And my leg is a bit sore again.*)
3 cough (*What about your cough?*)
4 medicine (*Have you taken your medicine?*)
5 temperature (*He had a temperature.*)

Speaking

5

- Explain that students are going to work in pairs to talk about the differences between the two pictures.
- Remind students to use *have / has got* and *there is / are*, and tell them to use them with the body-related words they have learnt to describe the differences.

- Go round the class monitoring students to make sure they are carrying out the task properly. Don't correct any mistakes at this stage, but make a note of any mistakes in structure and pronunciation.
- Ask each pair to tell the class one of the differences they found and repeat until each pair has had a turn.
- Write any structural mistakes that students made on the board, without saying who made them, and ask them to correct them. Deal with any problems in pronunciation.

Answers

In picture 1, there is one chair, but in picture 2, there are two chairs.
In picture 1, the boy has got a broken arm, but in picture 2, he hasn't.
In picture 1, the bed has got the name Mr Jones on it, but in picture 2, it has got the name Mr Smith.
In picture 1, the doctor has got a blue coat on, but in picture 2, he has got a white coat on.

Writing

Order of paragraphs

6

- Read the rules about the order of paragraphs to the class. Explain the meaning of any new vocabulary where necessary.
- Remind students that each paragraph will have a topic sentence that tells us what the rest of the paragraph will be about.

Teaching Tip

This is a good point to revise the phrases which students learnt to begin and end emails and letters to friends with in Unit 4, Lesson 3. Elicit the beginnings *Hi ...* and *Dear ...* and which name we use to write to friends (*first name*), then ask students to tell you the closing phrases (*Bye for now, Love from ...*).

7

- Explain that the beginning and ending of this email are in the correct place, but the four main paragraphs are mixed up. Ask students to read all the paragraphs to look for things that we write at the beginning of a letter and things we write at the end. Then tell them to find the middle paragraphs which give more detail about the topic and to look for time expressions to help them decide which order to put them in.
- Explain any words students don't understand.
- Ask students to do the task individually, but check the answers as a class.

Answers

3 (Paragraph 2 ended with by talking about another two days in bed and this paragraph started by talking about today.)

1 (We often begin letters with *How are you?* and this paragraph also gives us the reason for writing.)

4 (This paragraph concludes the letter and asks our friend to write back.)

2 (The end of paragraph 1 mentioned feeling awful and this paragraph goes on to explain what's been wrong and how Taylor has felt all week.)

Task

8

- Ask students to work in pairs to discuss ideas about what was wrong with them and what they did.
- Make sure students understand the paragraph plan on page 59. Remind them that each paragraph adds a different piece of information to the email to make it easy to follow.
- Ask students to use the plan to write an email like the one in *Writing 7*. Remind students that the email should open and close in a friendly way and it should have a beginning, a middle and an end.
- Alternatively, you could assign this task as homework.

Example answer

Hi (Samantha),

Hi! How are you? I'm fine. I'm writing because I didn't come to your basketball game yesterday. I went to the dentist.

I have had a sore mouth for three days. I usually play with my friends in the afternoon, but for three days, I just sat inside and read my comics. I didn't eat much even though I was hungry. The dentist was very nice. He said, 'Don't worry. You've just got toothache. Take this medicine and you'll soon be fine.' He was right. This morning I was able to eat all of my breakfast! After I ate, I went to school.

Well, I've got some homework to do now. Write soon and tell me who won the game.

See you soon!
Maggie

9

- Ask students to read back through their emails to make sure that it has a beginning, a middle and an end. If you ask them to write the email for homework, then give them a few minutes to do this at the beginning of the next lesson.

Extra Task (for early finishers)

See photocopiable material that can be found on the *Resource CD-ROM*.

Review 3

Objectives

- To revise vocabulary and grammar from Units 5 and 6
- Project – illness and health

Preparing for the review

- Explain to students that the tasks in *Review 3* revise the material they learnt in Units 5 and 6.
- Remind students that they can ask you for help with the exercises or look back at the units if they're not sure about an answer, as the review is not a test.
- Decide how you will carry out the review. You could ask students to do one task at a time and then correct it immediately, or ask students to do all the tasks and then correct them together at the end. If you do all the tasks together, let students know every now and again how much time they have got left to finish the tasks.
- Remind students not to leave any answers blank and to try to find any answers they aren't sure about in the units.
- Revise the vocabulary and grammar as a class before students do the review.

Vocabulary Revision

- Write the words *flash, show, real, show, die out* and *gigantic* on the board and ask students to give the meaning or an example sentence with each word.
- Ask students to tell you as many words and phrases as possible related to education. Make sure they revise *school term, uniforms, head teacher, lab, boarding school, library, marks, exams* and *report*. Ask students to use these words to tell you about their school.
- Ask students to tell you the meanings of *abroad, painted, colourful, documentary, handsome* and *tribe*. Ask them to make sentences using each of these words and phrases.
- Draw the outline of an animal's body on the board and get the students to come up and label the body parts they learnt in Unit 6, Lesson 1. Make sure they revise *ankle, chest, elbow, knee, shoulder, stomach, tail* and *throat*.
- Tell students to imagine they are ill and that you are the doctor. Get them to tell you what's wrong with them. Make sure they revise *burn, cough, headache, ill, pain, temperature, toothache, sneeze* and *sore*.

Grammar Revision

- Write *I, you, he / she / it,* and *we / you / they* one below the other on the board and ask a student to come and write the Present Perfect Simple affirmative forms of *finish* beside the subject pronouns. Ask the other students to help the student who's writing. Then ask individual students at random round the class to tell you the negative forms. Do the same for the question forms and short answers.
- Write *Lynne has been to university.* and *Lynne has gone to university.* Ask students if they can explain the difference between *have been* (when someone went somewhere and has returned) and *has gone* (when someone went somewhere and hasn't yet returned) to you.
- Write *for, since, already, just, never, ever* and *yet* on the board and then ask students to write down sentences with each word using the Present Perfect Simple.
- Ask students *How long have you been at this school?* and tell them to reply.
- Write *my, his, her, your, our* and *their* one below the other on the board. Write *mine* next to *my* and ask students to come up and fill in the other possessive pronouns. Make sure they remember that we use possessive adjectives before nouns and we use possessive pronouns to replace a possessive adjective and a noun.

Vocabulary

1

- Ask students to say each of the words as a class and then individually. Correct their pronunciation if necessary.
- Ask students to go to the first page of stickers at the back of the book and find the stickers for *Review 3*. Tell them to decide which thing each sticker shows and to stick it in the correct box.
- Check that students have put the correct stickers above each word.

2

- Ask students to read the words in the wordbank and make sure they understand the titles *Body, Education* and *Health*. Tell them to look back at Unit 5, Lessons 1 and 2 and Unit 6, Lesson 1 for a reminder if they need to.
- Accept the correct words in each column in any order when checking students' answers.

Answers		
Body	**Education**	**Health**
ankle	head teacher	burn
chest	library	pain
skin	report	temperature

3

- Ask students to read the whole dialogue and the possible options before circling the correct answers. After they have completed the exercise tell them to read the dialogue again to make sure their answers makes sense.

Answers
1 shoulders
2 cough
3 medicine
4 temperature
5 throat

Grammar
4

- Explain to students that they should read the sentences before trying to write the answers to decide whether the verb in brackets is regular or irregular and whether they need to write the affirmative, negative or question form. Tell them to find the subject of each sentence to help them get the correct form of the verb in brackets.
- Remind students to use the list of irregular verbs on pages 132 and 133 to find the past participles and tell them to look back at Unit 5, Lesson 1 grammar box for a reminder if they need to.

Answers
1 has / 's gone
2 has he had
3 have not / haven't read
4 has / 's been
5 Have they bought
6 have not / haven't finished

5

- Tell students to be careful about the word order in each sentence and to see if there is a time expression which the option matches before they circle the answer.
- Tell students to look back at the Unit 5, Lessons 1 and 2 grammar boxes for a reminder if they need to.

Answers
1 already
2 ever
3 since
4 never
5 for
6 yet

6

- Explain to students that they should read the webpage before trying to write the answers to decide whether to use the Present Perfect Simple or the Past Simple. Tell them to look for time expressions and to find the subject of each sentence to help them use the correct form of the verb in brackets.

- Remind students to use the list of irregular verbs on pages 132 and 133 and tell them to look back at the Unit 6, Lesson 1 grammar box for a reminder if they need to.

Answers
1 have / 've been
2 interviewed
3 has / 's taught
4 Have you had
5 did you come
6 have / 've already written

7

- Tell students to find out who something belongs to in each sentence and to see if the missing word comes before a noun or on its own to help them choose the correct word.
- Tell students to look back at the Unit 6, Lesson 2 grammar box for a reminder if they need to.

Answers
1a 2b 3b 4a 5a 6b 7b 8a

Project 3
1

- Explain to the students that they are going to do a project about illness and health. Ask them to say what illness they are going to pretend to have.
- Ask students to read the bullet points and explain that the advice they write must address these points.
- Read through the example advice with the class.
- Ask students to complete their projects. They can do this in the lesson or for homework.
- When the projects are complete, stick them on the classroom wall.

2

- Invite students to tell the class about the advice they gave as a doctor.

Teaching Tip
When checking students' answers to the review tasks, make a note of any problem areas in vocabulary and grammar that they still have. Try to do extra work on these areas so that your students progress well.

Way in

- If you assigned Unit 6, Lesson 3 *Writing 8* for homework, give students a few minutes to proofread their emails and to check that they have a beginning, a middle and an end. Then ask them to read each other's emails, or stick them on the wall so they can read them when they have time.
- Tell students that this unit is about nature. Ask them to say what they understand by the word *nature*.

Did you know?

- With books closed, ask students to think of places where they can see and/or learn about animals (they might suggest *zoo, wildlife park, TV, books, the Internet, DVDs, school*).
- Ask students to open their books at pages 62 and 63. Ask them to look at the picture and see if they know the name of the birds (*flamingos*). Ask what's unusual about flamingos (*they are pink*).
- Ask students to read the paragraph about flamingos on page 63. Explain that flamingos live in groups called colonies. They won't nest unless there are other flamingos around.
- Read the information from the *Did you know?* feature to the class. Ask students what else they think flamingos might eat (*small plants and insects that live in water*).
- Use the background information in the box below to give the students further information about flamingos if they are interested. Check if they have any questions. If they ask for information you don't have, refer them to the website in the Background Information box and ask them to feed back to you at the next lesson.

Background Information

Flamingos are found in Africa, Asia, North America, Central America, South America and Europe. They are very good at coping with different temperatures; they can live in hot volcanic lakes and in icy lakes in the Andean mountains. Flamingos eat with their head upside down in the water, so they can suck water and food in with the front of their bill. Mud and water drain out the back of their bill. Flamingos hold their breath when they are feeding. Flamingos run to gather speed when taking off. They can fly more than 120 kilometres to reach a new habitat. For further information, go to www.nationalgeographic.com and search for 'flamingos'.

Lesson 1

Objectives

Reading	the cartoon story – true or false
Vocabulary	text-related words; nature-related words
Grammar	be going to and future simple
Listening	changing words in bold
Speaking	asking and answering questions about a trip to the zoo

---

The cartoon story

- Ask students if they can remember what happened in the previous episode of the cartoon story (*Kristie and Mikey were looking at Beth's photos from when she had been abroad. Beth said she wanted to go to Africa so the children asked the magic globe to take them there. They went to an African village and saw people with painted bodies and colourful necklaces. The children went home and told Adam about their adventure.*).
- Ask students to look at the story pictures and suggest what might be happening.

1

- Please follow the procedure outlined in Unit 1, Lesson 1 on page 12 of this Teacher's Guide.

Answers

lizards – *reptiles with scaly skin and four legs*
natural environment – *the place where animals live in the wild*
frilled – *having a frill or collar of extra skin*
DVD recorder – *machine that plays and records DVDs*
second – *a unit of time; there are 60 seconds in one minute*

- Depending on whether you are using the DVD or the Audio CD, follow the relevant instructions.

For teachers using the DVD

- Make sure each child has a copy of Cartoon DVD Worksheet 7 that can be found on the *Resource CD-ROM*.
- Please follow the procedure outlined in Unit 1, Lesson 1 on page 12 of this Teacher's Guide for teachers using the DVD.

Before you watch

Answers
1 dark rain clouds, the garden
2 Mikey

While you watch

> **Answers**
> a2 b4 c5 d6 e1 f3

After you watch

> **Answers**
> 1 lizards
> 2 It's going to rain.
> 3 Australia
> 4 sandwiches
> 5 Mikey and Adam
> 6 angry

For teachers using the Audio CD

- Tell students to look at page 64 of their student's book and to work in pairs. Ask them to say who is playing with the globe at the start of the story (*Mikey*).
- Tell students they are going to listen to and read the story. Ask them to look at the pictures and to follow the story as they listen.
- Play the recording once and ask students what sort of lizards the children see (*frilled lizards*).
- Assign the roles of Kristie, Mikey and Adam to different students and ask them to read the story out loud. Time permitting, repeat until all students have had a turn.
- As a class, ask students the questions below to check their understanding of the episode.
  1 What does Mikey suggest doing? (*visiting lizards in their natural environment*)
  2 What sort of photos will Adam take? (*amazing photos*)
  3 What is the sun like in Australia? (*very bright*)
  4 Who wants to start the DVD recorder? (*Adam*)
  5 Why does Katie ask Mikey and Adam to wait? (*Because she doesn't want to stay in Australia on her own.*)

> **Teaching Tip**
> To encourage your less confident students to participate in dialogues, assign the shortest role to them. For example, in this episode, Kristie has the shortest role.

Comprehension

2

- Ask students to read sentences 1 to 5 so they know what information to look for when they read the cartoon story again. Ask them to decide if the sentences are true or false, using the information in the story.
- Ask students to do the task individually, but check the answers as a class. Encourage students to explain their answer choices by giving evidence from the story.

> **Answers**
> 1 F (Adam: *I want to take photos of lizards for the school magazine.*)
> 2 T (*My face will go red.*)
> 3 T (*I'm starving!*)
> 4 F (Adam: *I want to start the DVD recorder or I'll miss my favourite TV show.*)
> 5 T (*We've forgotten all about her!*)

> **Let's Talk**
> Put students into small groups. Ask them to take turns miming one of the sentences from the story. The others in the group have to guess the sentence.

Vocabulary

3

- Ask students to look at the words in the wordbank. Remind them that all the words are from the cartoon story on page 64 and point out that they already know the meaning of them. Check understanding of one or two of the words again if you think it's necessary.
- Ask students to do the task individually, but check the answers as a class.

> **Answers**
> 1 natural
> 2 lizard
> 3 environment
> 4 bright
> 5 second

4

- Ask students to look at pictures 1 to 6 and to tell you which of the things they see around them every day, sometimes or not at all. They can identify what they are talking about using the picture numbers.
- Explain to students that they have to match the words in the wordbank with pictures 1 to 6. Explain any vocabulary that students have not been taught yet or ask students to use a dictionary to find the meanings.
- Ask students to work in pairs to do the task, but check the answers as a class and correct pronunciation where necessary.

> **Answers**
> 1 branch   4 farm
> 2 leaves   5 stones
> 3 nest   6 soil

Grammar

Be going to

- Write on the board *I'm going to have a party on Saturday.* and tell students that *be going to* shows this is a plan you have made. Then write *We are going to have fun at the party.* and tell them that *be going to* can also show something is almost sure to happen, for example, because we usually have a great time with our friends at parties.

- Read the first part of the grammar box to the class and ask students to read the affirmative, negative and question forms with you. Read the short forms first and then the long forms. Then read the short answers.
- Ask students to look back at the cartoon on page 64 and to find three sentences with *be going to* (*It's going to rain. I'm not going to stay here on my own! She's going to be angry!*).
- Point out that *be going to* is followed by the main verb and that we only change the verb *be* to match the subject.
- Read the time expressions and explain that we normally put them at the end of the sentence. Refer students back to the first example sentence at the top of the grammar box.

Future Simple

- Read the uses of the Future Simple in the grammar box to the class and ask students to read the affirmative, negative and question forms with you. Then read the short answers.
- Ask students to look back at the cartoon episode on page 64 and to underline sentences with *will* (*I'll take the most amazing photos! My face will go red. I'll go back home and bring you some sun cream. Will you bring back some sandwiches, too? I'll come with you, Mikey. ... I'll miss my favourite TV show. We'll be back in a second!*).
- Draw students' attention to the time expressions and explain that we can use the same time expressions with *will* or *be going to*. Remind them that we normally put them at the end of the sentence.

Extra Class Activity
Ask students to work in pairs to make predictions about the cartoon story using *be going to* and *will*. Then ask each pair to tell the class one thing that *is going to happen* and one thing that *will happen*.

5

- Ask students to read each sentence to decide whether they need to use the correct form of *be going to* or *will* with the verb in brackets. Tell them to look back at the examples in the grammar boxes to see which rule matches each sentence.
- Explain that the answers include affirmative, negative and question forms.
- Ask students to do the task individually, but check the answers as a class.

Answers
1 is / 's going to bite
2 will be
3 will / 'll make
4 Will you help
5 Is he going to come

Listening

6

- Explain to students that they are going to listen to a teacher talking to her class about a school trip.

- Ask students to read the sentences before they hear the recording so that they know what information to listen for. Tell them that the words in bold are different from what the people say and that they have to write the correct word on each line.
- Play the recording to the end and ask students to fill in their answers. Ask them to work with a partner to check their answers and to justify any answers they have that are different.
- Play the recording again and ask students to check their answers and to fill in any missing information.

Turn to page 128 of this Teacher's Guide for the recording script.

Answers
1 rain (*I'm afraid it's going to rain ...*)
2 beach (*... we will go to the zoo and not to the beach today.*)
3 lunch (*We can have our lunch at the zoo.*)
4 three (*I've got three sandwiches ... you won't be hungry, Sam!*)
5 eleven (*... we'll leave at eleven o'clock, not ten o'clock ...*)

Speaking

7

- Explain that students are going to work in pairs to ask and answer questions about a visit to the zoo.
- Remind students that we use *be going to* and *will* to talk about the future, and tell them to use them to answer the questions. Tell them to use their imagination to think about all the things they can see or do at a zoo.
- Read through the *Express yourself!* box with students. Explain that this box provides useful language that will help them complete the Speaking task. Give one or two example sentences using the expressions in the box. When students are confident with the language, they can do the task in their pairs.
- Go round the class monitoring students to make sure they are carrying out the task properly. Don't correct any mistakes at this stage, but make a note of any mistakes in structure and pronunciation.
- Ask each pair to ask and answer one of the questions and repeat until each pair has had a turn.
- Write any structural mistakes that students made on the board, without saying who made them, and ask them to correct them. Deal with any problems in pronunciation.

Answers
Students' own answers

Extra Writing Task 7

- Make sure each student has a copy of Extra Writing Task 7 that can be found on the *Resource CD-ROM*.
- Explain to students that they are going to write a short paragraph about their plans for the weekend. Ask students to look at the rules about *be going to* and the Future Simple in the grammar box and ask them to try to use a mixture of both tenses in their paragraph. Remind them to proofread their sentences.
- Ask students to write their paragraphs in their notebooks. You could set this task for homework if you are short of time.
- If time allows, invite some of them to read their paragraphs to the rest of the class. Gently correct any mistakes.

Extra Task (for early finishers)

See photocopiable material that can be found on the *Resource CD-ROM*.

Lesson 2

Objectives

Reading	article – open-ended questions
Vocabulary	text-related words; nature-related words
Grammar	gerunds
Listening	completing sentences
Sounds of English	*ough* sounds

Way in

- Ask students at random to tell you the nature-related words they learnt in Lesson 1, Vocabulary 4 and get them to come up and write a word on the board. Correct their spelling and pronunciation where necessary.
- Go round the class asking students to tell you something they think will happen at the weekend or something they are going to do at the weekend.

Reading

1

- Tell students to look at the picture and ask them what they think it shows. Ask them who saw the frilled lizards in the cartoon story in Lesson 1 (*Adam*).
- Tell students they are going to listen to and read the article about frilled lizards. Ask them to follow the text as they listen.
- Remind them to focus on the meaning of the highlighted words. Play the recording once. Check the meaning of the highlighted words as a class. If students don't know, encourage them to guess from the context. Encourage students to help each other work out the meaning of unknown words.

Answers

neck – *part of the body immediately below the head*
display – *show*
creatures – *living things like animals*
beetles – *insects with six legs and often with a hard shell covering their back*
spotting – *seeing / noticing*
face – *meet face-to-face*
hissing – *making a noise like a snake*
collar – *a band of material round the neck*

2

- Explain that students are going to read the article again, this time to themselves. Ask students to tell you one fact they learned from the article that they didn't know before.
- Ask students to read the pre-reading question and to find the answer in the article.

Answer

They usually take the colour of the environment they live in.

Did you know?

- Ask students to read the information in the *Did you know?* feature and ask them what animal they would like to have as a mascot for their school.
- If students are interested, give them more information on frilled lizards using the Background Information box below.

Background Information

A frilled lizard can run standing up on its back legs, with its front legs and tail in the air. The lizard needs the sun to warm its blood so that it can feed and move quickly. To reduce the loss of water, the body of a frilled lizard is covered in scales. The lizard's frill can be as big as 30cm in diameter when it's opened out and can look quite scary. For further information, go to www.nationalgeographic.com and search for 'frilled lizards'.

Comprehension

3

- Ask students to read questions 1 to 5 before they read the text again so that they know what information to look for.
- Ask students to do the task individually, but check the answers as a class. Tell them to underline where they get the answers from in the text so they can justify their answers.
- Explain any vocabulary students don't know.

Answers

1 in the tropical and warm forests of Australia and New Guinea (*Frilled lizards live ... New Guinea.*)
2 the frill (*The frill is not usually on display and it's difficult to see its bright red and orange colour.*)
3 catching their food (*They're very good at catching their food ...*)
4 They open their mouth wide and their frill stands up. (*When they see danger, ... their frill stands up.*)
5 They run away. (*If the enemy is still there, then the lizard just runs away!*)

Vocabulary

4

- Explain that the words in the wordbank are all highlighted words in the article, so students should know them.
- Ask students to do the task individually, but check the answers as a class.

Answers

1 spot
2 hiss
3 neck
4 display
5 face

5

- Ask students to read through the paragraph and options.
- Explain that some of the options appear in the article on page 66. Explain any words students don't understand or tell them to use a dictionary to find the meanings.
- Ask students to work in pairs to do the task, but check the answers as a class and correct pronunciation where necessary.

Answers

1 wildlife
2 creatures
3 pond
4 fence
5 seeds

Teaching Tip

To make sure that students understand all the items and not only the correct options in two-option or multiple choice vocabulary tasks, ask them to write their own sentences using the options not chosen. Get them to exchange books with a partner to compare and proofread each other's sentences.

Grammar

Gerunds

- Read the uses of gerunds in the grammar box to students and ask them to read the examples with you.
- Explain that gerunds are formed by adding –*ing* to a verb. Draw their attention to the gerund in example *b* (*running*) and explain that we make the same spelling changes to some verbs before the –*ing* as we make when we write the Present Continuous.

6

- Ask students to look back at the article on page 66 to find the gerunds.
- Ask students to do the task individually, but check the answers as a class.

Answer
four
Students should underline the following: catching, Spotting, hissing, running

Extra Class Activity

After students have found the four gerunds, ask them which of the grammar rules these match (*a Spotting, b hissing, running, c catching*).

7

- Ask students to read the sentences to decide which verb fits each gap. Tell them to decide what they have to add to each verb to make the gerund.
- Ask students to do the task individually, but check the answers as a class.

Answers

1 taking
2 swimming
3 Staying
4 chasing
5 feeding

Listening

8

- Explain to students that they are going to listen to an interview with Brian and Alison about what they like doing at the weekend and that they are going to complete the sentences. Give students a few minutes to read the notes and then ask them which sentences they can complete with a gerund (*2, 3, 5*). Explain that after *go for* we can't use a gerund, but for example we can say *go for a swim / walk / ride*. Then ask what kind of word they will write in question 4 (*adjective*).
- Play the recording to the end and ask students to fill in their answers. Ask them to work with a partner to check their answers and to justify any answers they have that are different.
- Play the recording again and ask students to check their answers and to fill in any missing information.
- Once you have checked the answers, ask students whether they would like to do any of these things at the weekend.

Turn to page 128 of this Teacher's Guide for the recording script.

Answers

1 walks (*... I like watching TV and going for walks with my dog ...*)
2 walking (*I think walking is a waste of time ...*)
3 shopping (*I also love shopping!*)
4 boring (*... I hate shopping! I think it's very boring!*)
5 visiting (*I enjoy visiting the zoo.*)

Sounds of English

9

- Play the words on the recording and ask students to listen carefully.
- In pairs, ask students to say the words to each other and to work out which words rhyme with *bought* (*brought*, *thought*), then ask what rhymes with *dough* (*though*) and what rhymes with *rough* (*tough*).
- Play the recording again without stopping and ask students to repeat the words. Correct their pronunciation where necessary.

Answers

bought / brought / thought
dough / though
rough / tough

10

- Before you play the recording, explain what a tongue twister is. Elicit examples of tongue twisters in your students' L1.
- Play the first line of the tongue twister on the recording and ask students to repeat this. Play the rest of the tongue twister and ask students to repeat this.
- Play the recording again without stopping and then ask students to say the whole tongue twister.

Teaching Tip

Ask students to practise saying the tongue twister in pairs. Then get students to repeat it loudly as a class to encourage everyone to participate. Then ask for volunteers to say it individually. You could give a prize to the student who can say it the fastest.

Extra Task (for early finishers)

See photocopiable material that can be found on the *Resource CD-ROM*.

Lesson 3

Objectives

Reading	interview – missing sentences
Express yourself!	talking about pets
Grammar	question tags
Writing	punctuation; writing a postcard

Way in

- Check students' spelling of the words they learnt in Lesson 2 by asking them to write down the following words: *neck, display, creature, beetles, spotting, face, hissing, collar, wildlife, fence* and *seeds*. Then check that they remember the meanings by asking them to translate them into their own language, or to explain their meanings in English.

- Ask students how we form gerunds (by adding *–ing* to a verb) and which parts of a sentence we can use them for (*the subject or the object*). Then ask what verbs we can use gerunds after (*can't stand, dislike, enjoy, hate, like, love, miss, remember*) and what other kinds of words we can use them after (*prepositions*).

Teaching Tip

The topic of injured pets may be upsetting for young students whose pets have died. While it is good to raise students' awareness about caring for animals, it might be wise to avoid discussion on the tragic causes of injury and death, unless students themselves raise these subjects.

Reading

1

- Ask students to look at the pictures on page 68 and to say what is wrong with these animals (*the black dog has got sore ears and the other dog has got an injured head; the cat might have an injury on its body or a cut it shouldn't lick*).
- Ask students if they can remember the word for a doctor who takes care of animals (*vet*) and tell them that they are going to read an interview with a vet about a pet rescue centre. Ask them to listen to and read the interview. Play the recording and ask students to tell you the answer to the pre-reading question.

Answer

No, some of them do.

Comprehension

2

- Ask students to read the sentences and to complete the interview. Once they have finished, tell them to read back through the interview to make sure that they have put the sentences in the correct place.
- Ask students to do the task individually, but check the answers as a class.
- Explain any vocabulary students don't know.

Answers

1e 2c 3b 4d 5a

Let's Talk

Put students into pairs. Ask them to talk about whether or not they would like to work at the Pet Rescue Centre and to give their reasons.

Extra Class Activity

Ask students to work in pairs to practise the completed interview dialogue, taking turns at playing the roles of Liam and Dr Simmons. Ask some pairs to role play the interview in front of the class. Correct pronunciation and intonation where necessary.

Express yourself!

Talking about pets

- Ask students to work in pairs to read through the structures in *Talking about pets* and the description of a pet dog and a pet rabbit.

3

- Ask students to talk about their pets or, if they don't have any pets, to talk about a pet they know. Remind them to practise the language given in the box. Correct their pronunciation and intonation pattern if necessary.
- Ask each pair to perform their dialogue until all students have had the chance to speak.

> **Answers**
> Students' own answers

Grammar

Question Tags

- Read the rules in the grammar box to the class and ask them to read the example sentences with you. Explain the meaning of any grammar terms that students are not familiar with.
- Ask students to look back at the interview on page 68 and to find the question tags (*don't they?, isn't it?, don't they?*). Ask students if these question tags are affirmative or negative (*negative*) and then ask them to see if the main verbs in the sentence are affirmative or negative (*affirmative*).
- Explain that question tags are always in the same tense as the main verb. Write on the board *They went to England last year, ...?* and ask students what tense this is (*Past Simple*) and whether it is affirmative or negative (*affirmative*). Then ask students to tell you the correct question tag (*didn't they?*).
- Draw students' attention to the question tags used for *I* and *everyone* which are exceptions to the rules.

4

- Explain that numbers 1 to 5 are the first halves of sentences and that students have to match them with question tags a to e to make complete sentences. Tell them to find the verb in the first half of each sentence and to decide whether the question tag will be affirmative or negative. Then ask them to choose the correct question tag a to e.
- Ask students to do the task individually, but check the answers as a class.

> **Answers**
> 1d 2a 3e 4c 5b

5

- Ask students to read the first part of each sentence to find the verb and to see whether it is negative or affirmative. Tell them to compare the first part of each sentence with the examples in the grammar box and the sentences in *Grammar 4* to see which words they need to form the question tag.

- Ask students to do the task individually, but check the answers as a class.

> **Answers**
> 1 aren't you
> 2 can't you
> 3 is she
> 4 isn't it
> 5 have you

Writing

Punctuation

6

- Before reading the rules about punctuation, tell students to close their books and ask them when we use capital letters (*at the beginning of sentences and names*). Write their answers on the board without adding to them at this stage. Then ask them to come up and write the marks that we can use at the end of a sentence (*!* and *.*) and what we use at the end of a question (*?*). Write a comma on the board and ask students when we use commas (*to separate words in a list and question tags from the rest of the sentence*).
- Tell students to open their books and then read the punctuation rules to them. Emphasise any points that they have difficulty understanding and explain the meaning of any words they don't know.
- Write on the board *I feed my dog when I come home*. Draw students' attention to the fact that we always use a capital for the first person *I* even if it is in the middle of a sentence.

7

- Explain that the letters and punctuation marks in red are incorrect and that students have to correct these mistakes. Tell students that these are the only mistakes in the sentences. Ask students to read the sentences to see whether they are questions, statements or exclamations. Ask them to decide if they need to add or change any capital letters. Tell them to look for words which need to be separated by commas.
- Ask students to do the task individually, but check the answers as a class.

> **Answers**
> 1? 2T 3g 4, 5!

8

- Ask students to read the postcard to see where each sentence begins and ends and whether they are questions, statements or exclamations. Remind them to use capital letters to begin sentences and names. Then tell them to look for words which need to be separated by commas.
- Ask students to do the task individually, and then get them to exchange books with a partner to compare each other's punctuation. Check the answers as a class.

Answer

Hi Kevin,

How are you? Thanks for the photos of your holiday. What a great time you're having!

I'm writing this postcard from my holiday home. Yesterday I found a cat in the street and we're going to keep her and take her back home with us. Her name is Missy.

I've drawn a picture of Missy. She's lovely, isn't she? Missy's clever and cuddly. She's got small ears and a long tail. You will love her!

See you soon!
Ethan

Task

9

- Ask students to work in pairs to discuss which pet they will write about. Tell them to talk about where the pet came from and to describe it.
- Make sure students understand the paragraph plan on page 69. Point out that there is not much space to write on a postcard, so the paragraphs will be shorter than the paragraphs in a letter or an email.
- Ask students to use the plan to write a postcard like the one in *Writing 8*. Remind them to use capital letters where necessary and the correct punctuation marks.
- Alternatively, you could assign this task as homework.

Example answer

Hi Pete,

How are you? Thanks for the postcard about your holiday. What a beautiful island you went to!

I'm writing this from my uncle's farm in the village. Last month, my cousin's cat had three kittens. I'm going to take one of them home with me and keep her. Her name's Smoky.

I've drawn a picture of Smoky. She's great, isn't she? You can see she's grey and she's got blue eyes and white legs. You will love her!

See you soon!
Ben

10

- Remind students that the postcard should open and close in a friendly way and it should have a beginning, a middle and an end.
- Ask students to read back through their postcards to make sure that they have used the correct punctuation. If you ask them to write the postcard for homework, then give them a few minutes to do this at the beginning of the next lesson.

Extra Task (for early finishers)

See photocopiable material that can be found on the *Resource CD-ROM*.

The Environment

Way in

- If you assigned Unit 7, Lesson 3 *Writing 9* for homework, give students a few minutes to proofread their postcards checking the punctuation and capital letters. Then ask them to read each other's postcards, or stick them on the wall so they can read them when they have time.
- Explain to students that this unit is about the environment in general. Ask students to each say a sentence about the environment.

Did you know?

- With books closed, ask students to brainstorm recycling. Check they understand the meaning of the word, then ask them to list all the things that can be recycled. Ask if they recycle these things themselves.
- Ask students to open their books at pages 70 and 71. Ask them to look at the picture and see if they know the meaning of all the words on the bins.
- Ask students to read the paragraph about recycling on page 71. Explain that different sorts of materials are recycled in different ways, which is why they all go into different bins.
- Read the information from the *Did you know?* feature to the class. Ask students if they knew that recycling glass actually saved energy.
- Use the background information in the box below to give the students further information about recycling if they are interested. Check if they have any questions. If they ask for information you don't have, refer them to the website in the Background Information box and ask them to feed back to you at the next lesson.

Background Information

British people throw away 28 million tonnes of rubbish each year. That's the same weight as three and a half million double-decker buses – and that number of buses in a line would go around the world one and a half times! You can make 20 cans out of recycled material with the same amount of energy it takes to make one new one. Every ton of paper that's recycled saves 17 trees. In Britain, people use more than six billion glass bottles and jars. It would take more than three and a half thousand years to sing the whole of 'Six Billion Green Bottles'! For further information, go to www.nationalgeographic.com and search for 'recycling'.

Let's Talk

Put students into small groups. Ask them to talk about how they could do more to recycle the things they use at home and at school.

Lesson 1

Objectives

Reading	the cartoon story – completing sentences
Vocabulary	text-related words; environment-related words
Grammar	first conditional
Listening	completing sentences
Speaking	talking about recycling

The cartoon story

- Ask students if they can remember what happened in the previous episode of the cartoon story (*Adam wanted to take photos of lizards for the school magazine but it wasn't a nice day to go to the zoo. So the magic globe took the children to see lizards in their natural environment. They went to Australia and saw frilled lizards. Adam and Mikey asked the globe to take them home so they could get sun cream and sandwiches. They promised Kristie they would be back soon but started to watch a funny programme on TV and forgot about Kristie.*).
- Ask students to look at the story pictures and suggest what might be happening.

1

- Please follow the procedure outlined in Unit 1, Lesson 1 on page 12 of this Teacher's Guide.

Answers

litter bin – *large container for rubbish*
recycling – *use things again*
saving – *not wasting*
recycling plant – *place where things are used again*
take apart – *take to pieces*
separately – *not together, one by one*
protect – *keep safe; look after*
throw away – *put with the rubbish*

- Depending on whether you are using the DVD or the Audio CD, follow the relevant instructions.

For teachers using the DVD

- Make sure each child has a copy of Cartoon DVD Worksheet 8 that can be found on the *Resource CD-ROM*.
- Please follow the procedure outlined in Unit 1, Lesson 1 on page 12 of this Teacher's Guide for teachers using the DVD.

Before you watch

Answers

1 in Mikey's bedroom
2 putting things in a box

While you watch

Answers
1	Adam	4	Kristie
2	Mikey	5	Adam
3	Kristie	6	Kristie

After you watch

Answers
1	F	4	F
2	T	5	F
3	F	6	T

For teachers using the Audio CD

- Ask students to look at page 72 of their student's book and to work in pairs. Ask them to look at the pictures and say whose room the children are in at the end of the story (*Kristie's*).
- Tell students they are going to listen to and read the story. Ask them to look at the pictures and to follow the story as they listen.
- Play the recording once and ask students whether or not you can recycle anything that's electronic (*yes*).
- Put students into small groups of three and ask them to assign the roles of Kristie, Adam and Mikey within their groups. Ask them to read the story out loud in their groups.
- As a class, ask students the questions below to check their understanding of the episode.
  1 Did Mikey know you can recycle old TVs? (*No, he didn't.*)
  2 How many TVs are there at the recycling plant? (*thousands*)
  3 If we all recycle, what will we save? (*energy*)
  4 What will we protect if we recycle? (*the environment*)
  5 Which of Kristie's T-shirts has Adam got? (*her favourite T-shirt*)

Comprehension

2

- Ask students to read sentences 1 to 5 so they know what information to look for when they read the cartoon story again. Ask them to complete the sentences using information from the story.
- Ask students to do the task individually, but check the answers as a class. Encourage students to explain their answer choices by giving evidence from the story.

Answers
1 magazines (*I'm going to recycle my old books and magazines.*)
2 recycling plant (*This is an electronics recycling plant.*)
3 old TVs (*There are thousands of old TVs here!*)
4 old computer (*Can I recycle my old computer too?*)
5 T-shirt (*Hey! That's my favourite T-shirt!*)

Let's Talk

Put students into small groups. Tell them to plan something they could make out of rubbish (old bottles, cans, TVs, books, etc). It can be anything they like so encourage them to use their imagination. Time permitting, invite groups to share their ideas with the class.

Vocabulary

3

- Ask students to look at the words in the wordbank. Remind them that all the words are highlighted in the cartoon story on page 72 and point out that they already know the meaning of them.
- Ask students to do the task individually, but check the answers as a class.

Answers
1	away	4	litter
2	plant	5	apart
3	separately		

4

- Explain to students that they have to label the pictures 1 to 6 with the words in the wordbank. Explain any vocabulary that students have not been taught yet or ask students to use a dictionary to find the meanings.
- Ask students to work in pairs to do the task, but check the answers as a class and correct pronunciation where necessary.

Answers
1	litter bin	4	can
2	glass bottle	5	battery
3	plastic bag	6	newspaper

Extra Class Activity

Ask students to look at the words and pictures in *Vocabulary 4* and to tell you which of these things they see in the streets near their homes every day.

Grammar

First Conditional

- Read the first use of the First Conditional in the grammar box to the class and explain any grammar terms that students don't know. Ask students to read the example. Then ask them to find the verb in the *if* clause (*recycle*) and ask them what tense this is (*Present Simple*). Ask them what the verb is in the result clause (*will help*) and what tense it is (*Future Simple*).
- Read the rest of the grammar box to the class and ask different students to read out the examples. Draw students' attention to the note about punctuation and read through it with them.
- Ask students to look back at the cartoon episode on page 72 and to underline the First Conditional sentences in frame 2 (*If your TV doesn't work, they will take it apart. If we all recycle, we will save energy and we will protect the environment.*).

5

- Ask students to read through the sentences and options and find out whether the option is in the *if* clause or in the result clause. Remind them to choose the Present Simple in the *if* clause and the Future Simple in the result clause.
- Ask students to do the task individually. Then, when they are finished, give them a few minutes to compare their answers with a partner. Ask them to justify their answers if they are different.
- Check the answers as a class and ask students to justify the answers they give.

Answers
1 collect
2 don't use
3 will
4 don't go
5 will save

6

- Ask students to read each sentence to decide whether they need to use the Present Simple or the Future Simple of the verb in brackets. Tell them to think about whether the verb is in the *if* clause or in the result clause.
- Explain that the answers include affirmative, negative and question forms.
- Ask students to do the task individually, but check the answers as a class.

Answers
1 don't throw away
2 won't be
3 will recycle
4 will you take
5 don't protect

Listening

7

- Explain to students that they are going to listen to a teacher talking to a class and that they have to complete the sentences. Explain that they will hear some of the words from *Vocabulary 4*.
- Give students a few minutes to read the sentences to think about what information is missing.
- Play the recording to the end and ask students to fill in their answers. Ask them to work with a partner to check their answers and to justify any answers they have that are different.
- Play the recording again and ask students to check their answers and to fill in any missing information.

Turn to page 128 of this Teacher's Guide for the recording script.

Answers
1 recycling (*Today we're going to learn about recycling.*)
2 cans (*My parents recycle paper, glass and cans.*)
3 clothes (*And my mum recycles old clothes!*)
4 bin (*… Dad takes the other things to a special bin in the town centre.*)
5 boxes (*We've got some big green boxes just outside this classroom.*)

Speaking

8

- Explain that students are going to work in pairs to discuss the questions about the environment.
- Remind students to use the environment-related vocabulary that they have learnt so far to answer the questions.
- Read through the *Express yourself!* box with students. Explain that this box provides useful language that will help them complete the Speaking task. Give one or two example sentences, talking about when you did the things in the list. When students are confident with the language, they can do the task in their pairs.
- Go round the class monitoring students to make sure they are carrying out the task properly. Don't correct any mistakes in structure and pronunciation that you hear at this stage, but make a note of them.
- Tell each pair to ask and answer one of the questions and repeat until everyone has had a turn.
- Write any structural mistakes you heard on the board, without saying who made them, and ask students to correct them. Deal with any problems that arose with pronunciation.

Answers
Students' own answers

Teaching Tip
When students have expressed their opinions, add to the discussion by telling them your own answers to the questions. Let them know what you recycle and what more you'd like to do to help the environment.

Extra Writing Task 8

- Make sure each student has a copy of Extra Writing Task 8 that can be found on the *Resource CD-ROM*.
- Explain to students that they are going to write a short paragraph about why recycling is important. Encourage them to use as many of the words they learnt in Lesson 1 as possible. Before they write, put students into small groups to discuss their ideas.
- Ask students to write their paragraphs in their notebooks. You could set this task for homework if you are short of time.
- If time allows, invite some of them to read their paragraphs to the rest of the class. Gently correct any mistakes.

Extra Task (for early finishers)

See photocopiable material that can be found on the *Resource CD-ROM*.

Lesson 2

Objectives

Reading	article – true or false
Vocabulary	text-related words; environment-related words
Grammar	second conditional
Listening	multiple choice

Way in

- Write the words *litter bin, recycling, saving, take apart, throw away, separately* and *protect* on the board and tell students to write a sentence for each word. Then ask them to swap books with a partner to compare their sentences and check spelling. Ask different students to read one of their sentences to the class until all the words have been correctly used.
- Write *If* on the board and ask students to tell you a sentence in the First Conditional. Write two of their examples on the board and ask the class to correct them if necessary. Ask which tense we use in the *if* clause and which tense we use in the result clause.

Reading

1

- Tell students they are going to listen to and read the article. Ask them to follow the article as they listen.
- Play the recording once. Ask students to tell you one fact they learned from the article that they didn't know before.
- Ask students to read the pre-reading question and to find the answer in the article.

Answer

by turning off the TV, turning off lights, turning off the water while we brush our teeth

2

- Please follow the procedure outlined in Unit 1, Lesson 2 on page 15 of this Teacher's Guide.

Answers

solar power – *energy from the sun*
pollution – *dirt and unclean air, water, etc in the environment*
harms – *damages* panels - *a rectangular board usually made from wood, glass or metal*
electricity – *a form of energy*
in fact – *a way of introducing something that's true*
turned off – *stopped something working by stopping power going to it*
brushing – *cleaning with a brush*

Did you know?

- Ask students to read the information in the *Did you know?* feature and ask them what they think about the idea of making energy by dancing.
- If students are interested, give them more information about the sun and solar power using the Background Information box below.

Background Information

The sun is 109 times bigger than the Earth; its radius is 696,000km. The reason we can get energy from the sun is because the sun's average surface temperature is 5,700 degrees Celcius! The Earth's average temperature is only 20 degrees Celcius. Some people predict that 50% of the Earth's energy will come from solar power or other renewable energy sources by 2040. For further information, go to www.nationalgeographic.com and search for 'solar power'.

Let's Talk

Put students into small groups. Ask them to talk about other ideas for generating energy, similar to the Eco-club in the UK. Encourage them to use their imagination.

Comprehension

3

- Ask students to read sentences 1 to 5 so that they know what information to look for when reading the text again.
- Ask students to read the text again to find out if sentences 1 to 5 are true or false and then to write *T* or *F* in the boxes provided. Tell them to underline the information in the text that helps them to find the answers.
- Explain any vocabulary students don't know and correct their pronunciation if necessary.

Answers

1 T (*Solar power is 'clean' because it doesn't cause pollution that harms the environment.*)
2 F (*Solar panels turn electricity from the sun into electricity ...*)
3 F (*You may think that solar panels are only useful in countries with lots of sunshine all year round, like Spain ...*)
4 T (*... solar panels work better in colder temperatures.*)
5 F (*... there are many other things we can do too.*)

Vocabulary

4

- Remind students that the first letter of each word is given and that they must write one letter on each line to complete the word. Explain that the words appear in the article on page 74 and are highlighted words, so students should know the meaning. Explain any words they don't understand.

- Ask students to do the task individually, but check the answers as a class. Correct their pronunciation where necessary.

Answers
1 turn off
2 panel
3 electricity
4 solar power
5 pollution

Grammar

Second Conditional

- Read rules a to c in the grammar box to the class and explain any grammar terms that students don't know. Ask students to read the examples with you.
- Read the rest of the grammar box to the class and ask different students to read out the example sentences. Draw students' attention to the note and explain that we can use *were* instead of *was* after *he / she / it* in Second Conditional sentences.

5

- Ask students to look back at the article on page 74 and to underline all the Second Conditional sentences.
- Ask students to do the task individually, but check the answers as a class.

Answer
three
Students should underline the following:
If you wanted to protect the environment, what would you do?
... we would save energy if we turned off the TV and the light every time we left a room.
If we turned off the water while we were brushing our teeth, we would save water.

6

- Ask students to read each sentence to decide whether they need to use the Past Simple of the verb in brackets or *would* with the bare infinitive. Tell them to think about whether the verb is in the *if* clause or in the result clause.
- Explain that the answers include affirmative, negative and question forms.
- Ask students to do the task individually, but check the answers as a class.

Answer
1 Would we help, saved
2 Would I pay, had
3 would not / wouldn't harm, went
4 would you do, weren't
5 were, would recycle

Extra Class Activity

Ask students to work in pairs to write four sentences of their own using the Second Conditional. Give them time to write their sentences, and then ask them to swap books with another pair to check each other's sentences. Remind them to use the Past Simple in the *if* clause and *would* plus the bare infinitive of the main verb in the result clause. After students have checked each other's sentences, ask different students to read one of their sentences to the class.

Vocabulary

7

- Ask students to work in pairs to read the sentences and options and decide which options should fill the gaps. As most of the vocabulary is new, encourage students to use dictionaries, if they have them, as well as to look for clues in the general meaning of the sentence.
- Check the answers as a class and explain the meanings of the words where necessary.

Answers
1 pollute
2 rubbish
3 climate
4 empty
5 plant

Listening

8

- Ask students to read the questions and to choose the answers they think are correct before they listen to the recording.
- Explain to students that they are going to listen to a boy and a girl talking about recycling in Greece, and that the dialogue is in five parts with one question for each part.
- Play the recording once, stopping at the end of each part of the dialogue, and ask students to circle the correct answers.
- Give students a few minutes to compare their answers with a partner. Ask them to justify their answers if they are different.
- Play the recording again and ask students to check their answers and to fill in any missing information.
- Check the answers as a class and ask students to justify the answers they give.

Turn to page 129 of this Teacher's Guide for the recording script.

Answer
1 b (*No, it's 60%. We can recycle about 60% of the things in the rubbish.*)
2 a (*You must use the blue recycling bins.*)
3 c (*You must take batteries to the special bins in shops and supermarkets.*)
4 c (*...in Greece about 20% of waste is plastic.*)
5 c (*We make the bags in a minute and we use them for about twenty minutes, but they stay on land or in water for about 400 years.*)

Extra Task (for early finishers)

See photocopiable material that can be found on the *Resource CD-ROM*.

Lesson 3

Objectives

Reading	webpage – multiple matching
Express yourself!	talking about the environment
Listening	numbering pictures
Sounds of English	stressing different parts of a sentence
Speaking	talking about a picture
Writing	giving advice with conditional sentences; making a poster

Materials needed

Sheets of (coloured) paper for students to make posters.

Way in

- Check students' spelling of the words they learnt in Lesson 2 by asking them to write down the following words in their notebooks: *solar power, pollution, harm, panels, electricity, panel, in fact, turn off, brushing*. Check that they remember the meanings of the words by asking them to translate them into their own language, or to explain the meaning in English.
- Write on the board: *The town would be clean if we recycled our rubbish*. Ask students which tense the verb is in the *if* clause (*Past Simple*) and what word we use with the verb in the result clause (*would*). Remind them that this structure is called a Second Conditional and ask whether this is about something that is likely to happen in the future (*no*).

Reading

1

- Tell students that they are going to listen to and read a webpage with comments and tips that students from Greece have written about the environment. Ask them to follow the text on page 76 as they listen.
- Play the recording once. Ask students to tell you one fact they learned from the webpage that they didn't know before.
- Ask students to read the pre-reading question and to find the answer in the webpage.

Answer
Zoe

Comprehension

2

- Tell students to read questions 1 to 5 before they read the text again so that they know what information to look for.

- Ask students to do the task individually, but check the answers as a class. Ask students to underline where they get the answer from in the text so they can justify their answers.
- Explain any vocabulary students don't know and correct their pronunciation if necessary.

Answers
1 Z (*It takes energy to make the toys we play with, ...*)
2 P (*... my dad and I take them to the special recycling bins ...*)
3 N (*You can use the same plastic bags and the same glass bottles many times ...*)
4 A (*My friends and I clean the beaches at the beginning of the summer.*)
5 A (*If we pollute the beaches, sea turtles will die out.*)

Express yourself!

Talking about the environment

3

- Ask students to work in pairs to read the words and to complete the dialogue. Check answers as a class.

Answers
1 recycle
2 ride
3 waste
4 pollute
5 throw away

4

- Put students into pairs to practise the dialogue with their partner. Gently correct any errors of pronunciation.
- Invite some pairs to say the dialogue in front of the class.

Listening

5

- Ask students to look at pictures a to e and to tell you what they show (*a boy putting cans in a recycling bin, people talking about recycling, a boy taking a recycling bin, people putting recycling bins in front of a building, a boy putting a label on a recycling bin*).
- Explain to students that they are going to hear someone talking about recycling and that they are going to note down the order in which they hear about each thing. Tell students that they have to listen for the words that talk about what the people are doing in the pictures.
- Play the recording once and encourage students to number each object as they hear about it rather than try to find the answers from a to e respectively.
- Play the recording again and ask students to number the remaining things, then check the answers as a class. Ask students to justify their answers.

Turn to page 129 of this Teacher's Guide for the recording script.

Answers
a 5 (*When the bins are full, take them to a supermarket or your school's big recycling bins.*)
b 4 (*Next, tell the people in each house or flat about recycling.*)
c 1 (*... ask some neighbours for some rubbish bins.*)
d 3 (*... put the bins in a good place so everyone can see them ...*)
e 2 (*Use a special pen and write PAPER, PLASTIC, GLASS and CANS on the bins.*)

Extra Class Activity

Have a class discussion about what the boy in *Listening 5* did. Ask students whether they would do this where they live and whether they think it would be easy or not.

Sounds of English

6

- Tell students that they are going to listen to a sentence and that they should listen carefully to which words are stressed. Play the recording all the way through without stopping. Explain the meaning of any new vocabulary where necessary.
- Ask students what it means when we put the stress on the words shown (the stress on *If* shows we probably don't really care, and stress on *have* shows we have a lot of problems).
- Play the recording once more without stopping and then ask students to repeat the sentence as a class, stressing the words underlined.

Answer
Students should underline the following: If, have

7

- Play the recording once without stopping and ask students to listen carefully to which words are stressed this time.
- Check that students have circled the correct words and ask how the meaning of the sentence has changed.
- Play the recording once more without stopping and ask students to repeat the sentence as a class, stressing the words circled.

Answer
Students should circle the following: really, pollution

Suggested answer
The first time suggests that we might not have problems with pollution if we cared about the environment. The second time stresses that we don't care enough and that pollution is the result.

Speaking

8

- Tell students that they are going to work in pairs to talk about what they would do if they lived in the place in the picture.

- Remind students of the conditionals they learnt previously and tell them to use them to answer the questions.
- Go round the class monitoring students to make sure they are carrying out the task properly. Don't correct any mistakes at this stage, but make a note of any mistakes in structure and pronunciation.
- Write any structural mistakes that you heard on the board, without saying who made them, and ask students to correct them. Deal with any problems in pronunciation.

Suggested answers
If I lived there, I would ...
ride a bicycle / not throw things in the river / clean the park near the city / tell the boy to use a recycling bin / recycle the cans and bottles / plant more trees.

Writing

Giving advice with conditional sentences

9

- Ask students to read the three tips about the environment and explain the meaning of any words they don't know.
- Draw students' attention to the fact that each tip has two sentences and explain that the first tells us what to do and the second tells us the result of doing this.

10

- Explain that students have to complete the sentences to give the same tips as they read in *Writing 9*, but this time they will show each tip and its result in one sentence.
- Remind students to use the Past Simple in the *if* clause and *would* before the main verb in the result clause.
- Ask students to do the task individually, but check the answers as a class.

Answers
1 sent, wouldn't waste
2 turned off, would save
3 recycled, would help

11

- Ask students to read the poster to see whether the word in brackets is in the *if* clause or in the result clause, and then to complete the sentences using the second conditional.
- Ask students to do the task individually, but check the answers as a class.

Answers
1 threw away   5 put
2 would be   6 would have
3 stopped   7 would save
4 wouldn't pollute 8 recycled

Task

12

- Give students a piece of A3 paper to make their poster on. Ask students to work in pairs to discuss their answers to the questions on page 77 about each part of the poster. Tell them to use the ideas from the webpage on page 76 and the *Listening* and *Speaking* tasks.
- Make sure students understand the layout of the poster. Explain that they can write more than one tip and that each tip will come under a different heading.
- Ask students to use their answers to the questions to write a poster like the one in *Writing 11*. Remind students to use the Second Conditional to make sentences like the ones in *Writing 10* and the advice in *Writing 11*.
- Alternatively, you could assign this task as homework.

Example answer
Recycling
Recycle cans! If we recycled all our cans, we would save a lot of metal!

Water
Don't waste water. We would save a lot of water if we took showers and not baths.

Plastic bags
Take your own bags to the shops! If everyone used their own bags, we wouldn't need so much plastic.

13

- Ask students to look back through their posters to make sure that they have used the Second Conditional correctly. Tell them to make sure they have given a result for each piece of advice. If you ask them to make the poster for homework, then give them a few minutes to do this at the beginning of the next lesson.

Extra Task (for early finishers)

See photocopiable material that can be found on the *Resource CD-ROM*.

Review 4

Objectives

- To revise vocabulary and grammar from Units 7 and 8
- Project – wild animals

Preparing for the review

- Explain to students that the tasks in *Review 4* revise the material they learnt in Units 7 and 8.
- Remind students that they can ask you for help with the exercises or look back at the units if they're not sure about an answer, as the review is not a test.
- Decide how you will carry out the review. You could ask students to do one task at a time and then correct it immediately, or ask students to do all the tasks and then correct them together at the end. If you do all the tasks together, let students know every now and again how much time they have got left to finish the tasks.
- Remind students not to leave any answers blank and to try to find any answers they aren't sure about in the units.
- Revise the vocabulary and grammar as a class before students do the review.

Vocabulary Revision

- Check that students remember the text-related words and phrases from Unit 7, Lesson 1. Write the words *lizard, natural environment, frilled, DVD recorder* and *second* on the board and ask students to give the meaning or an example sentence for each one.
- Ask students to tell you as many nouns as possible related to nature. Make sure they revise *branch, farm, leaves, nest, soil* and *stones*.
- Write *neck, display, creatures, beetles, spot, face, hiss* and *collar* on the board and ask students to write down a sentence for each word in their notebooks. When they have finished, ask students at random to read out one of their sentences until all the words have been used correctly.
- Check that students remember the words related to the environment. Write the headings *verbs* and *nouns* on the board and ask students to tell you as many words as possible related to the environment. Invite them to come up to the board and write the words under the correct heading.

Grammar Revision

- Write *It's going to rain.* and *I think it will rain tomorrow.* on the board, and then ask students when we use *going to* and when we use *will* to talk about the future.
- Write *I love taking photos of lizards.* on the board and ask students which word is a gerund. Ask them to give other examples to show how we use gerunds as the subject of a sentence and after prepositions.

- Write *My dog is cute*, and *You like cats*, on the board and ask students to come up and add the question tags. Check that they remember how to make question tags when the verb is affirmative or negative.
- Write *use* and *pollute* on the board and ask a student to come and write a first conditional sentence with *If* and these verbs. Then ask a student to write a second conditional sentence with these words.

Vocabulary

1

- Ask students to say each of the words as a class and then individually. Correct their pronunciation if necessary.
- Ask students to go to the second page of stickers at the back of the book and find the stickers for *Review 4*. Tell them to decide which thing each sticker shows and to stick it in the correct box.
- Check that students have put the correct stickers above each word.

2

- Tell students to draw lines between words 1 to 5 and nouns a to e.
- Ask students to tell you which of these things is useful for us and which things are bad for the environment.

Answers
1d 2a 3b 4e 5c

3

- Explain to students that they should read the whole paragraph so that they understand the context for each of the missing words.
- Tell students they may need to look back at Unit 8, Lessons 2 and 3 for some of the answers as well as the *Vocabulary* tasks in both units.

Answers
1 environment
2 recycle
3 save
4 energy
5 bottles
6 plant

4

- Ask students to read the whole sentence and the possible options before circling the correct answer. After they have finished the exercise ask them to read the sentences again to make sure their answers make sense.

Answers
1 forecast
2 soil
3 green products
4 away
5 Pollution
6 treat

Grammar

5

- Explain to students that they should decide whether they need to make any spelling changes to the verb in brackets to make the gerund.
- Tell students to look back at the Unit 7, Lesson 2 grammar box for a reminder if they need to.

Answers
1 learning
2 Taking
3 looking after
4 spending
5 going
6 seeing

6

- Explain to students that they should read the sentences and the possible options before trying to choose the answers to decide whether we use *will* or *going to* in this context.
- Tell students to look back at Unit 7, Lesson 1 grammar boxes for a reminder if they need to.

Answers
1b 2b 3a 4a 5b 6a

7

- Tell students to look at the verb in the first part of each sentence to see which tense it is and whether it is affirmative or negative before they write the question tag.
- Tell students to look back at the Unit 7, Lesson 3 grammar box for a reminder if they need to.

Answers
1 do you
2 won't they
3 did you
4 hasn't she
5 has he
6 can't we

8

- Explain to students that they should read the sentences before trying to write the answers to decide whether to use the First or the Second Conditional. Tell them to look for verb tenses in the result clause or the *if* clause of each sentence to help them get the correct form of the verb in brackets.

- Remind students to use the list of irregular verbs on pages 132 and 133 and tell them to look back at the grammar boxes in Unit 8, Lessons 1 and 2 for a reminder if they need to.

Answers
1 would save
2 would ... die out
3 would go
4 do not / don't put
5 slept
6 will protect
7 would you do
8 don't leave

Project 4

1

- Explain to the students that they are going to make a page for a book about wild animals for their project. Ask them to say which wild animals they are going to write about.
- Point out that students should find photos of the animals they are going to have in their book or that they can draw and colour pictures of them.
- Ask students to read the bullet points and explain that the paragraph they write must address these points.
- Read through the example paragraph about an orangutan with the class.
- Ask students to complete their projects. They can do this in the lesson or for homework.
  When the projects are complete, stick them on the classroom wall.

2

- Invite students to tell the class about their wild animals. Find out which animal is the most popular.

Teaching Tip
When checking students' answers to the review tasks, make a note of any problem areas in vocabulary and grammar that they still have. Try to do extra work on these areas so that your students progress well.

In Town

Way in

- If you assigned Unit 8, Lesson 3 *Writing 12* as homework, give students a few minutes to proofread their posters and to check that it has headings, gives advice about the environment and says what would happen if we followed the advice. Ask students to read each other's posters, or stick them on the wall so they can read them when they have time.
- Ask students to read the title of the unit. Ask how they would describe a town. See if they know the difference between a town and a city.

Did you know?

- With books closed, ask students to brainstorm the advantages and disadvantages of living in a town or city.
- Ask students to open their books at pages 80 and 81. Ask them to look at the picture and see if they can guess which city it is (*Seattle*). Ask students if they would like to live in a city like this. Encourage them to give their reasons.
- Ask students to read the paragraph about Seattle on page 81. Tell students that in some countries, including England, there are a lot of tall buildings like this (explain that they are also called high rise buildings). Ask students why they think cities have high rise buildings (*to fit more people, more accommodation or more offices into the city*).
- Read the information from the *Did you know?* feature to the class. To give students an idea of how long 43 seconds is, count slowly to 43 (say *elephant* between each number so that you approximately count the rate of one number per second).
- Use the background information in the box below to give the students further information about the Space Needle in Seattle if they are interested. Check if they have any questions. If they ask for information you don't have, refer them to the website in the Background Information box and ask them to feed back to you at the next lesson.

Background Information
There are 848 steps from the bottom of the basement to the top of the Observation Deck in the Space Needle. It moves about 2.5cm for every 6 kilometres per hour of wind speed – so on a windy day it can feel a bit scary at the top! On a hot day, the Needle expands by about 2.5cm. The Space Needle was built in 1962 at a cost of 4.5 million dollars. In 2000, the Needle needed to be repaired and parts of it had to be replaced – that cost 20 million dollars! The first ever manager of the Needle, Hoge Sullivan, was afraid of heights, which must have made his job rather difficult. For further information, go to www.nationalgeographic.com and search for 'Seattle'.

Let's Talk
Put students into small groups. Ask them to talk about any other tall buildings that they know about in the world. If they don't know of any, ask them to research it; otherwise, bring some information about tall buildings to the lesson and let the students discuss it in their groups.

Extra Class Activity
Time permitting, provide the class with a roll of drawing paper and ask them to make a classroom frieze of a city skyline like Seattle's. They can draw and colour, paint, or use glue and stick magazine pictures onto the paper to make their collage.

Lesson 1

Objectives

Reading	the cartoon story – circling the correct words
Vocabulary	text-related words; directions
Grammar	have to; must
Listening	labelling a picture
Speaking	giving directions from one place to another

The cartoon story

- Ask students if they can remember what happened in the previous episode of the cartoon story (*Mikey tidied his bedroom and had a lot of things to throw away. Adam told Mikey he should recycle his old things. The magic globe took the children to a recycling plant so they could learn more about recycling. They learnt that they could recycle electronic things as well as clothes and books.*).
- Ask students to look at the story pictures and suggest what might be happening.

1

- Explain that students are going to listen to the words in the wordbank. Play the recording and ask them to point to each word as they hear it.
- Play the recording again and encourage students to repeat as a class. You could ask individual students to repeat on their own if you feel they are confident enough.
- Put the students in pairs and ask them to find the words in the story and underline them. When they have all found the words, work through them one at a time as a class, asking students to read out the sentences in the story containing the word. Ask students to say what the word means. If they don't know, encourage them to guess from the context.

2

- Depending on whether you are using the DVD or the Audio CD, follow the relevant instructions.

For teachers using the DVD

- Make sure each child has a copy of Cartoon DVD Worksheet 9 that can be found on the *Resource CD-ROM*.
- Please follow the procedure outlined in Unit 1, Lesson 1 on page 12 of this Teacher's Guide for teachers using the DVD.

Before you watch

> **Answers**
> 1 playing a board game
> 2 on the table

While you watch

> **Answers**
> 1 birthday
> 2 plane tickets
> 3 passport
> 4 restaurant
> 5 full circle
> 6 view

After you watch

> **Answers**
> 1 Kristie
> 2 Mikey
> 3 Beth
> 4 Mikey
> 5 Kristie
> 6 Mikey

For teachers using the Audio CD

- Tell students to look at page 82 of their student's book and to work in pairs. Ask students to say whose birthday it is (*Beth's*).
- Tell students they are going to listen to and read the story. Ask them to look at the pictures and to follow the story as they listen.
- Play the recording once and ask which restaurant they took Beth to (*SkyCity, at the top of the Space Needle in Seattle*).
- Put students into small groups of four and ask them to assign the roles of Kristie, Adam, Mikey and Beth within their groups. Ask them to read the story out loud in their groups.

- As a class, ask students the questions below to check their understanding of the episode.
  1 Who has a brilliant idea? (*Mikey*)
  2 Do the children have to book plane tickets? (*No, they don't.*)
  3 What do they have to buy? (*a present for Beth*)
  4 Where is the SkyCity restaurant? (*at the top of the Space Needle*)
  5 What can Adam take photos of? (*the whole city*)

> **Teaching Tip**
> Encourage students to answer the extra questions about the cartoon episode using complete sentences and to justify their answers wherever they can. This will help them practise producing correct structures and as much language as possible.

Comprehension

3

- Ask students to read sentences 1 to 5 so they know what information to look for when they read the cartoon story again. Ask them to circle the correct words using information from the story.
- Ask students to do the task individually, but check the answers as a class. Encourage students to explain their answer choices by giving evidence from the story.

> **Answers**
> 1 an e-card (*I must send her an e-card.*)
> 2 Mikey's (*Why don't we take her out to lunch for her birthday?*)
> 3 don't have (*We don't have to have a passport.*)
> 4 round in a circle (*It makes a full circle in 47 minutes.*)
> 5 doesn't like (*Stop it! I feel dizzy ...*)

> **Let's Talk**
> Put students into small groups. Tell them to imagine the magic globe could take them to the top of a building anywhere in the world. In their groups, ask them to talk about where they would go and why they would go there.

Vocabulary

4

- Ask students to look at the words in the wordbank. Remind them that all the words are from the cartoon story on page 82 and point out that they already know the meaning of them. Check understanding of one or two of the words again if you think it's necessary.
- Ask students to do the task individually, but check the answers as a class.

Answers
1 dizzy
2 book
3 magnificent
4 circle
5 passport

5

- Explain to students that they have to match pictures a to f with sentences 1 to 6. Tell students that we use these expressions to tell people how to go somewhere and then explain any vocabulary that students have not been taught yet.
- Ask students to work in pairs to do the task, but check the answers as a class and correct pronunciation where necessary.

Answers
1b 2e 3f 4d 5a 6c

Let's Talk

Put students into pairs. Ask them to describe a route they know to their partner – it could be their journey to school, a walk from their house to the shops, etc. Encourage them to use the expressions in *Vocabulary 5*.

Grammar

Have to

- Read the first part of the grammar box to the class and ask students to read the example sentences with you. Explain the grammar terms used if necessary.
- Read the affirmative, negative and question forms from the grammar box with the class. Ask them which word we put in front of *have to* in the negative (*don't / doesn't*). Then ask how we form questions (with *Do / Does* + subject + *have to* + infinitive).
- Ask students a few questions using *have to* to elicit short answers.
- Ask students to look back at the first frame of the cartoon episode on page 82 and to underline the sentences with *have to* (*We don't have to book plane tickets. We don't have to have a passport. But we have to buy her a present!*).

6

- Ask students to read each sentence to see whether it is in the affirmative, negative or question form and whether it is about the present or the past.
- Explain that the answers in the task include affirmative, negative and question forms.
- Ask students to do the task individually, but check the answers as a class.

Answers
1 have to
2 Did ... have to
3 don't have to
4 had to
5 Do ... have to

Must

- Read the first part of the grammar box to the class and ask students to read the example sentences with you. Draw students' attention to the fact that we never use *to* after *must*, but only the bare infinitive.
- Read the affirmative, negative and question forms from the grammar box with the class. Ask students a few questions using *must* to elicit short answers.

7

- Ask students to read through the sentences and options in the task. Ask them to decide whether each sentence is about an obligation, something that is or isn't necessary, or something we are not allowed to do. Then tell them to compare each sentence with the examples in the grammar box to see which grammar rule it matches.
- Give students a few minutes to compare their answers with a partner. Ask them to justify their answers if they are different.
- Check the answers as a class and ask students to justify the answers they give.

Answers
1 go out
2 mustn't
3 mustn't
4 have to
5 mustn't

Listening

8

- Explain to students that they are going to listen to a boy asking a girl how to get from the place that is shown on the map to another place in the town.
- Ask students to look at the list of places in the wordbank and to read the name of the streets on the map.
- Explain the meanings of any words that students don't know yet and tell them to look for any other things on the map that we can use to give directions. Ask them to listen to the recording all the way through and write the places in the correct boxes.
- Play the recording all the way through again and ask students to check their answers and to fill in any missing answers.

Turn to page 129 of this Teacher's Guide for the recording script.

Answers
Bottom left: supermarket (... *go down King Street for about two minutes. You'll pass the supermarket ...*)
Centre above Lang Road: restaurant (... *turn left into Lang Road. You'll see a restaurant on the left.*)
Centre of Hope Street: café (*Walk down Hope Street for a minute, past a café ...*)
Right above RECYCLING: library (*Walk down Cage Street for two minutes, and then you'll see the library on the right ...*)
Top right: school (... *you'll see the library on the right, opposite a school.*)

Speaking

9

- Explain that students are going to work in pairs to tell each other how to get from one place to another. Tell them they need to choose two places from *Listening 8* for their description.
- Remind students of the phrases they learnt for giving directions and ask them to use them to explain how to get from one place to another.
- Read through the *Express yourself!* box with students. Explain that this box provides useful language that will help students complete the Speaking task. When students are confident with the language, they can do the task in their pairs.
- Go round the class monitoring students to make sure they are carrying out the task properly. Don't correct any mistakes at this stage, but make a note of any mistakes in structure and pronunciation.
- Ask each pair to choose a different place on the map to give directions to and repeat until each pair has had a turn.
- Write any structural mistakes on the board, without saying who made them, and ask students to correct them. Deal with any problems in pronunciation.

Extra Class Activity

Ask students to work in pairs to draw a map of their neighbourhood and then to give each other directions from one place on their map to another. Tell them to take turns at giving directions to different places using the phrases they learnt in *Vocabulary 5*.

Extra Writing Task 9

- Make sure each student has a copy of Extra Writing Task 9 that can be found on the *Resource CD-ROM*.
- Explain to students that they are going to write a set of directions for someone coming to their house from their school. Make sure they know what the directions are before they start writing. They can draw a map to go with their work if they like.
- Ask students to write their directions in their notebooks. You could set this task for homework if you are short of time.
- If time allows, invite some of them to read their directions to the rest of the class. Gently correct any mistakes.

Extra Task (for early finishers)

See photocopiable material that can be found on the *Resource CD-ROM*.

Lesson 2

Objectives

Reading	travel article – completing sentences
Vocabulary	text-related words; town-related words
Grammar	can and could
Listening	circling the correct word
Sounds of English	different pronunciation of the same letter combinations

Way in

- Tell students to write the words *book, circle, dizzy, magnificent* and *passport* in their notebooks and to write one sentence for each word. Then ask them to swap books with a partner to compare their sentences and check their spelling. Ask students at random to read one of their sentences to the class until all the words have been correctly used.
- Write on the board: *You didn't … cross the road.* and ask students whether we can complete this with *have to* or *must* (*have to*). Remind them that we don't use *must* to talk about the past.

Reading

1

- Ask students to open their books at page 84 and explain that they are going to read an article about Tokyo. Ask them if they would like to visit Tokyo and why.
- Tell students they are going to listen to and read the article. Ask them to follow the article as they listen.
- Play the recording once. Ask students to tell you one fact they learned from the article that they didn't know before.
- Ask students what the capital city of Japan is (*Tokyo*).
- Ask students to read the pre-reading question and to find the answer in the article.

Answer
kite flying

2

- Please follow the procedure outlined in Unit 1, Lesson 2 on page 15 of this Teacher's Guide.

Answers
capital – *most important city in the country*
hire – *pay to borrow for a period of time*
tunnel – *path, road or river with a roof over it*
marine – *related to the sea*
patterns – *designs, often coloured*
mythology – *connected to old stories*
sightseeing – *looking at the main things to see in different places*
international – *connected with many different countries*

Did you know?

- Ask students to read the information in the *Did you know?* feature and ask if they know any other countries that have a lot of islands (*Greece, The Philippines*).
- If students are interested, give them more information about Tokyo using the Background Information box below.

> **Background Information**
>
> The word *Tokyo* means Eastern Capital. There are about 88,000 restaurants in Tokyo, and it has the largest number of top class restaurants in the world. People in Tokyo use trains a lot and there are more than 500 stations throughout the city! The streets in Tokyo have no names, only numbers, and the buildings are numbered by the order in which they were built. Earthquakes, fires and bombings in Tokyo mean that your chances of finding two buildings in a given street with consecutive numbers are next to nothing. For further information, go to www.nationalgeographic.com and search for 'Tokyo'.

> **Teaching Tip**
>
> You might find it useful to have a globe or a world map in the classroom so that you can show the positions of other countries and cities in the world when you need to. This will give students a clearer idea of where places are in relation to their own country and will also expand their general knowledge.

Comprehension

3

- Ask students to read sentences 1 to 5 so that they know what information to look for when reading the text again.
- Ask students to read the text again to find the words to complete the sentences.
- Explain any vocabulary students don't know and correct their pronunciation if necessary.

> **Answers**
> 1 1950s (*This tower opened in the 1950s ...*)
> 2 the Imperial Palace (*... the Imperial Palace, where the emperor lives.*)
> 3 22 metres (*... which has a 22-metre underwater tunnel.*)
> 4 national (*Kite flying is the national hobby of the Japanese ...*)
> 5 world (*... the world's largest fish market, ...*)

Vocabulary

4

- Explain that the words in the wordbank are all highlighted words in the article on page 84, so students should know them.
- Ask students to do the task individually, but check the answers as a class.

> **Answers**
> 1 hire
> 2 capital
> 3 marine
> 4 tunnel
> 5 international

Grammar

Can and Could

- Read the uses of *can* and *could* in the grammar box to the class and ask students to read the example sentences with you. Explain the grammar terms used if necessary.
- Read the affirmative, negative and question forms from the grammar box with the class. Then ask students to read the short answers.

5

- Ask students to read through the sentences and options and to find whether each one is about something in the present or in the past and if the meaning will be affirmative or negative. Tell them to compare each sentence with the examples in the grammar box to see which grammar rule it matches.
- Once students have finished, give them a few minutes to compare their answers with a partner. Ask them to justify their answers if they are different.
- Check the answers as a class and ask students to justify the answers they give.

> **Answers**
> 1 can't
> 2 Could
> 3 couldn't
> 4 can
> 5 can't

6

- Tell students that they have to use one of the four options given to complete the sentences. Ask students to read each sentence to see whether it is about the present or the past and whether the meaning is affirmative or negative.
- Ask students to do the task individually, but check the answers as a class.

> **Answers**
> 1 can   4 Could
> 2 can't   5 can
> 3 couldn't

> **Extra Class Activity**
>
> Ask students to work in pairs to make sentences using *can* or *could*:
>
> – about something they are able to do
> – asking for and giving permission
> – about something that is possible to do
>
> Then ask each pair to read their sentences to the class.

Vocabulary

7

- Explain to students that they have to label the pictures 1 to 6 with the words from the wordbank. Explain any vocabulary that students have not been taught yet.
- Ask students to work in pairs to do the task, but check the answers as a class and correct pronunciation where necessary.

Answers

1	museum	4	shopping centre
2	bank	5	skyscraper
3	square	6	fountain

Listening

8

- Before students listen to the recording, ask them to read through the sentences and options so they know what information to listen for.
- Explain to students that they are going to listen to a boy talking to his aunt about a visit to Athens.
- Play the recording and ask students to circle the correct answers.
- Give students a few minutes to compare their answers with a partner. Ask them to justify their answers if they are different.
- Play the recording again and ask students to check their answers and to circle any missing answers.
- Check answers as a class and ask students to justify the answers they give.

Turn to page 129 of this Teacher's Guide for the recording script.

Answers

1 2004 (*… I went to Athens for the Olympic Games in 2004 …*)
2 Parthenon (*… I've heard of the Parthenon. It's on a hill in the centre of the city, isn't it? … Yes, it is.*)
3 museum (*You must go to the museum there, too. They were still building it when we were there, so we couldn't go.*)
4 having lunch (*It says here that we're having lunch in Plaka.*)
5 theatre (*In the evening we're going to the cinema.*)

Sounds of English

9

- Explain that the words in each group have the same letters at the end, but one of the words in each group sounds different. Ask students to read the words and to circle the words they think are different. Explain the meaning of any new vocabulary.
- Play the recording once, stopping after each set of words to give students the chance to check their answers.
- Play the recording once more without stopping and ask students to repeat the words as a class.

Answers

1	eight
2	give
3	wind
4	home

10

- Ask students to work in pairs to practise saying the words in *Sounds of English 9* and then to think of some other words that rhyme with these sounds.
- Ask each pair to say one of the groups of words and to tell the class their rhyming words for this group. Write their ideas on the board as they say them.
- Repeat this until each pair has had a turn to say the words and to give their own ideas. Correct their pronunciation where necessary.

Suggested answers

1

(= sight, right)	fight, kite, light
(= eight)	gate, hate, late

2

(= give)	live
(= five, dive)	drive

3

(= wind)	binned, tinned
(= mind, find)	behind, underlined

4

(= some, come)	mum, gum
(= home)	comb, Rome

Extra Task (for early finishers)

See photocopiable material that can be found on the *Resource CD-ROM*.

Lesson 3

Objectives

Reading	letters to a magazine – multiple matching
Express yourself!	asking for and giving directions
Grammar	might; should
Writing	order of adjectives, writing a description

Way In

Teaching Tip

Now and then, both you and students might enjoy using different methods of practising vocabulary and spelling. For example, to revise the words from *Vocabulary 7* on page 85, write each of the words on a piece of card or thick paper and cut the words into letters so that one letter is on each piece of paper. Then, put the letters for each word into separate envelopes. Ask students to work in pairs and give each pair an envelope. Tell them to put the letters in the correct order to make the word, and then ask a student from each pair to write their word on the board.

- Check students' spelling of the words they learnt in Lesson 2 by asking them to write the following words in their notebooks: *capital, hire, international, marine, tunnel, bank, fountain, museum, shopping centre, skyscraper, square*. Then check that they remember the meanings by asking them to write a sentence for each one.
- Ask students to tell you sentences using *can* about something they are able to do, about something that it is possible to do now and to ask for or give permission. Then tell them to change the sentences about ability and possibility so that they are about the past. Ask them which word we use instead of *can* for the past (*could*) and what comes after *can* or *could* (*bare infinitive*).
- Ask students to look at the photos beside the letters on page 86 and to describe the places they can see using some of the words they learnt in Lesson 2.

Let's Talk

Put students into pairs. Ask them to take turns to describe either the place where they live or a city they have visited, using the words they have learned.

Reading

1

- Tell students that they are going to listen to and read letters that students have written to a magazine about the cities where they live. Ask them to follow the letters as they listen.
- Play the recording once. Ask students to tell you one fact they learnt from the article that they didn't know before.
- Ask students to read the pre-reading question and to find the answer in the article.

Answer
Toronto

Comprehension

2

- Ask students to read questions 1 to 5 before they read the letters for the second time so that they know what information to look for.
- Ask students to do the task individually, but check the answers as a class. Make sure students underline where they get the answers from in the text so they can justify their answers.
- Explain any vocabulary students don't know and correct their pronunciation if necessary.

Answers
1 K (*When you walk round the streets, you might hear people speaking different languages ...*)
2 H (*... enjoy a hot chocolate drink ...*)
3 F (*... bring their swimming costumes ... bring comfortable shoes and a camera!*)
4 H (*... violin concerts on street corners everywhere in the city!*)
5 K ('*Toronto' means 'meeting place'!*)

Express yourself!

Asking for and giving directions

- Ask students to work in pairs to read through the phrases and example sentences in *Asking for and giving directions*.

3

- Ask students to take turns asking for directions to their partner's house and to give directions to their house. Remind them to practise the language given in the box. Correct their pronunciation and intonation pattern if necessary.
- As a class, ask each pair to role-play their dialogue until all students have had the chance to speak.

Answers
Students' own answers

Grammar

Might

- Read the rule in the grammar box to the class and the example sentence. Explain that we use *might* to show that we are not sure if something will happen or not.
- Read the affirmative and negative forms from the grammar box with the class. Then draw students' attention to the fact that we rarely use *might* to make questions and we say *might not* instead of *mightn't*.

Should

- Read the first part of the grammar box to the class and ask students to read the example sentences with you.
- Read the affirmative, negative and question forms from the grammar box with the class. Then ask students to read the short answers.

4

- Ask students to read the sentences to decide which words fill the gaps.
- Tell students to decide whether each sentence is talking about a possibility or giving advice and whether it is affirmative, negative or a question form.
- Ask students to do the task individually, but check the answers as a class.

Answers

1	should	4	Should
2	shouldn't	5	might
3	might not		

5

- Ask students to look at the pictures and to read the sentences to decide whether the person is talking about a possibility or giving advice. Tell them to decide whether to write the affirmative or negative form.
- Ask students to do the task individually, but check the answers as a class.

Answers

1 might
2 Should
3 shouldn't
4 might not

Writing

Order of Adjectives

6

- Ask students to read the rules about the order of adjectives. Explain the meaning of any words they don't know.
- Tell students to look back at the first letter on page 86 to find the adjectives and see which of the categories 1 to 7 they match (*famous, beautiful, fantastic:* category 1).

Extra Class Activity

Ask students to work in pairs to think of as many adjectives as they can for each of the categories 1 to 7 to show that they have understood the meanings of these headings. Check their answers as a class.

7

- Explain that students have to complete the sentences with the adjectives in the correct order. Remind students to use the order of adjectives shown in *Writing 6*.
- Ask students to do the task individually, but check the answers as a class.

Answers

1 small Greek
2 beautiful old English
3 great new American

8

- Ask students to read the description of Brighton, and then to complete the sentences using the adjectives in brackets in the order they learnt in *Writing 6*. Ask students to pay attention to the order of the adjectives they use.
- Ask students to do the task individually, but check the answers as a class.

Answers

1 beautiful English
2 fantastic big
3 amazing glass
4 old metal
5 delicious fresh

Task

9

- Ask students to work in pairs to discuss ideas about the town they will write about. Tell them to use the letters on page 86 for ideas.
- Make sure students understand the plan for the description on page 87.
- Ask students to use the plan to write a description like the one in *Writing 8*.
- Alternatively, you could assign this task as homework.

Example answer

Edinburgh is an old Scottish city. Many people go there to visit the famous old castle. When the weather is good you can have a picnic in the beautiful big gardens in the centre near the castle. When the weather is bad, you can go to the amazing museums, and most of them are free. You can also eat tasty hot pies there. One kind of pie is called a *bridie*. You can also buy traditional Scottish clothes.

10

- Ask students to read back through their descriptions to make sure that they have put adjectives in the correct order. If you ask them to write the description for homework, then give them a few minutes to do this at the beginning of the next lesson.

Extra Task (for early finishers)

See photocopiable material that can be found on the *Resource CD-ROM*.

Way in

- If you assigned Unit 9, Lesson 3 *Writing 9* as homework, give students a few minutes to proofread their descriptions, checking the order of adjectives they used. Then ask them to read each other's descriptions, or stick them on the wall so they can read them when they have time.
- Write the following on the board:

  We might surf the Internet tonight.
  You shouldn't play computer games all day.

  Ask students why we use *might* in the first sentence (*to talk about a possibility*) and why we use *shouldn't* in the second sentence (*to give advice*).

Did you know?

- With books closed, ask students how they think the Internet has changed people's lives all over the world. Accept all reasonable answers and encourage students to elaborate on what they say.
- Ask students to open their books at pages 88 and 89. Ask them to look at the picture and say what they think of it. Are they surprised by it? How do they think the Internet has changed the life of the man in the picture?
- Ask students to read the sentences about technology on page 88. Ask for a show of hands from students who are in touch with people in different countries via the Internet. Invite them to say who they are in touch with and where they live.
- Read the information from the *Did you know?* feature to the class. Ask students if they are surprised by the numbers. Time permitting, have a class vote about the most popular websites students use.
- Use the background information in the box below to give the students further information about the Internet if they are interested. Check if they have any questions. If they ask for information you don't have, refer them to the website in the Background Information box and ask them to feed back to you at the next lesson.

> **Background Information**
> The parents of approximately 4 out of every 6 children don't know what their children surf on the Internet. Young people who use the Internet do so for an average of an hour a day and in America 87% of young people aged 12 to 17 use the Internet regularly. The Internet is more than 40 years old. A man called Tim Berners-Lee invented the phrase 'World Wide Web' (www) in 1990. Around 15 countries still have no Internet access at all. 70% of Internet users are boys / men while 30% are girls / women. It's thought that about 15 billion devices are connected to the Internet at any one time. And a couple of historical facts – the QWERTY keyboard layout is over 130 years old. The first mouse was ➡

> made of wood! For further information, go to www.nationalgeographic.com and search for 'Internet'.

> **Let's Talk**
> Put students into small groups. They take turns to talk about things they use a computer for on a regular basis (or that they would use a computer for if they had one).

Lesson 1

Objectives

Reading	the cartoon story – true or false
Vocabulary	text-related words; TV & radio-related words
Grammar	present simple passive
Listening	true or false
Speaking	talking about a game

The cartoon story

1

- Ask students if they can remember what happened in the previous episode of the cartoon story (*It was Beth's birthday so the children asked the magic globe to take them to Seattle to visit her. They wanted to take her out to lunch. They went to the SkyCity restaurant at the top of the Space Needle in Seattle. The restaurant moves in a circle and Adam took some great photos but Mikey felt dizzy.*).
- Ask students to look at the story pictures and suggest what might be happening.
- Please follow the procedure outlined in Unit 1, Lesson 1 on page 12 of this Teacher's Guide.

> **Answers**
> artist – *person with specific skills*
> designed – *made*
> levels – *parts of a game*
> screen – *part of a computer that shows pictures or words*
> program – *set of information telling a computer what to do*
> testers – *people who test things*
> grow up – *become an adult*

- Depending on whether you are using the DVD or the Audio CD, follow the relevant instructions.

For teachers using the DVD

- Make sure each child has a copy of Cartoon DVD Worksheet 10 that can be found on the *Resource CD-ROM*.

- Please follow the procedure outlined in Unit 1, Lesson 1 on page 12 of this Teacher's Guide for teachers using the DVD.

Before you watch

Answers
1 in Mikey's bedroom
2 Accept any logical answers based on what students can see in the picture.

While you watch

Answers
a2 b1 c3

After you watch

Answers
1	made	4	characters
2	artist	5	testers
3	levels	6	grows up

For teachers using the Audio CD

- Ask students to look at page 90 of their student's book and to work in pairs. Ask if they can guess what job Fred (the man wearing the cap in frames 2 and 3) does (*video artist*).
- Tell students they are going to listen to and read the story. Ask them to look at the pictures and to follow the story as they listen.
- Play the recording once and ask students what happens to a video game once it is created (*It is tested.*).
- Put students into small groups of four and ask them to assign the roles of Kristie, Adam, Mikey and Fred within their groups. Ask them to read the story out loud in their groups.
- As a class, ask students the questions below to check their understanding of the episode.
  1 What has Mikey got? (*a new video game*)
  2 What does Mikey want the globe to show him? (*how video games are made*)
  3 Where does Fred work? (*Game Power*)
  4 Is the character's hair designed before the face? (*No, it isn't.*)
  5 What does Adam ask to do? (*test the new game*)

Comprehension

2

- Ask students to read sentences 1 to 5 so they know what information to look for when they read the cartoon story again. Ask them to decide if the sentences are true or false, using information from the story.
- Ask students to do the task individually, but check the answers as a class. Encourage students to explain their answer choices by giving evidence from the story.

Answers
1 F ('*Hi, Mikey! Is this your new video game?*' '*Yes, it's great.*')
2 T (*... I don't work alone.*)
3 T (*After that, a computer program is created.*)
4 F (*We run lots of tests before the game is ready to go to the shops.*)
5 F (*I want to be a video game tester!*)

Let's Talk

Put students into small groups and ask them to develop an idea for a computer game. Time permitting, invite groups to present their ideas to the rest of the class.

Vocabulary

3

- Ask students to look at the words in the wordbank. Remind them that all the words are highlighted in the cartoon story on page 90 and point out that they already know the meaning of them.
- Ask students to do the task individually, but check the answers as a class.

Answers
1	screen	4	program
2	artist	5	level
3	grow up		

Grammar

Teaching Tip

It is a good idea to regularly review all the tenses which students have learnt so far, to help them remember how to form them and when to use them. You can use examples from whichever lesson you are currently working on.

Present Simple Passive

- Write the following sentences on the board to show the difference between the passive and the active voice:
  Fred makes video games. (active voice)
  Video games are made by Fred. (passive voice)
  Explain that the first sentence tells us that Fred, who is the subject, does something, and this is called the active voice. In the next sentence, Video games, which are the subject, don't do anything, but something happens to them. Tell students we call this the passive voice.
- Read the first part of the grammar box to the class and ask students to read the example sentences with you. Then read the affirmative, negative, question and short forms from the grammar box with the class.
- Ask students to look back at frames 2 and 3 in the cartoon story on page 90 and to underline the sentences in the passive voice (*... the story is drawn in pictures. Games are designed to have many different levels. The body and face are designed first. Then, the hair and the clothes are added. After that, a computer program is created. ... it is tested by our testers.*)

4

- Ask students to read each sentence and to find the subject of each missing verb. Remind them that the subjects will help them decide on the correct form of the Present Simple Passive each time. Ask students to use the list of irregular verbs on pages 132 and 133 to find the past participles of any irregular verbs they come across.
- Ask students to do the task individually, but check the answers as a class.

Answers
1 are made
2 is written
3 are not / aren't designed
4 is used
5 Are ... tested

5

- Ask students to read the sentences and to find the subject of each missing verb.
- Tell students to think about which words they need to use to form the passive.
- Ask students to decide whether each verb is regular or irregular and then to look at the list of irregular past participles on pages 132 and 133 if they need to.
- Ask students to do the task individually, but check the answers as a class.

Answers
1 are used   4 is visited
2 is paid   5 are played
3 are given

Let's Talk

Put students in pairs. They take turns to say Present Simple Passive sentences to their partner. Encourage them to make up their own sentences rather than using the ones from the lesson.

Vocabulary

6

- Explain to students that they have to label the pictures 1 to 6 with the words in the wordbank. Explain any vocabulary that students have not been taught yet or ask students to use a dictionary to find the meanings.
- Ask students to work in pairs to do the task, but check the answers as a class and correct pronunciation where necessary.

Answers
1 web camera   4 screen
2 printer   5 keyboard
3 mouse   6 laptop

Listening

7

- Explain to students that they are going to hear Brenda and Jeremy talking about a new video game. Tell them to read sentences 1 to 5 before they listen to the recording, so they know what information to listen for. Remind them that they have to write *T* if the sentence is correct and *F* if it is incorrect. Remind students to listen carefully for meaning as well as actual words.
- Play the recording to the end and ask students to compare their answers with a partner. Ask them to justify any answers that are different. Play the recording a second time and ask them to check their answers or fill in any missing information.
- Check the answers as a class and make sure students can justify their answers.

Turn to page 130 of this Teacher's Guide for the recording script.

Answers
1 F (*'Is this a new video game?' 'Actually, ... It's a program that comes with the laptop.'*)
2 T (*You can create your own game.*)
3 F (*Then a robot chases them ...*)
4 F (*They can stop the robot ...*)
5 F (*... if you catch the robot, you get points ...*)
6 F (*I've only created the first level.*)

Speaking

8

- Explain that students are going to listen to Brenda and Jeremy again and are then going to use the information in *Listening 7* to talk about a game they would like to make.
- Read through the *Express yourself!* box with students. Explain that this box provides useful language that will help students complete the Speaking task. When students are confident with the language, they can do the task in their pairs.
- Go round the class monitoring students and make sure they're carrying out the task properly. Don't correct any mistakes at this stage, but make a note of any mistakes in structure and pronunciation.
- Ask each pair to tell the rest of the class about their video game.
- Write any mistakes that you heard on the board, without saying who made them, and ask students to correct them. Deal with any problems in pronunciation.

Answers
Students' own answers

Extra Class Activity

Ask students to talk about video games they play. Encourage them to describe the game, talk about the different levels, describe the characters, etc.

Extra Writing Task 10

- Make sure each student has a copy of Extra Writing Task 10 that can be found on the *Resource CD-ROM*.
- Explain to students that they are going to write six sentences about gadgets they have got or that they would like to have, using the vocabulary from Lesson 1 and also the Present Simple Passive. Before they write, put students into pairs to discuss their ideas and work out what they are going to write in their sentences. Point out that students can look back at the grammar box if they need reminding how to form the Present Simple Passive.
- Ask students to write their sentences in their notebooks. You could set this task for homework if you are short of time.
- If time allows, ask each student to read one of their sentences to the class.

Extra Task (for early finishers)

See photocopiable material that can be found on the *Resource CD-ROM*.

Lesson 2

Objectives

Reading	article – missing sentences
Vocabulary	text-related words; computer-related words
Grammar	past simple passive
Listening	numbering sentences

Way in

- Tell students to write the words *keyboard, laptop, monitor, mouse, printer* and *web camera* in their notebooks and to write one sentence for each word. Then ask them to swap books with a partner to compare sentences and check their spelling. Ask students at random to read one of their sentences to the class until all the words have been correctly used.
- Ask students how we make the Present Simple Passive (with *am, are, is* and the past participle). Write the verbs *play, show* and *watch* on the board and ask students to make a sentence for each verb using the passive voice.

Teaching Tip
Use word scrambles as an alternative to dictation to help students remember vocabulary. For example, write *okdebayr, platpo, imoront, seoum, nrtprie* and *bew macrea* on the board and ask students to unscramble these to make the computer-related words from Lesson 1. Ask them to copy down the scrambled words in their notebooks and to write the correct word next to each one. Check the answers as a class and also check that they understand the meanings.

Reading
1
- Explain that students are going to listen to the words in the wordbank. Play the recording and ask them to point to each word as they hear it.
- Play the recording again and encourage students to repeat as a class. You could ask individual students to repeat on their own if you feel they are confident enough.
- Put the students into pairs and ask them to find the words in the article on page 92. When they have all found the words, work through them one at a time as a class, asking students to read out the sentences in the article containing the word. Ask students to say what the word means. If they don't know, encourage them to guess from the context.

2
- Tell students they are going to listen to and read the article. Ask them to follow the article as they listen.
- Play the recording once.
- Ask students to tell you one fact they learned from the article that they didn't know before.
- Ask students what high-speed Internet has changed (*the way we work and communicate*).
- Ask students to read the pre-reading question and to find the answer in the article.

Answer
in the early 1990s

Did you know?
- Ask students to read the information in the *Did you know?* feature and ask if they are surprised by the information. Ask students if they think it's a good thing that children know more about computers than about things like tying shoelaces or riding a bike.
- If students are interested, give them more information on how the Internet has changed our lives using the Background Information box below.

Background Information
People say the Internet has re-sized the world and made it much smaller. They say this because now people all over the world can talk to each other whenever they want to, if they have access to the Internet. The Internet also means that anybody with an Internet connection can get information about anything with the click of a mouse. One problem with that is that people tend to believe everything they read on the Internet but not all of it is true. For further information, go to www.nationalgeographic.com and search for 'Internet'.

Comprehension
3
- Ask students to read the missing sentences before they read the text for the second time. This way they will have more of an idea about what information is missing and where it may be likely to go.

- Once they have filled the gaps tell students to read back through the article to make sure that they have chosen the correct sentences.
- Ask students to do the task individually, but check the answers as a class.
- Explain any vocabulary students don't know and correct their pronunciation where necessary.

Answers
1b 2d 3c 4a

Vocabulary
4

- Explain that the words are grouped but that one word in each group is the odd one out. Point out that all the words are in the article on page 92.
- Ask students to find the odd words and to think about why they don't fit with the other two words in the row.
- Ask students to do the task individually, but check the answers as a class.

Answers
1 work (*the other two are connected to 'the Internet'*)
2 communicate (*the other words are synonyms*)
3 show (*you can have a blog or a site on the Internet*)
4 change (*the other two are connected to 'email'*)
5 speed (*the other two are gadgets*)

5

- Explain that the words in the wordbank appear in the article on page 92. Ask students to find the words in the text and to underline them. Explain any words again if necessary.
- Ask students to do the task individually, but check the answers as a class.

Answers
1	receive	4	visit
2	download	5	online
3	surf	6	upload

Let's Talk

Put students into pairs. Ask them to talk about the Internet and how they use it (or would use it if they had access to it), using the words from the wordbank.

Grammar
Past Simple Passive

- Remind students that we form the Present Simple Passive with *am*, *are* or *is* and the past participle of the main verb, and make sure they remember the uses of the passive voice (*when we are more interested in the action than the person who does it, when we don't know who does the action or when it's obvious who does the action*).
- Read the first part of the grammar box to the class and ask students to read the example sentences with you.

- Read the affirmative, negative, question and short forms from the grammar box with the class.

6

- Ask students to read each sentence in the task and to find the subject of each missing verb. Remind them that the subjects will help them decide on the correct form of the Past Simple Passive each time. Tell them to see whether the subject is singular or plural and whether the verb is regular or irregular. Remind them to use the list of irregular verbs on pages 132 and 133 to find the past participles of any irregular verbs.
- Explain that the answers include affirmative, negative and question forms.
- Ask students to do the task individually, but check the answers as a class.

Answers
1 was visited
2 was ... sent
3 were not / weren't booked
4 Were ... taken
5 was sold
6 was tested
7 was not / wasn't used
8 were invented

Extra Class Activity

Ask students to write three examples of their own using the Past Simple Passive. Ask them to write one affirmative sentence, one negative sentence and one question. Check their answers as a class.

Listening
7

- Explain to students that they are going to listen to someone talking about how technology has changed the world of music. Ask students to read sentences a to f before they listen to the recording. Point out that they won't hear exactly the same words on the recording; they must listen for meaning. Remind them that they have to number the sentences according to the order they hear them on the recording.
- Play the recording to the end and ask students to compare their answers with a partner. Ask them to justify any answers that are different. Play the recording a second time and ask them to check their answers or fill in any missing information.
- Check the answers as a class and make sure students can justify their answers.

Turn to page 130 of this Teacher's Guide for the recording script.

Answers

a 4 (*After that, they upload their songs onto websites.*)
b 1 (*These days, new musicians often meet online for the first time.*)
c 3 (*Then, the band will record their songs.*)
d 5 (*... the songs can be downloaded by thousands or even millions of people.*)
e 6 (*This way, they can become famous in a few weeks.*)
f 2 (*Then they decide they want to play music together and form a band.*)

Extra Task (for early finishers)

See photocopiable material that can be found on the *Resource CD-ROM.*

Lesson 3

Objectives

Reading	magazine article – multiple matching
Express yourself!	expressing preferences
Listening	multiple matching
Speaking	asking and answering questions about TV
Sounds of English	similar-sounding words
Writing	spelling; writing a review

Way in

- Check students' spelling of the words they learnt in Lesson 2 by asking them to write down the following words in their notebooks: *download, online, receive, surf* and *upload*. Check that they remember the meanings by asking students to translate them into their own language.
- Write the following sentence on the board: *That game was created in Japan.* Ask students which tense the verb is in (*Past Simple*) and what kind of word comes after *was* (*past participle*). Remind them that this structure is called the passive voice and ask them why we use it here (*because it's obvious who does the action*).

Reading

1

- Tell students that they are going to listen to and read a magazine article about which video games some children like. Ask them to open their books at page 94 and to follow the article as they listen.
- Play the recording once. Ask students to tell you one fact they learnt from the article that they didn't know before.
- Ask students to read the pre-reading question and to find the answer in the article.

Answer

He likes that he can make the race exactly as he wants it.

Let's Talk

Put students into pairs. They take turns to pretend to be one of the children from the magazine article, talking about the same video game but using their own words.

Comprehension

2

- Tell students to read questions 1 to 5 before they read the text again so that they know what information to look for.
- Ask students to underline where they get the answers from in the text so they can justify their answers.
- Ask students to do the task individually, but check the answers as a class.
- Explain any vocabulary students don't know and correct their pronunciation where necessary.

Answers

1 J (*I can't stand most video games because they are usually boring.*)
2 A (*... I can go to the next level quite easily.*)
3 H (*I prefer playing real football ...*)
4 J (*I lose if I crash my plane, but that's fun too!*)
5 H (*... you get better as you play.*)

Express yourself!

Expressing preferences

- Ask students to work in pairs to read through the phrases and example sentences in *Expressing preferences.*

3

- Ask students to complete the dialogue with some of these phrases. After they have completed the dialogue, ask them to take turns to read out the parts of Tina and Josh to practise the language given. Correct their pronunciation and intonation pattern if necessary.
- Ask each pair to role-play their dialogue until all students have had the chance to speak.

Answer

1 My favourite
2 can't stand
3 Do you prefer
4 prefer

Listening

4

- Explain to students that they are going to hear five descriptions of different kinds of video game and that they have to match descriptions 1 to 5 with the games a to e. Tell students that they have to listen for the words that talk about each kind of game.

- Play the recording to the end of the first description and ask students what they think the correct answer is. Play the rest of the recording and ask students to number the remaining games. Encourage students to match each description to the video game as they hear about them rather than trying to remember all the answers until the end.
- Play the recording again and ask students to check their answers and fill in any missing answers. Then check the answers as a class. Ask students to justify their answers.

Turn to page 130 of this Teacher's Guide for the recording script.

Answers
a 2 (*... like bungee jumping or sky diving. They're too dangerous to do in real life ...*)
b 4 (*You can choose to play the drums, the guitar or the piano ...*)
c 1 (*You can get a new car every time ... other drivers.*)
d 5 (*It's like living someone else's life for a while.*)
e 3 (*You are an explorer and you have to ...*)

Speaking

5

- Explain that students are going to work in pairs to ask and answer questions about video games. Remind students of the video game-related words that they have already learnt and tell them to use them to answer the questions.
- Read through the *Express yourself!* box with students. Explain that this box provides useful language that will help students complete the Speaking task. When students are confident with the language, they can do the task in their pairs.
- Go round the class monitoring students to make sure they are carrying out the task properly. Don't correct any mistakes at this stage, but make a note of any mistakes in structure and pronunciation.
- As a class, ask each pair to ask and answer one of the questions and repeat until each pair has had a turn.
- Write any mistakes you heard on the board, without saying who made them, and ask them to correct them. Deal with any problems in pronunciation.

Answers
Students' own answers

Sounds of English

6

- Ask students to work in pairs to say the pairs of words to each other. Then tell them to write *S* if they think the pairs of words sound the same and *D* if they think they sound different.
- Give students time to read the words and write down their answers, but don't check their answers until they have heard the recording.

Answers
1D 2S 3S 4D 5S

7

- Play the recording once, stopping after each pair of words to give students time to check their answers. Draw students' attention to the different sounds of *s* and *sh* in question 1, and *i* and *ee* in question 4. Explain that the words in questions 2 and 5 sound the same although the spelling is different, and that in question 3, the *k* in *knows* is a silent letter, so the word sounds like *nose*.
- Play the recording once more without stopping and ask students to repeat the words as a class.

Writing

Spelling Mistakes

8

- Ask students to read the sentences carefully. Explain that there is one spelling mistake in each sentence and that they have to correct it. Tell students that there could be a letter missing, an extra letter or just the wrong letter altogether.
- Ask students to do the task individually, but check the answers as a class.

Answers
1 think
2 business
3 download
4 receive
5 racing
6 designed
7 Were
8 address
9 Where
10 communicate

9

- Ask students to read the review of a mobile phone game carefully to find the spelling mistakes. Explain that there are eight spelling mistakes in the review and that they have to correct them.
- Ask students to do the task individually, but check the answers as a class.

Answers

Paragraph 1	line 3 called
	line 3 fun
Paragraph 2	line 1 beginning
	line 7 too
	line 8 careful
	line 10 lose
Paragraph 3	line 2 exciting
	line 2 difficult

Teaching Tip

Keep notes of the common spelling mistakes that your students make in their writing. Spend time going over these now and again to focus on the correct spelling. Write the incorrect spellings on the board and ask students to come up and correct them. This should help students avoid repeating the same mistakes.

Task

10

- Ask students to work in pairs to discuss ideas about the mobile phone game they will write their review about. Tell them to use the ideas from the article on page 94.
- Make sure students understand the paragraph plan for the review on page 95. Ask students to use the plan to write a review like the one in *Writing 9*. Tell them to be extra careful with their spelling.
- Alternatively, you could assign this task as homework.

Example answer

My favourite mobile phone game is called *Nice Town*. You can play it on your own or with friends.

In the game, you make a town and then you choose the people who live in the town. You can choose from hundreds of funny characters or you can design characters of your own. Then you decide what the people do every day. They can do crazy things but they always have to be nice. That's why it's called *Nice Town*! There are lots of different levels in the game and you move to the next level by making everyone who lives in your town happy.

I like the game because it always makes me smile and when I play it with my friends, we have lots of fun. Even my mum likes it!

11

- Ask students to read back through their reviews to make sure that they have spelt everything correctly. If you ask them to write the review for homework, then give them a few minutes to do this at the beginning of the next lesson.

Extra Class Activity

Put students into small groups. Ask them to list the good and the bad things about playing video games. Then get groups to share their opinions and discuss them.

Extra Task (for early finishers)

See photocopiable material that can be found on the *Resource CD-ROM*.

Review 5

Objectives

- To revise vocabulary and grammar from Units 9 and 10
- Project – my favourite piece of technology

Preparing for the review

- Explain to students that the tasks in *Review 5* revise the material they learnt in Units 9 and 10.
- Remind students that they can ask you for help with the exercises or look back at the units if they're not sure about an answer, as the review is not a test.
- Decide how you will carry out the review. You could ask students to do one task at a time and then correct it immediately, or ask students to do all the tasks and then correct them together at the end. If you do all the tasks together, let students know every now and again how much time they have got left to finish the tasks.
- Remind students not to leave any answers blank and to try to find any answers they aren't sure about in the units.
- Revise the vocabulary and grammar as a class before students do the review.

Vocabulary Revision

- Ask students to write sentences using the words *book, circle, dizzy, magnificent* and *passport*.
- Tell students to work in pairs and to look at the map on page 83. Ask them to give each other directions to various places on the map. Make sure they revise *turn right, turn left, cross the road, go round the corner* and *go straight ahead*.
- Ask students if they know what a skyscraper is and then ask them to write down all the other words related to towns which they learnt in Unit 9.
- Ask students to tell you as many words related to computers and technology as possible. Make sure they revise the words they learnt in the vocabulary tasks in Unit 10, Lessons 1 and 2 and any other related words from the unit.

Grammar Revision

- Write *We have to buy tickets.* on the board, and then ask students to write the negative and question forms and to give short answers. Ask students which tenses we can use with *have to*.
- Ask students to give example sentences with *must* in the affirmative, negative and question forms. Check that students can remember the difference between *don't have to* and *mustn't* (we use *don't have to* to show that something isn't necessary but we can choose to do it if we want, but we use *mustn't* when we want to say we are not allowed to do something or it is necessary that we don't)

- Ask students to give example sentences with *can, could, might* and *should* in the affirmative and negative. Check that students remember to use the bare infinitive with these modal verbs.
- Write *People make video games in Japan.* on the board and ask a student to come and rewrite the sentence using the passive voice. Then ask a student to write the same sentence with the Past Simple Passive.

Vocabulary

1

- Ask students to say each of the words as a class and then individually. Correct their pronunciation if necessary.
- Ask students to go to the second page of stickers at the back of the book and find the stickers for *Review 5*. Tell them to decide which thing each sticker shows and to stick it in the correct box.
- Check that students have put the correct stickers above each word.

2

- Tell students to think about how the words in each group are related to one another so that they can decide which word doesn't belong in the group.
- When checking students' answers, ask them to tell you why each of the words are odd.

Answers

1 screen (*the other two are buildings*)
2 artist (*the others are things used with computers*)
3 web camera (*the others are things used when travelling*)
4 pattern (*the other two are found in towns or cities*)
5 level (*the other two are connected to the Internet*)

3

- Ask students to read the whole paragraph and the possible options to themselves before they choose the correct answers. After they have finished circling the answers tell them to read the paragraph again to make sure their answers make sense.

Answers

1 download
2 fan
3 invent
4 designed
5 level
6 prefer

Grammar

4

- Explain to students that they should read the sentences and the possible options before trying to choose the answers to decide which one matches the structure and meaning of each sentence.
- Tell students to look back at the grammar boxes in Unit 9, Lessons 1, 2 and 3 for a reminder if they need to.

Answers
1a 2b 3b 4a 5b 6b

5

- Point out to students that they should read the whole dialogue before trying to fill the gaps to decide which word matches the context and whether they need to choose the affirmative or the negative form.
- Tell students to look back at the grammar boxes in Unit 9, Lessons 1, 2 and 3 for a reminder if they need to.

Answers

1	shouldn't	5	might not
2	couldn't	6	might
3	should	7	can
4	can't	8	have

6

- Tell students to look at the verb in bold in the first sentence to see which tense it is in and whether it is affirmative or negative before they write the answer.
- Tell students to look back at the grammar boxes in Unit 10, Lessons 1 and 2 for a reminder if they need to.

Answers

1	are fed	5	Are ... sold
2	wasn't used	6	were sent
3	Are ... made	7	was visited
4	is watched	8	weren't uploaded

Project 5

1

- Explain to the students that they are going to do a project about their favourite piece of technology. Ask them to say what piece of technology they are going to make a poster about.
- Point out that students should find photos of the item they are going to write about or that they can draw and colour pictures of it.
- Ask students to read the bullet points and explain that the paragraph they write must address these points.
- Read through the example poster about a television with the class.
- Ask students to complete their projects. They can do this in the lesson or for homework.
- When the projects are complete, stick them on the classroom wall.

2

- Invite students to tell the class about their favourite piece of technology.

Way in

- If you assigned Unit 10, Lesson 3 *Writing 9* for homework, give students a few minutes to proofread their reviews and check their spelling. Then ask them to read each other's reviews, or stick them on the wall so they can read them when they have time.
- Explain that this unit is about different kinds of transport. Then ask students to name all the types of transport they can think of.

Did you know?

- With books closed, ask students to brainstorm the advantages and disadvantages of different types of transport. You could write their views on the board then have a class vote to find the most popular form of transport.
- Ask students to open their books at pages 98 and 99. Ask them to look at the picture and see if they know the name of the train (*bullet train* or *Shinkansen*). Ask them to guess why it's called the bullet train (*because it goes very fast*).
- Ask students to read the paragraph about bullet trains on page 99. Explain that technology in Japan is very advanced and they have found a way to make really fast trains.
- Read the information from the *Did you know?* feature to the class. To help students understand how many people use the train each year, ask them what the population of their country is (or tell them that the population of England is only about 55 million).
- Use the background information in the box below to give the students further information about bullet trains if they are interested. Check if they have any questions. If they ask for information you don't have, refer them to the website in the Background Information box and ask them to feed back to you at the next lesson.

> **Background Information**
> Bullet trains have been running in Japan for more than 40 years. There are almost 2,500 kilometres of track for bullet trains in Japan. In 1999, many old bullet trains were phased out to make way for the new 700 series Nozomi trains, which travel at 285kph compared to 210kph for the old bullet trains. The Shinkansen is famous for reliability, safety and punctuality. The average delay is only about 10 seconds, apart from in 2004, when the average delay increased to 42 seconds as a result of typhoons, earthquakes and some other problems. Bullet trains are very safe and there has never been a serious accident involving a bullet train. For further information, go to www.nationalgeographic.com and search for 'bullet train'.

Lesson 1

Objectives

Reading	the cartoon story – open-ended questions
Vocabulary	text-related words; means of transport
Grammar	comparatives and superlatives
Listening	circling the correct answers
Speaking	comparing different means of transport

The cartoon story

- Ask students if they can remember what happened in the previous episode of the cartoon story (*The children wanted to know how video games were made so they asked the magic globe to show them. The globe took them to a place called Game Power, where they met a man called Fred who makes video games. Fred explained how the games are made and who does what. Fred showed the children a new video game and he said the children could test the game.*).
- Ask students to look at the story pictures and suggest what might be happening.

1

- Please follow the procedure outlined in Unit 1, Lesson 1 on page 12 of this Teacher's Guide.

> **Answers**
> means of transport – *forms of transport*
> comfortable – *not causing any pain or awkwardness*
> passengers – *people travelling*
> wander – *walk around without a purpose* aisle - *the corridor on a plane*
> adventurous – *creating adventures*

- Depending on whether you are using the DVD or the Audio CD, follow the relevant instructions.

For teachers using the DVD

- Make sure each child has a copy of Cartoon DVD Worksheet 11 that can be found on the *Resource CD-ROM*.
- Please follow the procedure outlined in Unit 1, Lesson 1 on page 12 of this Teacher's Guide for teachers using the DVD.

Before you watch

> **Answers**
> 1 playing basketball
> 2 Accept any logical answers based on what students can see in the picture.

While you watch

> **Answers**
> a2 b6 c5 d1 e4 f3

After you watch

Answers
1b 2b 3a 4b 5b

For teachers using the Audio CD

- Ask students to look at page 100 of their student's book and to work in pairs. Ask them to say how the children are travelling at the end of the story (*by hot air balloon*).
- Tell students they are going to listen to and read the story. Ask them to look at the pictures and to follow the story as they listen.
- Play the recording once and ask students what Adam hates (*travelling by plane*).
- Assign the roles of Kristie, Mikey and Adam to three different students and ask them to read the story out loud. Time permitting, repeat until all students have had a turn.
- As a class, ask students the questions below to check their understanding of the episode.

  1 What does Mikey say about stopping when you travel by car? (*you can stop wherever you like*)
  2 What does Adam say about planes? (*they are faster but more expensive than trains or cars*)
  3 What do passengers have to do on a plane, according to Adam? (*sit down*)
  4 What do the children think is the easiest way to travel? (*by globe*)
  5 Why do they like travelling by globe? (*It's cheap, easy and adventurous.*)

Comprehension

2

- Ask students to read sentences 1 to 5 so they know what information to look for when they read the cartoon story again. Ask them to write their answers, using the information in the cartoon story.
- Ask students to do the task individually, but check the answers as a class. Encourage students to explain their answer choices by giving evidence from the story.

Answers
1 means of transport (*I'm doing a project on means of transport.*)
2 Because you can stop wherever you like. (*... you can stop wherever you like.*)
3 travelling by plane (*... travelling by plane is faster than travelling by train or car, ...*)
4 wander up and down the aisle (*Passengers can't just wander up and down the aisle.*)
5 He thinks it's cheap, easy and adventurous. (*It's the cheapest, easiest and most adventurous way to travel!*)

Let's Talk

Put students into small groups. Ask them to choose one person to be the interviewer; he/she then interviews the others in the group about different means of transport. Encourage them all to use their own ideas rather than to copy what the children in the story say.

Extra Class Activity

Ask students to close their books and to work in pairs to talk about what might happen in the next episode of the cartoon story. Tell them to see how many different endings they can think of for the story and whether it is likely to be happy or sad. Then ask them to share their ideas as a class.

Teaching Tip

Explain to students that although *means* in *means of transport* ends with an –s, we can use it as a singular noun (*This is an expensive means of transport.*) or as a plural (*The best means of transport are trams.*).

Vocabulary

3

- Ask students to look at the words in the wordbank. Remind them that all the words are from the cartoon story on page 100 and point out that they already know the meaning of them. Check understanding of one or two of the words again if you think it's necessary.
- Ask students to do the task individually, but check the answers as a class.

Answers
1 means
2 comfortable
3 aisle
4 wander
5 adventurous

4

- Explain to students that they have to label pictures 1 to 6 with the words from the wordbank. Explain any vocabulary that students have not been taught or ask them to look up the words in their dictionaries.
- Ask students to work in pairs to do the task, but check the answers as a class and correct pronunciation where necessary.

Answers
1 passenger
2 check-in desk
3 seat belt
4 motorbike
5 coach
6 metro

Grammar

Comparatives and Superlatives

- Read the rules in the grammar box to the class and ask students to read the example sentences with you. Explain the meaning of any grammar terms that students are not familiar with.
- Ask students to look back at the cartoon episode on page 100 and to find the comparatives (*faster than, more expensive, more comfortable than*). Then ask them to find the superlatives (*cheapest, easiest, most adventurous*), pointing out that this form is used because they are talking about more than two things or actions.
- Draw students' attention to the fact that *good*, *bad* and *many / much* are irregular adjectives and tell students they have to learn these comparatives and superlatives by heart.

5

- Tell students that they have to complete each of the sentences and ask them to read each sentence to decide whether they need to use the comparative or superlative of the adjective in brackets.
- Tell them to look for other words in each sentence that we use with a comparative or a superlative and to look back at the grammar box to see whether they need to make changes to the adjectives and what other words they may need to use.
- Ask students to do the task individually, but check the answers as a class.

Answers
1. faster
2. as cheap
3. the most popular
4. the best
5. safer

6

- Ask students to read the speech bubbles to decide which adjective should fill the gap in each one.
- Tell students to decide whether each adjective will be comparative or superlative. Ask them to make any changes necessary to the adjective and to add the other words they need to make the comparative or superlative structures.
- Ask students to do the task individually, but check the answers as a class.

Answers
1. the most frightening
2. as good as
3. bigger than
4. the cheapest

Listening

7

Teaching Tip
When students do listening exercises, tell them to write down the key words they hear, as this can help them find the answers. When you check the answers with them, the words they have written down can sometimes help to identify misunderstandings which lead to their mistakes.

- Explain to students that they are going to listen to Jim talking to Ann about going on a trip to London. Ask students to read through the sentences and options.
- Play the recording and ask students to circle the correct answers.
- Give students a few minutes to compare their answers with a partner. Ask them to justify their answers if they are different.
- Play the recording again and ask students to check their answers and to circle any missing answers.
- Check the answers as a class and ask students to justify the answers they give.

Turn to page 130 of this Teacher's Guide for the recording script.

Answers
1. grandparents (*Are you going with your parents? … No, with my grandparents.*)
2. train (*… the train is more exciting than the coach.*)
3. fast (*… the coach isn't as fast as the train.*)
4. £30 (*Train tickets are £30 each.*)
5. coach (*We should go by coach.*)

Speaking

8

- Explain that students are going to work in pairs to compare different means of transport. Remind students of the comparatives and superlatives that they have learnt, and tell them to use them to compare things.
- Read through the *Express yourself!* box with students. Explain that this box provides useful language that will help them complete the Speaking task. Give one or two example sentences, talking about your views on means of transport. When students are confident with the language, they can do the task in their pairs.
- Go round the class monitoring students to make sure they are carrying out the task properly. Don't correct any mistakes at this stage, but make a note of any mistakes in structure and pronunciation.
- As a class, ask each pair to answer one of the questions and repeat until each pair has had a turn.
- Write any mistakes you heard on the board, without saying who made them, and ask students to correct them. Deal with any problems in pronunciation.

Answers
Students' own answers

Extra Writing Task 11

- Make sure each student has a copy of Extra Writing Task 11 that can be found on the *Resource CD-ROM*.
- Explain to students that they are going to write a short review about their favourite means of transport. Ask them to use comparatives and superlatives in their review.
- Ask students to write their reviews in their notebooks. You could set this task for homework if you are short of time.
- If time allows, invite some students to share their reviews with the class. Gently correct any mistakes.

Extra Task (for early finishers)

See photocopiable material that can be found on the *Resource CD-ROM*.

Lesson 2

Objectives

Reading	article – completing sentences
Vocabulary	text-related words; transport-related words
Grammar	both, either and neither
Listening	true or false
Sounds of English	*th* sounds

Way in

- Ask students to write down all the means of transport-related words they can remember from Lesson 1. Then ask them to swap books with a partner to compare what they have remembered. Check their answers as a class to make sure they have learnt *aisle, check-in desk, coach, metro, motorbike, passenger* and *seat belt*.
- Write the following on the board: *good, bad* and *many / much* and ask students to tell you the comparative and superlative forms. Write the answers on the board as they give them and ask the rest of the class whether these are correct.

Reading

1

- Ask students to open their books at page 102 and explain that they are going to listen to and read an article about travel in the 19th century. Ask them to follow the text as they listen.
- Remind them to focus on the meaning of the highlighted words. Play the recording once. Check the meaning of the highlighted words as a class. If students don't know, encourage them to guess from the context. Encourage students to help each other work out the meaning of unknown words.

Answers
coach – *a carriage pulled by horses*
uncomfortable – *causing pain and discomfort*
thieves – *robbers*
afford – *have enough money to pay for*
dining car – *part of a train where people can eat meals*
carriages – *sections of a train*
benches – *wooden seats*
journey – *the experience of travelling from one place to another*

2

- Explain that students are going to read the article again, this time to themselves. Ask students to tell you one fact they learned from the article that they didn't know before.
- Ask students to read the pre-reading question and to find the answer in the article.

Answer
Because there were thieves along the way.

Did you know?

- Ask students to read the information in the *Did you know?* feature and ask them what they like to do when they travel. Do they read? Play games? Send text messages?
- If students are interested, give them more information on transport in the 19th century using the Background Information box below.

Background Information
In the 19th century there were lots of different types of carriages pulled by horses – some had two wheels and others had four; some were covered in and weather-proof, while others were open to the elements. The first bus appeared in London in 1829 and carried 22 passengers. For further information, go to www.nationalgeographic.com and search for 'transport'.

Let's Talk

Put the students into pairs. They take turns to ask each other questions about the information in the article.

Comprehension

3

- Ask students to read questions 1 to 5 before they read the text again so that they know what information to look for.
- Ask students to underline where they get the answer from in the text so they can justify their answers.
- Ask students to do the task individually, but check the answers as a class.
- Explain any vocabulary students don't know and correct their pronunciation if necessary.

Answers
1 cars (*There are neither planes nor cars yet, ...*)
2 two days (*Travelling by coach and horses takes two days, ...*)
3 benches (*Second class passengers sat on benches instead of seats.*)
4 stand (*Third class passengers had to stand during the journey!*)
5 two hours (*The journey from Leeds to London now takes two hours.*)

Vocabulary

4

- Explain that the words in the wordbank are all highlighted words in the article on page 102, so students should know them.
- Ask students to do the task individually, but check the answers as a class. Correct their pronunciation where necessary.

Answers
1 journey
2 uncomfortable
3 afford
4 bench
5 coach

5

- Explain to students that they have to label pictures 1 to 6 with the words from the wordbank. Encourage students to use dictionaries or explain any vocabulary that students have not been taught yet.
- Ask students to work in pairs to do the task, but check the answers as a class and correct pronunciation where necessary.

Answers
1 timetable
2 ticket machine
3 inspector
4 street sign
5 escalator
6 luggage

Grammar

Both, Either and Neither

- Read the rules in the grammar box to the class and ask them to read the example sentences with you.
- Draw students' attention to the fact that we can use affirmative verbs with *both*, *either* or *neither*. Ask them which word we can also use with negative verbs (*either*).

Extra Class Activity

Tell students to close their books. Write the following on the board:

1 Both Athens ___ Paris have Metros. (*and*)
2 You either get off here ___ at the next station. (*or*)
3 I can't see either ___ the street signs. (*of*)
4 Neither Bill ___ Nick have got tickets. (*nor*)
5 Neither ___ those cars is very fast. (*of*)

Then ask students to come up to the board and fill in the missing words.

6

- Ask students to read the sentences and options and to find out whether the verbs are affirmative or negative. Tell them to look for other words in the sentence that we can use after *either*, *neither* or *both*. Tell them to compare each sentence with the examples in the grammar box to see which answer matches.
- Give students a few minutes to compare their answers with a partner. Ask them to justify their answers if they are different.
- Check the answers as a class and ask students to justify their answers.

Answers
1 neither
2 Both
3 either
4 Neither
5 or

7

- Ask students to read the sentences to decide which word best fills the gap.
- Tell them to decide whether each sentence is affirmative or negative and to look for words in the sentence which go with *both*, *either* or *neither* (*and*, *or*, *nor*, *of*).
- Ask students to do the task individually, but check the answers as a class.

Answers
1 Both
2 either
3 Neither
4 either
5 Neither

Listening

8

- Explain to students that they are going to listen to Lisa and Gary talking about a new car. Ask students to read sentences 1 to 6 quickly to find what each one says about a car. Then ask them to underline the adjectives and colours in the sentences (*new, small, more expensive, fast, blue, red, or black, new*).
- Remind students that they have to write *T* if the sentence is true or *F* if it is false.

- Play the recording once and then ask students to compare their answers with a partner. Ask them to justify any answers that are different. Play the recording a second time and ask them to check their answers or fill in any missing information.
- Check the answers as a class and make sure students can justify their answers.

Turn to page 131 of this Teacher's Guide for the recording script.

Answers
1 F (*Hi, Gary. Wow! Look at your mum's new car!*)
2 T (*It's really small!*)
3 F (*… it's cheaper than a lot of other cars.*)
4 F (*… it isn't a fast car, is it? … Well, no, but it's great for the city.*)
5 F (*No, but you can get blue … or black. … Don't they make them in red? … I don't think so.*)
6 T (*Dad is going to buy a new car …*)

Let's Talk
Put students into pairs and ask them to practise a dialogue of their own about a new car, similar to the one described in *Listening 8*. Encourage them to use their own words and their imagination! Invite different pairs to come to the front of the class to act out their dialogue.

Sounds of English
9
- Ask students to work in pairs to say the words to each other and to see if they recognise the difference in the sounds of *th* in each pair.
- Explain that the *th* in *this* is a hard sound and *th* in *thin* is a soft sound and say the words stressing the *th* sounds.

Answers
In *this*, *either* and *there*, the *th* is a hard sound.
In *thin*, *both* and *thing*, the *th* is a soft sound.

10
- Play the first three words on the recording and ask students to repeat the words and to put them in the correct column. Play the rest of the recording to the end and ask students to repeat the words and to fill in the rest of their answers.
- Play the recording again without stopping and check students' answers.

Answers
brother	tooth
1 mother	4 bath
2 neither	5 cloth
3 other	6 thank

Teaching Tip
There are many popular songs about travelling by different means of transport. To expand students' vocabulary on the topic, you might like to bring in some songs with this theme for students to listen to. Alternatively, you could note down the lyrics to some of the songs and give them to the students.

Extra Task (for early finishers)
See photocopiable material that can be found on the *Resource CD-ROM*.

Lesson 3

Objectives

Reading	travel guide entries – true or false
Express yourself!	talking about transport
Grammar	too and enough
Writing	headings; writing a report about transport in your area

Way in
- Check students' spelling of the words they learnt in Lesson 2. Ask them to write down the following words: *coach, uncomfortable, thieves, afford, dining car, carriage, benches, journey, escalator, inspector, luggage, street sign, ticket machine* and *timetable*. Then check that they remember the meanings by asking them to write a sentence for each word.
- Write the following on the board: *both, either, neither*. Ask students which words sometimes follow each of these words in a sentence (*and, or, nor, of*). Then ask them which word we can use with affirmative and negative verbs (*either*) and which word has a negative meaning (*neither*).

Reading
1
- Tell students that they are going to listen to and read three entries about different places in a travel guide. Ask them to open their books at page 104 and follow the entries as they listen.
- Play the recording once. Ask students to tell you one fact they learnt from the travel guide that they didn't know before.
- Ask students to read the pre-reading question and to find the answer in the article.

Answer
Beijing

Let's Talk
Have a class discussion about the three cities. Ask students which of the three cities they would prefer to visit. Have a class vote to find out which is the most popular.

Comprehension

2

- Ask students to read sentences 1 to 6 so that they know what information to look for when they read the text again.
- Ask students to read the text again to find out if the sentences are true or false and to write *T* or *F* in the boxes provided. Tell them to underline the information in the text that helps them to find the answers.
- Explain any vocabulary students don't know and correct their pronunciation if necessary.

Answers
1 T (*In the summer, you can take the river or lake buses ...*)
2 F (*They are never more than 30 second late!*)
3 T (*... except during weekends when it's too crowded.*)
4 F (*Metro trains run every four or five minutes daily, ...*)
5 F (*The city centre is a 'car-free' area ...*)
6 F (*... but they're too expensive for others.*)

Express yourself!

Talking about transport

- Ask students to work in pairs to read through the phrases and example sentences in *Talking about transport*.

3

- Ask students to take turns to ask and answer questions about transport in their own area. Remind them to practise the language given in the box. Correct their pronunciation and intonation pattern if necessary.
- As a class, ask each pair to read out their dialogue until all students have had the chance to speak.

Answers
Students' own answers

Grammar

Too and Enough

- Read the rules in the grammar box to the class and ask students to read the example sentences with you.
- Ask students to find examples of *too* followed by an adjective in the entries on page 104 (*too crowded, too expensive*). Explain that *too* gives the adjective a negative meaning. Ask them to compare these with the examples of *enough* from the grammar box.

4

- Ask students to read the sentences to decide which word best fits the gap.
- Tell students to see whether the word before or after the gap is an adjective or a noun.
- Ask students to do the task individually, but check the answers as a class.

Answers
1 enough   4 enough
2 too   5 enough
3 too

5

- Tell students that they have to put the words given into the correct order to make a sentence.
- Tell students to decide which word is the subject of each sentence. Then tell them to find the adjective or noun and to decide whether this goes before or after *enough* or *too*.
- Tell students to make questions if a question mark is given.
- Ask students to do the task individually, but check the answers as a class.

Answers
1 Buses aren't fast enough.
2 This bike is too expensive for me.
3 Are there enough tickets for everyone?
4 On Sundays the metro is too crowded.

Extra Class Activity

Ask students to write two sentences using *too* and two sentences using *enough*. Ask them to swap books with a partner to compare each other's sentences. Then ask them to read them to the class.

Writing

Headings

6

- Ask students to read about how to use headings and explain the meaning of any words they don't know.
- Explain that we can write reports without headings, but headings help us to put the information in order in a report and this makes it easier to read.

7

- Explain to students they have to match headings 1 to 4 with extracts a to d. Tell them to read each extract to find words which match the meaning of the heading or which refer to words in the heading.
- Ask students to do the task individually, but check the answers as a class.

Answers
1 c (*... clean ... find a seat.*)
2 a (*... you can get them ... They cost ...*)
3 d (*... at weekends ... 24 hours a day.*)
4 b (*... too slow.*)

8

- Ask students to read the headings and then the report and to find the information which relates to each heading.
- Ask students to do the task individually, but check the answers as a class. When you have checked the answers, ask students what public transport is like in their area.

Answers
Paragraph 1 b
Paragraph 2 c
Paragraph 3 d
Paragraph 4 a

Task

9

- Ask students to work in pairs to discuss what they are going to include in their report about transport in their area and to say why.
- Make sure students understand the paragraph plan on page 105. Remind them that each paragraph should add a different piece of information to the description to make it easy to follow.
- Ask students to use the plan to write their report and ask them to write a clear heading for each paragraph like the ones in *Writing 8*.
- Alternatively, you could assign this task as homework if you are short of time.

Example answer
Public transport in Athens
Kinds of public transport
There are many kinds of public transport in my area as it is near the centre of Athens. You can either take a bus or a taxi to almost any part of the city, or you can go by tram, train, trolley or metro to some areas.

Cost
At the moment, you can buy a ticket for €1 and this lasts for 90 minutes. This ticket is for all kinds of public transport apart from taxis and 90 minutes is usually enough time to get from one side of the city to the other. You can also buy cheap travel passes too. Taxi rides are too expensive for most people to take every day.

Problems
There is too much traffic in Athens so the buses can be very slow. Also there aren't enough buses to some parts of Athens and people have to wait a long time at the bus stops. The metro is faster than the bus, but there aren't enough metro stations for the whole city.

Which means of transport is the best?
As the buses to the centre of the city are too slow, I think the best way to get around the centre of Athens at the moment is to take the metro and then walk from the metro station, if it's not too far, of course!

10

- Ask students to read back through their reports to make sure that they have used headings correctly. If you ask them to write the report for homework, then give them a few minutes to do this at the beginning of the next lesson.

Extra Task (for early finishers)

See photocopiable material that can be found on the *Resource CD-ROM*.

Jobs

Way in

- If you assigned Unit 11, Lesson 3 *Writing 9* for homework, give students a few minutes to proofread their reports, checking the headings. Then ask them to read each other's reports, or stick them on the wall so they can read them when they have time.
- Write *too* and *enough* on the board and ask students to give you sentences using these words. Write their answers on the board as they give them and ask the class to correct them when necessary. Make sure they have understood the difference in meanings and remind them that *too* is followed by an adjective while *enough* comes after an adjective or before a noun.

Did you know?

- With books closed, ask students to brainstorm different jobs. Write their suggestions on the board and then ask students to say which of the jobs are dangerous.
- Ask students to open their books at pages 106 and 107. Ask them to look at the picture and see if they can guess what job the men are doing (*rescuing someone from a mountain*).
- Ask students to read the paragraph about rescuers on page 107. Explain that when people are injured on mountains it is usually very difficult for rescue teams to reach them and that they often have to use helicopters to get to the injured person.
- Read the information from the *Did you know?* feature to the class. Ask students if they can think of any other places where people might be injured that are difficult to get to (they might suggest *at sea, in deep snow, down a mine, in a cave*; accept any reasonable suggestions).
- Use the background information in the box below to give the students further information about mountain rescue teams if they are interested. Check if they have any questions. If they ask for information you don't have, refer them to the website in the Background Information box and ask them to feed back to you at the next lesson.

> ### Background Information
> Mountain rescue teams risk their lives to go and help people who have fallen, been injured or have got stuck in bad weather whilst climbing. One of the biggest problems is that people often go walking or climbing without checking the weather forecast and then get stranded in fog or snow. Lots or mountain rescue team members are volunteers but they all have to have special training for the job. Some teams use dogs to help them find people who are injured or lost – especially in heavy rain or snow when it's hard to see properly. For further information, go to www.nationalgeographic.com and search for 'mountain rescue'.

> ### Let's Talk
> Put students into small groups. Ask them to talk about whether or not they would like to be a member of a mountain rescue team. Encourage them to give their reasons.

Lesson 1

Objectives

Reading	the cartoon story – circling the correct words
Vocabulary	text-related words; jobs
Grammar	adverbs of manner
Listening	multiple matching
Speaking	asking and answering questions about jobs

The cartoon story

- Ask students if they can remember what happened in the previous episode of the cartoon story (*Kristie was doing a project on means of transport. She interviewed Mikey and Adam about different means of transport and asked them about their favourite way to travel. Then the globe took the children up in a hot air balloon. The children all agreed that the magic globe is the best way to travel!*).
- Ask students to look at the story pictures and suggest what might be happening.

1
- Please follow the procedure outlined in Unit 1, Lesson 1 on page 12 of this Teacher's Guide.

> ### Answers
> rescue – *the act of saving people in danger*
> admire – *have respect for*
> in action – *whilst doing something*
> grab – *get hold of quickly*
> slipping – *moving without intending to*
> panic – *worry and get upset*
> instructions – *statements about what to do*

- Depending on whether you are using the DVD or the Audio CD, follow the relevant instructions.

For teachers using the DVD
- Make sure each child has a copy of Cartoon DVD Worksheet 12 that can be found on the *Resource CD-ROM*.
- Please follow the procedure outlined in Unit 1, Lesson 1 on page 12 of this Teacher's Guide for teachers using the DVD.

Before you watch

Answers
1 a cliff / a mountain
2 Mikey falls down the cliff.

While you watch

Answers
1 Adam
2 Kristie
3 Mikey
4 Adam
5 Mikey
6 Kristie

After you watch

Answers
1 programme
2 cliff
3 real life
4 plan
5 hand
6 globe

For teachers using the Audio CD

- Ask students to look at page 108 of their student's book and to work in pairs. Ask them to say where the globe is at the beginning of the story (*on top of the TV*).
- Tell students they are going to listen to and read the story. Ask them to look at the pictures and to follow the story as they listen.
- Play the recording once and ask students who tells Mikey not to worry (*the rescue man*).
- Assign the roles of Kristie, Mikey, Adam and the rescue man and woman to different students and ask them to read the story out loud and to act it out. Time permitting, repeat until all students have had a turn.
- As a class, ask students the questions below to check their understanding of the episode.
  1 What is 'The Rescue'? (*a programme about a team of rescuers*)
  2 What does Adam say about the man climbing down the cliff? (*It looks dangerous!*)
  3 Who does Mikey admire? (*rescuers*)
  4 Why does Adam want Mikey to climb a little higher? (*So he can grab his hand.*)
  5 What does the woman say Mikey has to do if he wants to train to be a rescuer? (*work really hard*)

Comprehension

2

- Ask students to read sentences 1 to 5 so they know what information to look for when they read the cartoon story again. Ask them to circle the correct words using information from the story.
- Ask students to do the task individually, but check the answers as a class. Encourage students to explain their answer choices by giving evidence from the story.

Answers
1 a documentary (*The camera follows them around as they do their job.*)
2 real life (*I'd love to see them in action in real life!*)
3 can't (*Oh no! I'm slipping!*)
4 did (*... you followed our instructions carefully.*)
5 saved (*You saved my life.*)

Let's Talk

Put students into small groups. Ask them to take turns telling each other about things that happened in the story, using their own words.

Extra Class Activity

As a class, ask students to read out the whole cartoon story (all the episodes), from the beginning to the end. Assign the roles of Kristie, Mikey, Adam, Beth, Diana, Fred, the rescue man and the rescue woman to different students. If you have a large class, you could ask different students to play the roles from Unit 6 onwards so that all students will have a turn.

Vocabulary

3

- Ask students to read the definitions, then to find the words in the story that match. Explain that that all the answers are highlighted words in the story.
- Ask students to do the task individually, but check the answers as a class. Correct their pronunciation where necessary.

Answers
1 grab
2 panic
3 rescue
4 admire
5 instructions

4

- Explain to students that they have to label pictures 1 to 6 with the words in the wordbank. Encourage them to use their dictionaries to look up any vocabulary they don't know.
- Ask students to work in pairs to do the task, but check the answers as a class. Correct their pronunciation where necessary.

Answers
1 sailor
2 detective
3 artist
4 chef
5 mechanic
6 photographer

Grammar

Adverbs of Manner

- Write the sentence *I wasn't thinking clearly.* on the board and explain that *clearly* is an adverb which tells us how the action *thinking* was done.

- Read the rules in the grammar box to the class and ask them to read the example sentences with you. Explain the meaning of any grammar terms that students are not familiar with.
- Draw students' attention to the irregular adverbs and tell students that they have to learn these by heart.

5

- Tell students that they have to complete the sentences by making adverbs from the adjectives in brackets.
- Ask students to read each sentence to see whether the adjective is regular or irregular. Tell them to look back at the grammar box to see whether they need to make changes to the adjective to make it an adverb.
- Ask students to do the task individually, but check the answers as a class.

Answers
1	carefully	4	easily
2	quickly	5	quietly
3	slowly		

6

- Tell students that they have to complete the sentences with words from the wordbank.
- Tell them to decide whether each adverb is regular or irregular, and to think about all the changes they need to make to the regular adjectives.
- Ask students to do the task individually, but check the answers as a class.

Answers
1	well	4	slowly
2	comfortably	5	angrily
3	fast		

Teaching Tip
For further practice on adverbs, ask students to work in pairs to write down as many adjectives as they can remember, and then tell them to write down the adverbs from these adjectives. Ask them to come up and write their adjectives and adverbs on the board to share their answers with the class.

Listening

7

- Explain to students that they are going to hear five people talking about their jobs and that they have to match speakers 1 to 5 with the jobs in pictures a to e. Tell students that they have to listen for the words that talk about the jobs in the pictures.
- Encourage students to match each speaker to their job as they hear about them rather than trying to remember the answers at the end. Do the first one together as a class.
- Play the rest of the recording all the way to the end. Then play the recording a second time and ask students to check their answers or fill in any missing information.

- Check the answers as a class and make sure students can justify their answers.

Turn to page 131 of this Teacher's Guide for the recording script.

Answers
- a 3 (*I'm very good at cooking and I work in a restaurant.*)
- b 4 (*I work in a hospital and I wear a uniform, ...*)
- c 2 (*... I paint pictures and I sell them ...*)
- d 1 (*I spend a lot of time at the police station. ... Protecting people makes me feel good!*)
- e 5 (*Last week we saved a young skier from danger.*)

Speaking

8

- Explain that students are going to work in pairs to ask and answer questions about jobs.
- Remind students of the adverbs of manner they learnt and tell them to use them with the work-related words to answer the questions.
- Read through the *Express yourself!* box with students. Explain that this box provides useful language that will help them complete the Speaking task. Give one or two example sentences, talking about your job as a teacher. When students are confident with the language, they can do the task in their pairs.
- Go round the class monitoring students to make sure they are carrying out the task properly. Don't correct any mistakes at this stage, but make a note of any mistakes in structure and pronunciation.
- As a class, ask each pair to ask and answer one of the questions and repeat until each pair has had a turn.
- Write any mistakes that students made on the board, without saying who made them, and ask them to correct them. Deal with any problems that arose in pronunciation.

Answers
Students' own answers

Extra Writing Task 12

- Make sure each student has a copy of Extra Writing Task 12 that can be found on the *Resource CD-ROM*.
- Explain to students that they are going to imagine they have a job they don't like and they are going to write a short email to a friend telling them about their job. Encourage them to use their imagination! Ask students to try to use adverbs in their email.
- Ask students to write their emails in their notebooks. Remind them to proofread their emails carefully once they have finished, checking that they have used a range of vocabulary and a variety of adverbs. Remind them to check their spelling too. You could set this task for homework if you are short of time.
- If time allows, invite some of them to read their emails to the rest of the class. Gently correct any mistakes.

See photocopiable material that can be found on the *Resource CD-ROM*.

Lesson 2

Objectives

Reading	article – true or false
Vocabulary	text-related words; job-related words
Grammar	relative clauses
Listening	true or false
Sounds of English	*t* and *d* sounds

Way in

- Check students' spelling of the words they learnt in Lesson 1 by asking them to write the following words in their notebooks: *rescue, admire, in action, grab, slipping, panic* and *instructions*. Then check that they remember the meanings by asking them to translate the words into their own language.
- Ask students to come up and write the words for the different jobs they learnt in Lesson 1 (*artist, chef, photographer, rescuer, detective, mechanic, nurse, sailor*) on the board. Ask the class to correct their spelling where necessary.
- Write the adjectives *beautiful, clear, easy* and *quick* on the board and ask students how to make adverbs from these. Elicit the irregular adverbs for the adjectives *hard, fast, high, right, wrong* and *good*.

Reading

1

- Ask students to open their books at page 110 and explain that they are going to read an article about Patrick, a conservationist. Ask them if any of them would like to be a conservationist and if yes, ask why.
- Tell students they are going to listen to and read the article. Ask them to follow the article as they listen.
- Play the recording once. Ask students to tell you one fact they learned from the article that they didn't know before.
- Ask students to read the pre-reading question and to find the answer in the article.

Answer
Because he loves his job.

2

- Please follow the procedure outlined in Unit 1, Lesson 2 on page 15 of this Teacher's Guide.

Answers
endangered species – *types of animal that are in danger of becoming extinct*
population – *number of people or animals living in a place*
conservationist – *person who works to save animals*
prevent – *stop from happening*
dead – *no longer alive*
involves – *includes*
career – *job*
wildlife – *animals and birds living wild in an area*

Did you know?

- Ask students to read the information in the *Did you know?* feature and ask them how they feel about the enormous decrease in the number of lions over the past 70 years.
- If students are interested, give them more information about endangered species using the Background Information box below.

Background Information
Since the year 1500, more than 800 species of plants and animals have become extinct. This is only counting the animals and plants we know of. At the moment, there are more than 1,100 species of animal worldwide that are endangered and half of these are in the United States. People and global warming are the two biggest threats to animal species. For further information, go to www.nationalgeographic.com and search for 'endangered species'.

Let's Talk
Put students into small groups. Ask them to talk about their ideas for saving endangered species.

Comprehension

3

- Ask students to read sentences 1 to 5 so that they know what information to look for when reading the text again.
- Tell them they have to work out if the sentences are true or false and to write *T* or *F* in the boxes provided. Tell them to underline the information in the text that helps them to find the answers.
- Explain any vocabulary students don't know and correct their pronunciation if necessary.

Answers
1 F (*If we don't protect them, their population will get smaller.*)
2 T (*My job is to find out ... where they are.*)
3 T (*... we try to find out what has caused them to die ...*)
4 F (*... this is the place where I grew up.*)
5 T (*... I feel like the luckiest guy on earth!*)

Vocabulary

4

- Explain that the words in the wordbank are all highlighted words in the article, so students should know them.
- Ask students to do the task individually, but check the answers as a class.

Answers
1 conservationist
2 dead
3 wildlife
4 prevent
5 population

5

- Ask students to read the sentences and the options and to pick the option which completes the sentence. Encourage students to use their dictionaries to look up any unknown vocabulary.
- Check the answers as a class and explain the meanings of the words where necessary.

Answers
1 manager
2 part-time
3 career
4 employees
5 qualifications
6 species

Let's Talk

Put students into pairs. They take turns to make their own sentences using the words they learnt in *Vocabulary 5*. Make sure they use both word options, not just the one which was the correct answer option.

Grammar

Relative Clauses

- Read the rules in the grammar box to the class and ask them to read the example sentences with you. Explain the meaning of any grammar terms that students are not familiar with.
- Ask students to look back at the article on page 110 and to find two sentences with relative clauses. Ask them what each of the relative clauses tells us about *Patrick Kimenyi is a biologist and part-time conservationist who is working to prevent this from happening. [Patrick Kimenyi]; It's a career which is difficult ... [the career].*

6

- Ask students to read through the sentences and options and to find out whether the relative pronoun or adverb is about a person, an animal, a thing or a place. Tell them to compare each sentence with the examples in the grammar box to see which relative pronoun fits.
- Give students a few minutes to compare their answers with a partner. Ask them to justify their answers if they are different.
- Check the answers as a class and ask students to justify the answers they give.

Answers
1 which
2 who
3 which
4 where
5 which
6 who

7

- Before they fill in the gaps, ask students to read the sentences to decide whether the relative pronoun is about a person, an animal or thing, or a place.
- Ask students to do the task individually, but check the answers as a class.

Answers
1 who
2 which
3 which
4 where
5 who

Listening

8

- Explain to students that they are going to hear Kate and Ollie discussing their weekends and the new employee in the office.
- Tell them to read sentences 1 to 5 before they listen to the recording, so they know what information to listen for. Remind them that they have to write *T* if the sentence is correct and *F* if it is incorrect. Remind students to listen carefully for meaning as well as actual words.
- Play the recording to the end and ask students to compare their answers with a partner. Ask them to justify any answers that are different. Play the recording a second time and ask them to check their answers or fill in any missing information.
- Check the answers as a class and make sure students can justify their answers.

Turn to page 131 of this Teacher's Guide for the recording script.

Answers
1 F (*Oh, I didn't go out. I stayed at home and watched TV.*)
2 T (*... she started last Tuesday. She's been here for a few days.*)
3 T ('*Well, my son was sick so I had to stay at home ...*)
4 F (*She's got a full-time job here, of course.*)
5 T (*I haven't spoken to her yet.*)

Sounds of English

9

- Ask students to work in pairs to say the words to each other and to see if they know the difference in the sounds of the last letters in each pair.
- Ask students to say *lit* and *lid* and to tell you which words they think end with the same sound as *lit* (*mat, foot, cut, but*) and which end with the same sound as *lid* (*mad, food, could, bad*).

10

- Play the recording, stopping after each word for students to tick the word they hear.
- Play the recording again without stopping and ask students to repeat the words as a class.

> **Answers**
> Students should tick the following:
> **1** lit
> **2** mad
> **3** food
> **4** cut
> **5** bad

> **Extra Class Activity**
> Ask students to work in pairs to write down as many words as they can which end with *d* or *t*. Ask them to practise saying these words to each other. Correct pronunciation where necessary. Then ask them to use their words to write a short rhyme. Ask them to take turns at reading their rhymes to the class.

> **Extra Task (for early finishers)**
> See photocopiable material that can be found on the *Resource CD-ROM*.

Lesson 3

Objectives

Reading	comments about jobs – circling the correct words
Express yourself!	talking about jobs
Listening	circling the correct answers
Speaking	talking about jobs
Writing	making notes; writing an article

Way in

- Write the following on the board: *conservationist, population, prevent, employee, manager, part-time, career* and *qualifications* and ask students to write a sentence for each one in their notebooks. When they have finished, ask them to swap books with a partner to compare their sentences and check the spelling. Ask students at random to read one of their sentences to the class until all the words have been correctly used.
- Write the words *who*, *which* and *where* on the board and ask students which word we use to begin relative clauses about people (*who*), things (*which*), animals (*which*) or places (*where*). Ask them to give you sentences with relative clauses and write one of their examples on the board for each relative pronoun or adverb to check that they have used the correct sentence structure.

Reading

1

- Tell students that they are going to listen to and read three comments about what different teenagers want to be. Ask them to open their books at page 112 and follow the comments as they listen.
- Play the recording once. Ask students to tell you who has a job that makes them sad sometimes (*Christopher*).
- Ask students to read the pre-reading question and to find the answer in the article.

> **Answer**
> Alicia – she wants to open her own restaurant

> **Let's Talk**
> Put students into small groups and ask them to compare the three jobs in the article, saying what they think is good and bad about each one.

Comprehension

2

- Tell students to read the sentences and both answer options before they read the text again so that they know what information to look for.
- Ask students to do the task individually, but check the answers as a class. Ask students to underline where they get the answer from in the text so they can justify their answers.
- Explain any vocabulary students don't know and correct their pronunciation if necessary.

> **Answer**
> **1** has (*I've thought a lot about my future.*)
> **2** technology (*My friends say that I know so much about technology that I will probably invent the new smart phones!*)
> **3** seven (*You have to go to university and study for about seven years to become a vet.*)
> **4** can (*You can find a part-time job in pet rescue centres when you are a student.*)
> **5** be famous like (*... and be a famous chef like Jamie Oliver!*)

> **Teaching Tip**
> Now that students have almost completed their elementary level course, they should be able to consolidate their vocabulary through brainstorming sessions. For example, draw two circles near the centre of the board and write the headings *indoors* and *outdoors* in the circles, and then ask students to say all the jobs they can think of that link to these categories. Invite students to come up and write their answers on the board around each category. This will help give students ideas for the speaking and writing tasks which follow.

Express yourself!

Talking about jobs

- Ask students to work in pairs to read through the question and phrases with the example answers in *Talking about jobs*.

3

- Ask students to take turns to ask and answer the question about what they want to be. Remind them to practise the language given in the box. Correct their pronunciation and intonation pattern if necessary.
- As a class, ask some of the pairs to say their dialogue out loud.

Answer
Students' own answers

Listening

4

- Ask students to read through the sentences and options.
- Explain to students that they are going to listen to two friends talking about jobs.
- Play the recording and ask students to circle the correct answers.
- Give students a few minutes to compare their answers with a partner. Ask them to justify their answers if they are different.
- Play the recording again and ask students to check their answers and to circle any missing answers.
- Check the answers as a class and ask students to justify the answers they give.

Turn to page 131 of this Teacher's Guide for the recording script

Answers
1 doctor (… *Oh, I want to be a doctor …*)
2 qualifications (*My teacher told me that you have to study for many years and get good qualifications …*)
3 dad (*My dad is a doctor …*)
4 taxi driver (*When I was younger, I used to think I wanted to be a taxi driver, but now I want to be a pilot.*)
5 enjoys (*He earns quite a lot of money and he has a lot of days off, so he's happy.*)
6 manager (*My sister Anna is a manager in a supermarket.*)

Speaking

5

- Explain that students are going to work in pairs to explain what the people in the pictures are good at and what is good and bad about their jobs.
- Remind students of the job-related words that they learnt and tell them to use them to answer the questions.

- Go round the class monitoring students to make sure they are carrying out the task properly. Don't correct any mistakes at this stage, but make a note of any mistakes in structure and pronunciation.
- Ask each pair to talk about one of the pictures and repeat until each pair has had a turn.
- Write any mistakes you heard on the board, without saying who made them, and ask students to correct them. Deal with any problems that arose in pronunciation.

Answers
Students' own answers

Extra Class Activity

Divide the class into teams to play a *Guess the job* game. Give the teams a few minutes to decide which jobs they will describe, and then ask the teams in turn to describe the job without saying what it is. Tell them to say what is good and bad about the job and what the person has to do in this particular job. The team which guesses the most answers correctly is the winner.

Writing

Making Notes

6

- Ask students to read the advice about making notes.
- Explain that notes are not full sentences and that they are short phrases or words which we can write down to help us remember the main points we want to include in our writing.

7

- Ask students to read the headings on the notebook to decide which notes fit the meaning. Explain that some headings match more than one note.
- Ask students to do the task individually, but check the answers as a class.

Answers
Why is it bad?
long hours, dangerous
One good thing: good money
Why is it good?
don't have to travel, you decide what to do, you make beautiful things
One bad thing: not much money

8

- Ask students to read the article and to find the sentences which relate to each of the notes in *Writing 7* and to underline them.
- Ask students to do the task individually, but check the answers as a class.
- When you have checked the answers, ask students whether they agree with what the writer says about these jobs.

Answers

Paragraphs 2 and 3 / They appear in the second and third paragraphs.

Students should underline the following:

Paragraph 2

You can make beautiful things

you don't have to travel

You decide what to paint and when to paint it.

artists don't make much money

Paragraph 3

You have to work long hours

It's too dangerous.

pilots are paid a lot of money

Task

9

- Ask students to work in pairs to discuss what jobs they are going to write about in their articles.
- Make sure students understand the paragraph plan on page 113. Remind them that each paragraph adds a different piece of information to the description to make it easy to follow.
- Ask students to make notes like the ones in *Writing* 7 to help them make their plan before they write the article. Then tell them to use their plan to write an article like the one in *Writing 8*.
- Alternatively, you could assign this task as homework.

Example answer

Notes

Worst job: taxi driver

Why is it bad?

long hours

too much traffic

customers get angry

One good thing: talking to customers

Favourite job: teacher

Why is it good?

work with children

meet new students every year

easy to find a job

One bad thing: qualifications

The best and the worst jobs

There are lots of jobs in the world. It isn't easy to find a job in my country, but there are some jobs that many people can do.

I would like to be a teacher. I think it's the best job for me because I love children and I think I'd be good at teaching them. It is also interesting to meet new students every year and every one is different. There are schools everywhere, so it's quite easy to find a job as a teacher. The worst thing is that you need a lot of qualifications so you have to study hard to become a teacher. ➡

The worst job I can think of is a taxi driver. They have to work long hours and they have to wait in traffic to take people to different parts of the city. Customers often get angry with taxi drivers when they have to wait too long. However, the good thing is that they can have interesting chats with some nice customers.

In conclusion, I think both these jobs are quite easy to find in my country, but I think that teachers have the best job.

10

- Ask students to read back through their articles to make sure that they have included all the information from their notes. If you ask them to write the article for homework, then give them a few minutes to do this before they do *Review 6*.

Extra Task (for early finishers)

See photocopiable material that can be found on the *Resource CD-ROM*.

Objectives

- To revise vocabulary and grammar from Units 11 and 12
- Project – my ideal job

Preparing for the review

- Explain to students that the tasks in *Review 6* revise the material they learnt in Units 11 and 12.
- Remind students that they can ask you for help with the exercises or look back at the units if they're not sure about an answer, as the review is not a test.
- Decide how you will carry out the review. You could ask students to do one task at a time and then correct it immediately, or ask students to do all the tasks and then correct them together at the end. If you do all the tasks together, let students know every now and again how much time they have got left to finish the tasks.
- Remind students not to leave any answers blank and to try to find any answers they aren't sure about in the units.
- Revise the vocabulary and grammar as a class before students do the review.

Vocabulary Revision

- Ask students to tell you as many words as possible related to transport. Make sure they revise the words they learnt in the vocabulary tasks in Unit 11, Lessons 1 and 2 and any other words related to transport from the unit.
- Check that students remember the text-related words from Unit 12, Lesson 1. Say the words *rescue, admire, in action, grab, slip, panic* and *instructions* and ask students to give the meaning or an example sentence with each word after you say each one.
- Write the following jumbled words on the board and ask students to unscramble them to find words from Unit 12, Lesson 1.

  - evitceted   (*detective*)
  - efhc   (*chef*)
  - tistrat   (*artist*)
  - laisro   (*sailor*)
  - rehotohprgap   (*photographer*)
  - cinchema   (*mechanic*)
  - esurn   (*nurse*)

- Write the words *career, employee, experience, manager, parttime, qualifications* and *staff* on the board and ask students to write a sentence for each word in their notebooks. Ask students at random to read out one of their sentences until all the words have been used correctly.

Grammar Revision

- Ask students to tell you when we use the comparative (*to compare two or more people, animals, things*) and what word is often used after the comparative (*than*). Then ask them when we use the superlative (*to compare a person, an animal or thing with many other people, animals or things*).
- Write *both, either* and *neither* on the board. Ask students which words we use with each of them (*both – and, either – or / of, neither – nor / of*) Then ask them which word we can use with both affirmative and negative verbs (*either*).
- Check that students remember the different meanings of *too* and *enough* (*too* shows that there is more of something than we need and that this is a problem, *enough* shows there is as much of something as we need). Ask students at random to give you a sentence using either *too* or *enough*.
- Ask students what we use relative clauses for (*to give more information about people, animals or places*). Ask them which relative pronoun or adverb we use when talking about people (*who*), animals (*which*) and places (*where*). Tell students to write a sentence for each in their notebooks.
- Write *quick, angry, good* and *fast* on the board and ask a student to come and write the adverbs next to them.

Vocabulary

1

- Ask students to say each of the words as a class and then individually. Correct their pronunciation if necessary.
- Ask students to go to the second page of stickers at the back of the book and find the stickers for *Review 6*. Tell them to decide which thing each sticker shows and to stick it in the correct box.
- Check that students have put the correct stickers above each word.

2

- Tell students to think about how the words in each group are related to one another so that they can decide which word doesn't belong in the group.
- When checking students' answers, ask them to tell you why each of the words are odd.

> **Answers**
> 1 photographer (*the other two words are to do with airports*)
> 2 timetable (*the other two words are jobs*)
> 3 instruction (*the other two words are to do with jobs*)
> 4 transport (*the other two words are jobs*)
> 5 flight (*the other two words are means of transport*)

3

- Ask students to read the whole sentence and the possible options before circling the correct answer and to read the sentences again to make sure their answer makes sense when they have finished.

Answers

1	inspector	6	panic
2	career	7	part-time
3	population	8	adventurous
4	manager	9	transport
5	admire	10	afford

Grammar

4

- Explain to students that they should read the sentences before trying to write the answers to decide whether to use the comparative or the superlative. Tell them to decide whether the adjective is regular or irregular to help them get the correct form of the adjective in brackets.
- Tell students to look back at the Unit 11, Lesson 1 grammar box for a reminder if they need to.

Answers

1	the best	5	the most comfortable
2	more interesting than	6	the worst
3	as cheap	7	as big
4	slower than	8	more expensive than

5

- Point out to students that they should read the sentences first before trying to fill the gaps and to look for any words that we use with one of the words in the wordbank and to decide which word matches the context.
- Tell students to look back at the grammar boxes in Unit 11, Lessons 2 and 3 for a reminder if they need to.

Answers

1 either
2 too
3 neither
4 enough
5 both

6

- Tell students to decide whether the adverb is regular or irregular and to think about whether they need to make any extra spelling changes to help them form the adverb of manner of the adjective in brackets.
- Tell students to look back at the Unit 12, Lesson 1 grammar box for a reminder if they need to.

Answers

1	well	5	lazily
2	fast	6	beautifully
3	quietly	7	carefully
4	rudely	8	badly

7

- Explain to students that they should read the sentences and the possible options before trying to choose the answers to find out whether the relative pronoun is about a person, a thing or a place.
- Tell students to look back at the Unit 12, Lesson 2 grammar box for a reminder if they need to.

Answers

1 which
2 where
3 who
4 which
5 who
6 where

Project 6

1

- Explain to the students that they are going to do a project about their ideal job. Ask them to say what job they are going to write about.
- Ask students to read the bullet points and explain that the email they write must address these points.
- Read through the example email with the class.
- Ask students to complete their projects. They can do this in the lesson or for homework.
- When the projects are complete, stick them on the classroom wall.

2

- Invite students to read their emails to the class. Have a class vote to find the most interesting job.

National Geographic DVD Worksheets

General Note

The National Geographic DVDs can be used as an interesting way to introduce your students to other cultures. They are authentic National Geographic DVDs and it is not necessary for students to understand everything they hear to benefit from them. Some of the tasks focus on the visual aspects of the videos, so students can concentrate more on what they see than on what they hear. They are also a good way to encourage your students to watch TV programmes and films in English so that they can get used to the sound of the language. The more students are exposed to English, the easier it will be for them to pick up the language.

DVD 1: Farley the Red Panda

* Explain to students that they are going to watch a DVD about a red panda. Ask them what colour pandas usually are (*black and white*). Tell them that the red panda on the DVD has lived in both the cities marked on the globe. Draw their attention to the cities (*San Diego* and *New York*) and ask what country they are in (*America*). Ask students if they think pandas come from America (*No, they don't.*). See if they know what countries pandas live in in the wild (*China and some other countries in Asia, especially Nepal in the case of red pandas*).
* Use the background information in the box below to give students further information if they are interested.

> ### Background Information
> Red pandas are related to the more common black and white giant pandas from China. Red pandas are a lot smaller – not much bigger than a large cat, but with a bushy tail which makes them look a little larger. Baby red pandas aren't red at all; they're grey! They spend many hours in trees and often sleep in the trees, too. As well as bamboo, red pandas like to eat fruit, roots, acorns and eggs. They don't live for a very long time – the average age for a red panda is between 8 and 12 years. Because of humans cutting down trees, red pandas are an endangered species. For more information go to www.nationalgeographic.com and search for 'pandas'.

1 Before you watch

* Ask students to read the questions. Ask them to think about their answers.
* Put students into pairs and ask them to take turns asking and answering the questions with their partner. Allow a few minutes for this. When they have finished, encourage some pairs to share their answers with the class.

> ### Answers
> Students' own answers

* Write the following words on the board and explain that students will hear them while they watch the DVD: *concerned, nutrition, hypothermic, playmates* and *bond*. If they don't know the words, either encourage students to look them up in a dictionary to find the meaning, or explain the meaning of each one and check understanding before going on to watch the DVD.

2 While you watch

* Explain to students that you want them to keep their books closed while they watch the DVD for the first time. Tell them not to worry if they don't understand everything.
* Play the DVD through the first time without stopping, then encourage students to tell the class about something they saw or heard on the DVD.
* Ask students to open their books and read the sentences before they watch the DVD again so that they know what information to listen out for. Explain any words that students have difficulty with.
* Play the DVD until you hear the information about where Farley was born and elicit that he was born at San Diego Zoo.
* Play the rest of the DVD and ask students to do the rest of the task. Then ask them to discuss their answers with a partner and to justify any answers they have that are different.
* Check the answers as a class.

> ### Answers
> | | | | |
> |---|---|---|---|
> | 1 | Zoo | 4 | day |
> | 2 | three | 5 | climber |
> | 3 | care | 6 | youngsters |

> ### Extra Class Activity
> Put students in small groups to do a mini project on red pandas. They should write down any facts they can remember about red pandas from the DVD. If you have an Internet connection available, allow them to do some more research on pandas. Encourage them to draw pictures or find magazine pictures to illustrate their projects. Ask the groups to present their projects to the class.

3 After you watch

* Ask students to read the words in the wordbank and then to read the sentences and complete them with the words.
* Ask students to do the task individually. Then play the DVD again and check the answers as a class.

> ### Answers
> | | | | |
> |---|---|---|---|
> | 1 | hours | 4 | friendly |
> | 2 | sick | 5 | zoo |
> | 3 | hospital | 6 | playmate |

DVD 2: Dangerous Dinners

- Explain to students that they are going to watch a DVD about a dangerous food. Ask if they can guess what sort of food it is (*fish*). Explain that the fish is popular in Japan and draw their attention to Tokyo on the map. See if they can remember anything about Tokyo from Unit 9 in the student's book.
- Use the background information in the box below to give students further information if they are interested.

Background Information

The puffer fish gets its name from the fact that when it needs to defend itself against enemies, it drinks large amounts of water – this makes its stomach puff up, making it look a lot bigger and scarier. The puffer fish also has spikes on its stomach, which makes them hard for predators to eat. The flesh, skin and fins of the puffer fish are not poisonous but the eyes, intestines and liver are all extremely toxic. In the last ten years, 26 people in Japan have died from eating the fish. If someone who is not trained to cook them catches and cooks a puffer fish to eat, they have a 90% chance of dying. The Emperor of Japan is forbidden from eating the fish for his own safety. For more information go to www.nationalgeographic.com and search for 'puffer fish'.

1 Before you watch

- Ask students to look at the pictures. Invite them to guess how the pictures might be connected with the DVD. Don't say whether their guesses are right or not at this stage; they will find out when they watch.
- Ask students to read the words in the wordbank and explain that they are going to label the pictures with these words. Ask them to work in pairs. Check the answers as a class.

Answers

1	rubbish bin	4	fish
2	chef	5	heart
3	medicine	6	restaurant

- Present and check understanding of *licence, toxin, cyanide, milligram* and *funeral* as in DVD 1 on page 121 of this Teacher's Guide.

2 While you watch

- Explain to students that you want them to keep their books closed while they watch the DVD for the first time. Tell them not to worry if they don't understand everything.
- Play the DVD through the first time without stopping, then encourage students to tell the class about something they saw or heard on the DVD.
- Ask students to open their books and read the sentences before they watch the DVD again so that they know what information to listen out for. Explain any words that students have difficulty with.

- Make sure students understand that they should write *T* or *F* in the boxes provided to show whether the sentences are true or false according to what they see and hear on the DVD. Play the DVD until you hear the information about fish being a popular food in Japan and elicit that sentence 1 is true. Ask students to write *T* in the box.
- Play the rest of the DVD and ask students to write *T* or *F* next to the rest of the sentences. Then ask them to discuss their answers with a partner and to justify any answers they have that are different.
- Check the answers as a class.

Answers

1 T (*Fish is a very popular food in Japan.*)
2 T (*Eating this fish is like playing a dangerous game.*)
3 F (*... puffer fish is on more than 80 menus ...*)
4 T (*Chefs had to get a licence to say they can prepare and serve puffer fish.*)
5 T (*A tiger fugu has enough toxin to kill 30 people.*)
6 F (*A puffer fish meal is usually eight different dishes, ...*)

3 After you watch

- Ask students to read the whole sentence and both answer options before they choose their answer and then to read the sentence again with their answer to make sure it is correct.
- Ask students to do the task individually. Then play the DVD again and check the answers as a class.

Answers

1a 2b 3a 4b

DVD 3: Dinosaurs

- Explain to students that they are going to watch a DVD about dinosaurs. As a class, brainstorm dinosaurs and make a list of facts that students know about them. For example, list the names of different dinosaurs, when they lived, how big they were, what they ate, etc. Ask students to think of any films they have seen with dinosaurs in them (lifelike or cartoons) and to say what they remember about them.
- Use the background information in the box below to give students further information if they are interested.

Background Information

The word 'dinosaur' means 'terrible lizard' and was invented in 1842 by Sir Richard Owen to describe the creatures that roamed the Earth up to 65 million years ago. The largest dinosaurs were over 30 metres long and the smallest were the size of a chicken. Dinosaurs like the massive Tyrannosaurus Rex were carnivores that ate meat, but around 65% were herbivores that only ate plants. Most dinosaurs hatched from eggs. Scientists are sure there are lots of dinosaurs we still haven't found out about. For more information, go to www.nationalgeographic.com and search for 'dinosaurs'.

1 Before you watch

- Ask students to read the questions. Ask them to think about their answers.
- Put students into pairs and ask them to take turns asking and answering the questions with their partner. Allow a few minutes for this. When they have finished, encourage some pairs to share their answers with the class.

Answers
Students' own answers

- Present and check understanding of *throat, crush* and *comet* as in DVD 1 on page 121 of this Teacher's Guide.

2 While you watch

- Explain to students that you want them to keep their books closed while they watch the DVD for the first time. Tell them not to worry if they don't understand everything.
- Play the DVD through the first time without stopping, then encourage students to tell the class about something they saw or heard on the DVD.
- Ask students to open their books and read the sentences before they watch the DVD again so that they know what information to listen out for. Explain any words that students have difficulty with.
- Make sure students understand that they should write *T* or *F* in the boxes provided to show whether the sentences are true or false according to what they see and hear on the DVD. Play the DVD until your hear the information about when dinosaurs first walked on Earth and elicit that sentence 1 is false. Ask students to write *F* in the box.
- Play the rest of the DVD and ask students to write *T* or *F* next to the rest of the sentences. Then ask them to discuss their answers with a partner and to justify any answers they have that are different.
- Check the answers as a class.

Answers
1 F (*... the first dinosaurs walked on Earth about 225 million years ago.*)
2 F (*The biggest were the sauropods.*)
3 T (*... most dinosaurs laid eggs.*)
4 T (*... dinosaurs lived in groups, called herds ...*)
5 T (*So ... why did the dinosaurs die? We don't really know for sure.*)
6 F (*Scientists think that birds are similar to dinosaurs.*)

3 After you watch

- Ask students to read the whole sentence and both answer options before they choose their answer and then to read the sentence again with their answer to make sure it is correct.
- Ask students to do the task individually. Then play the DVD again and check the answers as a class.

Answers
1b 2b 3a 4a

Extra Class Activity
Ask students to work in pairs to talk about the two photos on page 118. Encourage them to take turns to say one thing each about the pictures and to speculate about the dinosaurs shown.

DVD 4: Antarctica

- Explain to students that they are going to watch a DVD about Antarctica and draw their attention to its position on the map on page 119. Ask students if they think Antarctica is at the North Pole or the South Pole (*the South Pole*). Ask what sorts of things students might expect to see in the DVD about Antarctica.
- Use the background information in the box below to give students further information if they are interested.

Background Information
Antarctica is the highest, driest, windiest, emptiest, coldest place on earth. It covers an area of 14 million square kilometres. An ice sheet covers more than 97% of Antarctica. This constitutes 90% of the world's ice and it is also 70% of the world's fresh water. There are lots of penguins, whales, seals, krill (the main food for whales) and even fish in Antarctica's waters, but there are no land mammals and, as far as scientists know, no native people. Eskimos and polar bears are not found in the Antarctic; they are found on the other side of the world in the Arctic region. For more information go to www.nationalgeographic.com and search for 'Antarctica'.

1 Before you watch

- Ask students to look at the pictures. Invite them to guess how the pictures might be connected with the DVD. Don't say whether their guesses are right or not at this stage; they will find out when they watch.
- Ask students to read the words in the wordbank and explain that they are going to label the pictures with these words. Ask them to work in pairs. Check the answers as a class.

Answers
1	tourist	4	iceberg
2	whale	5	scientists
3	penguins	6	explorer

- Present and check understanding of *continent, orca* and *awesome* as in DVD 1 on page 121 of this Teacher's Guide.

2 While you watch

- Explain to students that you want them to keep their books closed while they watch the DVD for the first time. Tell them not to worry if they don't understand everything.
- Play the DVD through the first time without stopping, then encourage students to tell the class about something they saw or heard on the DVD.

- Ask students to open their books and read the sentences before they watch the DVD again so that they know what information to listen out for. Explain any words that students have difficulty with.
- Play the DVD until you hear the information about Antarctica really being a huge desert and elicit that the correct word in sentence 1 is *desert*.
- Play the rest of the DVD and ask students to do the rest of the task. Then ask them to discuss their answers with a partner and to justify any answers they have that are different.
- Check the answers as a class.

Answers

1	desert	4	taller
2	Chile	5	penguins
3	Antarctica's	6	explorers

3 After you watch
- Ask students to read the words in the wordbank and then to read the sentences and complete them with the words.
- Ask students to do the task individually. Then play the DVD again and check the answers as a class.

Answers

1	continent	4	whale
2	boat	5	food
3	summer	6	famous

DVD 5: Loch Ness Mystery
- Explain to students that they are going to watch a DVD about Loch Ness in Scotland and draw their attention to its position on the map on page 120. Explain that *loch* is the Scottish name for *lake*. Ask students if they have heard of Loch Ness and if they know anything about it.
- Use the background information in the box below to give students further information if they are interested.

Background Information

The first recorded sighting of the Loch Ness Monster was in 565 AD by St Columba, who said he saw the monster twice in that year. The monster was first seen in the River Ness before being seen in the loch itself. The next sighting of the monster was in 1933, when a Mr and Mrs Spicer said they saw a large animal crossing the road in front of their car. Nessie, as the Loch Ness Monster is affectionately called, is usually described as having a small head, long neck, broad body, four flippers and a long tail. The scientific name for the Loch Ness Monster is a 'plesiosaur', which is a type of carnivorous aquatic, usually marine, reptile. Nessie is the most famous cryptid in the world. The word 'cryptid' refers to a hidden creature or living creature which might exist. For more information, go to www.nationalgeographic.com and search for 'Loch Ness'.

1 Before you watch
- Ask students to look at the pictures. Invite them to guess how the pictures might be connected with the DVD. Don't say whether their guesses are right or not at this stage; they will find out when they watch.
- Ask students to read the words in the wordbank and explain that they are going to label the pictures with these words. Ask them to work in pairs. Check the answers as a class.

Answers

1	doctor	4	monster
2	lake	5	submarine
3	newspaper	6	photo

2 While you watch
- Explain to students that you want them to keep their books closed while they watch the DVD for the first time. Tell them not to worry if they don't understand everything.
- Play the DVD through the first time without stopping, then encourage students to tell the class about something they saw or heard on the DVD.
- Ask students to open their books and read the sentences before they watch the DVD again so that they know what information to listen out for. Explain any words that students have difficulty with.
- Play the DVD until you hear that Nessie's history goes back more than a thousand years and elicit that the correct word in sentence 1 is *thousand*.
- Play the rest of the DVD and ask students to do the rest of the task. Then ask them to discuss their answers with a partner and to justify any answers they have that are different.
- Check the answers as a class.

Answers

1	thousand	4	step-father
2	Newspapers	5	job
3	certain	6	photo

3 After you watch
- Ask students to read the whole sentence and both answer options before they choose their answer and then to read the sentence again with their answer to make sure it is correct.
- Ask students to do the task individually. Then play the DVD again and check the answers as a class.

Answers
1a 2b 3b 4a

Extra Class Activity

Ask students to work in pairs to discuss whether or not they believe Nessie is real. Encourage them to give reasons for their opinions.

DVD 6: New York City

- Explain to students that they are going to watch a DVD about New York City. Draw their attention to New York's position on the map on page 121. Explain that although New York is not the capital city of America (that's Washington DC), it is one of the most famous cities in the United States. Ask students if they know anything about New York. Have they seen it in films? Ask if they would like to go there and if so, why?
- Use the background information in the box below to give students further information if they are interested.

Background Information

It's said that a Dutch explorer called Peter Minuit bought the island of Manhattan (actually its southern tip) from the Algonquin tribe for trinkets worth about $24. That's why Manhattan used to be called *New Amsterdam*. Although New York is not the capital of America now, it was the capital from 1789 to 1790. New York is the most densely populated city in America. More than 26,000 people live in each square mile of New York City and over 45 million people visit the city each year. There are over 18,000 restaurants in the city. For more information go to www.nationalgeographic.com and search for 'New York'.

1 Before you watch

- Ask students to look at the pictures. Invite them to guess how the pictures might be connected with the DVD. Don't say whether their guesses are right or not at this stage; they will find out when they watch.
- Ask students to read the words in the wordbank and explain that they are going to label the pictures with these words. Ask them to work in pairs. Check the answers as a class.

Answers

1	crown	4	train
2	ambulance	5	jogging
3	crowd	6	statue

- Present and check understanding of *liberty* and *subway* as in DVD 1 on page 121 of this Teacher's Guide.

2 While you watch

- Explain to students that you want them to keep their books closed while they watch the DVD for the first time. Tell them not to worry if they don't understand everything.
- Play the DVD through the first time without stopping, then encourage students to tell the class about something they saw or heard on the DVD.
- Ask students to open their books and read the sentences before they watch the DVD again so that they know what information to listen out for. Explain any words that students have difficulty with.
- Play the DVD until you hear that there is a great view of the whole city from the Statue of Liberty and elicit that the correct word in sentence 1 is *city*.

- Play the rest of the DVD and ask students to do the rest of the task. Then ask them to discuss their answers with a partner and to justify any answers they have that are different.
- Check the answers as a class.

Answers

1	city	4	park
2	ferry	5	amazing
3	Yellow	6	sleeps

3 After you watch

- Ask students to read the whole sentence and both answers options before they choose their answer and then to read the sentence again with their answer to make sure it is correct.
- Ask students to do the task individually. Then play the DVD again and check the answers as a class.

Answers
1b 2a 3a 4b

Extra Class Activity

Ask students to work in pairs to discuss whether or not they would like to live in New York. Encourage them to give reasons.

Recording Script

Unit 1

Lesson 1

1

I love my grandparents. I visit them <u>on Tuesdays and on Sundays</u>. That's <u>twice a week</u>.

2

Every Saturday after football I go with my best friend Tom for ice cream. Tom likes chocolate ice cream but <u>I *always* have a *banana* ice cream</u>.

3

My dad often goes on holiday but <u>he never goes to the sea</u>. He loves the mountains. He usually goes to the mountains once a year.

4

On Mondays I take my dog Tilly to the beach and <u>on Saturdays we go to the park</u>. She really loves the park!

Lesson 2

Dan	Hi, Helen.
Helen	Hi. What are you doing tomorrow?
Dan	Tomorrow? <u>We're going shopping</u> for a present for my grandma because it's her birthday.
Helen	It's your grandma's birthday? How old is she?
Dan	She's 60! Then, after lunch, I'm meeting my friend Toby in the park. We're playing football.
Helen	Oh, football in the park! Can I come? I love football.
Dan	Yes, OK. <u>We're meeting at three o'clock</u>.
Helen	Great. <u>I'm going to a party tomorrow evening</u>. Do you want to come with me?
Dan	No, sorry. I like parties but <u>my family and I are taking Grandma out for dinner</u>.
Helen	<u>OK, never mind. See you in the park at three o'clock tomorrow</u>.
Dan	OK, bye.

Unit 2

Lesson 1

Jemma	Hi, Carl.
Carl	Hi, Jemma. Did you move into your new flat yesterday?
Jemma	Yes, we did. <u>First we moved the beds in</u>. My bed is next to the wardrobe.
Carl	What did you do after that?
Jemma	<u>Then</u> we moved the things into the sitting room. <u>I helped Dad with the chairs and the sofa</u>.
Carl	Really? Sofas are very heavy!
Jemma	It's only a small sofa. After that we wanted some food, so Mum phoned for a pizza.
Carl	Where did you eat it?
Jemma	At the table. <u>Dad carried *that* in</u>. After lunch, we cleaned the kitchen. Then, <u>at two o'clock, some men arrived with our new fridge</u>.
Carl	Did a new oven arrive too?
Jemma	No, the oven didn't arrive yesterday. It's coming this afternoon.
Carl	Well, I hope you like your new home.
Jemma	Yes, I do, thanks. See you later!

Lesson 2

Neil	Tell me about your holiday home, Lara.
Lara	Well, last summer we went to Greece for a holiday and <u>we stayed for three months</u>!
Neil	For three months? Really?
Lara	Yes. We really liked it there. We lived in a fantastic old house.
Neil	Did you like your bedroom?
Lara	Oh, yes! It was blue and white, just like the house, and it was huge. It had a balcony with a great view of the sea. <u>Every morning I had breakfast on the balcony and I looked out at the sea</u>.
Neil	Breakfast on the balcony … very nice.
Lara	The only bad thing was that we didn't have a washing machine! <u>We cleaned our clothes in a bucket on the floor!</u>
Neil	A bucket on the floor? That's hard! Are you going back again next year?
Lara	<u>No. Next year we're going to Italy!</u>
Neil	Oh, Italy's very nice. Are you going for three months again?
Lara	No, not this time. I've got lots of work now. <u>We're going for two weeks in July</u>.
Neil	Oh, well. Two weeks is OK. I'm going to France for two weeks in August.
Lara	Oh, that's sounds nice. Well, see you later …
Neil	Bye.

Lesson 3

Paula	Yesterday <u>we visited my cousin's new cottage</u>. It's in a village. She moved in two days ago.
Billy	Oh, is it nice? I like cottages.
Paula	<u>No, it's awful!</u>
Billy	Why is it so awful?
Paula	<u>First of all, it's very dirty</u>.
Billy	Oh, no! Are the rooms big? My grandma's cottage has got huge rooms.
Paula	<u>No, the rooms are really small</u> with <u>very old furniture</u>.
Billy	Old furniture? Didn't your cousin take her own furniture there?
Paula	No, she didn't have any and she likes the old furniture. But <u>she doesn't like the garden! It's full of rubbish</u>.
Billy	Rubbish? Yuk. Why did she buy it?
Paula	I don't know.

Unit 3

Lesson 1

Sandy Hello, Annabel. You look happy this morning.

Annabel Hi, Sandy. Yes, I am. I had a great evening yesterday.

Sandy What were you doing?

Annabel Well, from six o'clock till seven I was listening to my favourite show, *Hot Hits*, on the radio. They play really good music and I was dancing all around the kitchen. At the same time I was helping Dad with dinner.

Sandy Oh, I like *Hot Hits* too, but I wasn't listening to the radio last night. I was out with my mum. What did you do at seven o'clock?

Annabel At seven I had dinner with my parents and my brother Toby. After that, at seven thirty, Toby and I were talking about our holiday in Paris last June. We had a great time there.

Sandy Yes, Paris is incredible.

Annabel Then, at eight o'clock, my cousin Larry arrived. We were trying out my new computer game and he was talking about his new hobby, golf.

Sandy It sounds like you had a good time. I must go now because …

Lesson 2

Here's a photo of my family. We were in the park last Tuesday when the rain started and we were all doing different things. My sister Daisy was riding her bike. She loves her bike! My brother Tommy likes bikes too, but he wasn't riding his bike yesterday. He was sleeping because he was very tired. There he is, under the tree. My other brother, Mark, was sliding down a hill with his friend Lucy. Mark always slides down the hill in the park. My cousin Adam was showing off and he fell in the water. He's very silly because he can't swim! You can see my uncle shouting at him. And me? You can't see me, but I was laughing when I took the photo!

Unit 4

Lesson 1

Shopkeeper Good morning.

Woman Hello. I need a few eggs. Have you got any? I need six.

Shopkeeper Of course. Here you are, six eggs.

Woman Can you also give me three bottles of lemonade? We drink a lot of lemonade. Oh, and a little vanilla ice cream too. And a few of those delicious doughnuts.

Shopkeeper How many doughnuts?

Woman Four, please.

Shopkeeper Here you are!

Woman Thank you. How much is that all together?

Shopkeeper That's eleven euros, please.

Woman Right. Thank you.

Shopkeeper Thanks! Goodbye.

Lesson 2

Here's a quick and easy recipe for spaghetti with tomato sauce. First, boil some water in a pan. Then add a packet of spaghetti and boil for ten minutes. While the spaghetti is boiling, chop an onion and fry it in a little oil. After that, add a tin of tomatoes to the onions and cook for five minutes. Then add the spaghetti to the sauce and mix together. Add lots of cheese and enjoy your meal!

Lesson 3

Hello, I'm Tom. In my family, we all like different things. My daughter, Anna, really likes prawns, but she hates cheese! My son Jimmy likes honey. He thinks it's delicious. He eats honey every morning with his breakfast, but he never eats ice cream. He doesn't like it at all. My wife, Susie, likes raw carrots, but she doesn't like fried food. She thinks fried eggs are disgusting! And me? Well, I love spaghetti, but I don't like sweet things. I don't like cakes at all.

Unit 5

Lesson 1

Lucy Hello, Mr Jackson, we've done everything you asked. We're ready for the school dance now.

Mr Jackson That's good! Who helped?

Lucy Everybody helped. Bill moved the desks and Andrew cleaned the floor.

Mr Jackson Oh, Bill moved all the desks? Very good. Did anyone help Andrew with the floor?

Lucy No, but we were all busy! Jane brought the balloons in and …

Mr Jackson Where did Jane find balloons?

Lucy The head teacher gave them to her.

Mr Jackson Oh, OK. Who took the chairs to the other classrooms?

Lucy Ada took the chairs away.

Mr Jackson Oh, well done, Ada. And what did you do, Lucy?

Lucy Me? I watched the other kids, Mr Jackson!

Lesson 2

Miss Andrews Good morning, Class. I'm Miss Andrews. I'm teaching you this week because Mr Rogers is away. Now, let's see. Henry, has the class done exercise five on page fifty yet?

Henry Yes, Miss Andrews.

Miss Andrews What about the text on the next page? Have you read that?

Henry No, we haven't read that yet.

Miss Andrews Mm, OK. Everybody turn to the article on page fifty-one. What's the article about?

Henry It's about people in Thailand.

Miss Andrews No, it isn't. Denise, what do you think it's about?

Denise It's about elephants.

Miss Andrews That's right, it's about elephants. Denise, can you read it for us please?

Denise	Oh, please, Miss Andrews, I've already read something three times this week!
Miss Andrews	Well, Henry, you read it, then.
Henry	OK, Miss Andrews.

Unit 6

Lesson 1

Polly	Hi, Mum!
Mum	Hello, Polly. What are you doing?
Polly	I'm making animals with paper.
Mum	Oh, really? What have you made?
Polly	I've made an elephant.
Mum	It's a very funny elephant!
Polly	Yes, I know. I didn't have a good picture and I haven't seen a real elephant.
Mum	Where's the tail?
Polly	I put the tail on an hour ago but it's already fallen off.
Mum	And it hasn't got any legs.
Polly	I haven't finished the legs yet.
Mum	Oh, well. Maybe it will be nice when it's got legs and a new tail!
Polly	I hope so!

Lesson 2

Doctor	Good morning, Doctor Kipling here.
Woman	Hello, Doctor. This is Mrs Myers.
Doctor	Mrs Myers! What can I do for you today?
Woman	Well, everyone in the family is sick.
Doctor	Everyone? Oh dear. What's the matter with them?
Woman	The twins have got a temperature and they're in bed.
Doctor	They've got a temperature, huh? Poor kids! Who else is ill?
Woman	Well, Grandad's in bed with a really bad cough. I've given him some medicine but it hasn't helped very much. And my husband spent all day in the garden yesterday and he's got sunburn.
Doctor	And what about you, Mrs Myers? Have you got a headache again?
Woman	Yes, Doctor, I've got a very bad headache. Can you visit us at home this afternoon?
Doctor	Er … OK. How about four o'clock?
Woman	Well, er … can you come at five o'clock? Grandad usually sleeps in the afternoon.
Doctor	OK, five o'clock. That's fine.
Woman	OK, Doctor. Thank you. Goodbye.
Doctor	Goodbye.

Lesson 3

Lizzie	What's wrong, Grandma? Are you OK?
Grandma	Well, I've got a pain in my finger.
Lizzie	Oh dear.
Grandma	And my leg is a bit sore again.
Lizzie	Yes, it's been sore for a while. What about your cough? Have you taken your medicine?
Grandma	Yes, I took my medicine this morning. Grandad took his medicine too. He had a temperature.
Lizzie	Oh dear. I hope he's OK.
Grandma	Yes. Don't worry. He's fine now!

Unit 7

Lesson 1

Miss Brown	Listen, everybody. I'm afraid it's going to rain, so I think we will go to the zoo and not to the beach today. Is that OK with everyone?
Boy	But I don't like the zoo, Miss Brown. I like the beach! I want lunch on the beach!
Miss Brown	Don't worry. We can have our lunch at the zoo. We'll go to the beach another day. At the zoo we can see lots of animals – lions, elephants, everything! And we can go inside when the rain starts. Now, I see you've all got coats. Has everybody brought sandwiches?
Kids	Yes, Miss Brown.
Boy	I've got *three* sandwiches, Miss Brown!
Miss Brown	Three? Well, *you* won't be hungry, Sam! Now, the zoo isn't far away so we'll leave at eleven o'clock, not ten o'clock as we said yesterday. Did everyone hear that? We'll leave the school at eleven o'clock, after the morning break.
Kids	Yes, Miss Brown.
Miss Brown	Good. I'll see you at the school gates at ten to eleven, then. Don't be late!

Lesson 2

Interviewer	Today we're talking to some young people about what they like doing at the weekend. Brian, what do you like doing at the weekend?
Brian	Well, I like watching TV and going for walks with my dog, Barney.
Interviewer	Alison, what about you? Do you go for walks?
Alison	No, I don't like going for walks. I think walking is a waste of time, but I love watching birds. We've got three nests in our garden. I also love shopping!
Interviewer	OK. And you, David? Do you like shopping too?
David	No, I *hate* shopping! I think it's very boring! I enjoy visiting the zoo. The lions are my favourite animals. I often go to the zoo on Saturdays with my Grandad.

Unit 8

Lesson 1

Teacher	Good morning. Today we're going to learn about recycling. What do you know about recycling?
Johnny	Well, recycling helps the environment. If we recycle things, we won't have so much rubbish. We can use lots of things again.

Teacher	That's right, Johnny. What can we recycle, Susie?
Susie	My parents recycle paper, glass and cans.
Teacher	Well done, Susie. What else can we recycle, Johnny?
Johnny	We can recycle batteries and plastic things too. And my mum recycles old clothes!
Teacher	Clothes too? Very good, Johnny. Where do you recycle your things?
Johnny	Some people come and collect paper and glass from our house, but Dad takes the other things to a special bin in the town centre.
Teacher	Very good! And from today you can recycle things at school too. We've got some big green boxes just outside this classroom.
Susie	That's great, Mr Davids.
Teacher	OK. Let's open our books and read about recycling in London …

Lesson 2

1

Boy	Jackie, do you know how much rubbish from a litter bin we can recycle?
Girl	No – maybe 30%?
Boy	No, it's 60%. We can recycle about 60% of the things in the rubbish.
Girl	Wow, that's a lot!

2

Girl	So where can we recycle things in this area? Do we put things in green recycling bins?
Boy	No. In this area, the green bins are for rubbish. You must use the *blue* recycling bins.
Girl	Where can I find them?
Boy	They are in streets or outside supermarkets, usually next to rubbish bins.

3

Girl	Can I recycle batteries in the blue recycling bins in the street?
Boy	No, you can't. You must take batteries to the special bins in shops and supermarkets.
Girl	Are they just for batteries, or can you put other things in too?
Boy	They're just for batteries.

4

Girl	How much of the waste in litter bins in Greece is plastic?
Boy	What do you *think*?
Girl	I don't know. About 5%?
Boy	No. In some countries it's only 2%, but in Greece about 20% of waste is plastic.

5

Girl	How long can a plastic bag pollute the environment?
Boy	A very long time! We make the bags in a minute and we use them for about twenty minutes, but they stay on land or in water for about 400 years.
Girl	400 years! That's terrible!

Lesson 3

Everyone can help the environment. One thing you can do is make a recycling centre for your street or block of flats! Here's what you must do: ask some neighbours for some rubbish bins. You will need four. Use a special pen and write PAPER, PLASTIC, GLASS and CANS on the bins. Then you must put the bins in a good place so everyone can see them – maybe on the corner of your street or near the door of your block of flats. Next, tell the people in each house or flat about recycling. Tell them how important it is so that they recycle lots of things! Take your mum or dad with you, though! When the bins are full, take them to a supermarket or your school's big recycling bins. Go green! It's easy!

Unit 9

Lesson 1

Boy	Excuse me. I'm looking for the library. Can you tell me where it is?
Girl	Let's see. The library, yes. You have to go down King Street for about two minutes. You'll pass the supermarket and then at the traffic lights turn left into Lang Road. You'll see a restaurant on the left. Turn left after the restaurant into Hope Street and then cross the road, but be careful because it's a very busy street. Walk down Hope Street for a minute, past a café, and then turn right into Merry Lane. Turn right again into Cage Street. Walk down Cage Street for two minutes, and then you'll see the library on the right, opposite a school.
Boy	OK, let me just check. So I walk down King Street for two minutes. I pass a supermarket and then turn left at the traffic lights into Lang Road. Then I turn left again after the restaurant into Hope Street. I cross the road and walk down Hope Street, past a café, and then turn right into Merry Lane and right again into Cage Street. The library will be on my right, opposite a school. That's right, isn't it?
Girl	Yes, that sounds right to me.

Lesson 2

Aunt Helen	Hello Josh, you look happy.
Josh	Hello, Aunt Helen. I *am* happy! We're going on a school trip tomorrow – to Athens, in Greece. Didn't you go there in 2006?
Aunt Helen	No, I went to Athens for the Olympic Games in 2004 with your uncle. We stayed in a great hotel in the centre. Well, you'll have to visit the Parthenon.
Josh	Oh, yes, I've heard of the Parthenon. It's on a hill in the centre of the city, isn't it?
Aunt Helen	Yes, it is. We went there and I loved it. You can see far away from the top of the hill. It's beautiful. You must go to the museum there, too. They were still building it when we were there, so we couldn't go.
Josh	Oh, yes. I'm sure the museum will be very interesting. It says here that we're having lunch in Plaka. What's that? Is it a restaurant?

Aunt Helen	No, it's a district with lots of shops, cafés and restaurants. You can do all your shopping there and you can eat some delicious Greek food. Be careful, though. It's quite expensive.
Josh	<u>In the evening we're going to the cinema.</u> It's outside in a big park. I've never been to a cinema like that before. Have you?
Aunt Helen	Yes, I have. I went to a cinema in a park when *I* was in Athens. It was great! I saw a play at an ancient theatre too.
Josh	It sounds brilliant! I'm so excited!

Unit 10

Lesson 1

Jeremy	Hi Brenda. Is that your new laptop?
Brenda	Yeah, I got it last week.
Jeremy	So what are you doing now? <u>Is this a new video game?</u>
Brenda	Actually, it's better than that. <u>It's a program that comes with the laptop.</u>
Jeremy	What does it do?
Brenda	It's really great. <u>You can create your own game.</u>
Jeremy	Create your own game?
Brenda	Look, I'll show you. In my game, there are some kids with super powers. I call them 'Super Teens'. <u>Then a robot chases them</u> and makes them disappear. But Super Teens are clever. <u>They can stop the robot</u> and then catch it.
Jeremy	This sounds exciting!
Brenda	Yes, and in the end the robot can become their friend!
Jeremy	How do you win the game?
Brenda	Well, <u>if you catch the robot, you get points.</u> And this way you move on to the next level.
Jeremy	What happens in the next level?
Brenda	I don't know, I haven't thought about it yet! <u>I've only created the first level.</u>

Lesson 2

Welcome back to our show. Tonight on 'New Technologies', we talk about how the Internet has changed the world of music. Take, for example, a pop band. <u>These days, new musicians often meet online for the first time.</u> <u>Then they decide they want to play music together and form a band.</u> When the band is formed, they make their own music using modern computer technology. <u>Then, the band will record their songs.</u> To do so, most bands use special computer programs on the Internet. <u>After that, they upload their songs onto websites.</u> If they're lucky, people will find them interesting and start downloading the music. In a short time, <u>the songs can be downloaded by thousands or even millions of people.</u> <u>This way, they can become famous in a few weeks.</u> Success can come really fast on the Internet!

Lesson 3

1

What's great about this game is the speed. <u>You can get a new car every time and see if you can go faster than the other drivers.</u> Going to the next level is not easy because the race gets faster every time you win.

2

We can all play football or go swimming but there are some things that I prefer playing on my computer, <u>like bungee jumping or sky diving. They're too dangerous to do in real life but</u> they're great on this game.

3

In this game, there are gold coins somewhere in an old castle. <u>You are an explorer and you have to</u> go and find them. On the way, you have to be careful not to get lost or let the castle dragon catch you. Scary!

4

Even if you can't play a real instrument, you can make your own pop band with this game. <u>You can choose to play the drums, the guitar or the piano</u> and you can even have your own concert. Cool, isn't it?

5

This is a game for older teens or adults. You can choose to play the pop star or the reporter. You must find the right people and ask them the right questions. <u>It's like living someone else's life for a while.</u>

Unit 11

Lesson 1

Jim	I'm going on a trip to London next week.
Ann	A trip to London! Great! <u>Are you going with your parents?</u>
Jim	<u>No, with my grandparents.</u>
Ann	Oh, that's nice. Are you going by train?
Jim	Well, we don't know yet. We can't decide, but <u>the train is more exciting than the coach.</u>
Ann	Yes, I agree. The train is much more exciting. And you can walk around on the train, but you have to stay in your seat on a coach.
Jim	Yes, and <u>the coach isn't as fast as the train.</u> The coach takes three and a half hours.
Ann	Three and a half hours! That's a long time. How long does the train take?
Jim	The train takes two and a half hours.
Ann	That's better. What about price? Which is the cheapest?
Jim	Well, the coach is the cheapest. The tickets are only £13 each.
Ann	Oh, £13? That's good. And what about the train tickets?
Jim	<u>Train tickets are £30 each.</u>
Ann	That's a big difference!
Jim	Yes, it is. I don't think my grandparents can afford the train, really.
Ann	Well, I think you should take the coach then!
Jim	Yes, I think you're right. <u>We should go by coach.</u>

Lesson 2

Lisa Hi, Gary. Wow! Look at your mum's new car! It's really small!

Gary Yes, it is. It's a really special car too because it uses very little energy.

Lisa Oh, really? That's good. Is it really expensive, though?

Gary No, it isn't. In fact it's cheaper than a lot of other cars.

Lisa But it isn't a *fast* car, is it?

Gary Well, no, but it's great for the city. It can travel at about 70 kilometres per hour.

Lisa That's good. Can you get a lot of different colours?

Gary No, but you can get blue, like Mum's car, or black.

Lisa Don't they make them in red? I prefer red cars.

Gary No, I don't think so.

Lisa Oh, well, it doesn't matter. Dad is going to buy a new car, so I'll tell him about this kind. I think they're a really good idea.

Gary Yes, they are.

Lisa OK, Gary, I have to go now. See you later.

Gary OK, Lisa. Bye.

Unit 12

Lesson 1

Speaker 1

My job isn't easy, but I enjoy it. The worst thing is that I have to work long hours and I don't see my family much. I spend a lot of time at the police station, but I also get out a lot. My team and I caught a very dangerous thief last week. Protecting people makes me feel good!

Speaker 2

I love my job. I work at home and I paint pictures and then I sell them – well, I want to sell them but it isn't always easy. This year I've only sold two pictures. Sometimes I work in a shop too, just for a bit more money.

Speaker 3

I wear a white uniform. I'm very good at cooking and I work in a restaurant. I have a team of cooks and they help me in the kitchen. I start work at 12 o'clock and I go home late at night. I love making new kinds of food. I think my job's great.

Speaker 4

I work in a hospital and I wear a uniform, but I'm not a doctor. Sometimes I have to work at the weekends or at night. I look after sick people. My job is tiring, but I like helping people. When I'm at work, the time always goes fast because I'm so busy.

Speaker 5

My job is very difficult but I love it. It's not tiring and I don't have to work every day. I like the people I work with. Last week we saved a young skier from danger. He was skiing down a hill and fell off a cliff! It took us one hour to pull him up! I always feel good when I save somebody's life.

Lesson 2

Ollie Good morning, Kate. It's Monday again! Did you have a nice weekend?

Kate Yes, thanks, Ollie. I went shopping on Saturday and then I went out for dinner with my husband on Sunday night. What about you?

Ollie Oh, I didn't go out. I stayed at home and watched TV. My friend came round yesterday and we watched the football together.

Kate Oh, that's nice.

Ollie Oh, look – there's Jan.

Kate Who's Jan? Do you mean that woman in the white dress?

Ollie No, that's Helen! You know Helen! Jan is the one with the red top on. She's the new employee.

Kate Oh, that's right. Did she start this morning?

Ollie No, she started last Tuesday. She's been here for a few days.

Kate Oh, right, I wasn't at work last week, so I didn't meet her.

Ollie Oh, yes, that's right. Where did you go last week?

Kate Well, my son was sick so I had to stay at home with him.

Ollie Is your son OK now?

Kate Yes, he's fine now. He felt a lot better on Friday. Anyway, what were we talking about? Oh, yes, the new employee. Is she nice?

Ollie Well, the manager is very happy with her. She's very good at her job and she's got a lot of experience, but she was only part-time in her last job. She's got a full-time job here, of course.

Kate We've all got full-time jobs here! Is she friendly?

Ollie Well, she's very quiet. I haven't spoken to her yet.

Kate Maybe you should try! It isn't easy when you start a new job, you know.

Ollie That's true. But what can I talk about?

Kate What a silly question! Just say who you are and have a chat.

Ollie OK, let's go and talk to her together.

Kate Come on, then.

Lesson 3

Kevin What do you want to be when you grow up, Jenny?

Jenny Oh, I want to be a doctor because I enjoy helping people. I want to work in a hospital. My teacher told me that you have to study for many years and get good qualifications, though, so I'm going to study hard. What do you want to be, Kevin?

Kevin Well, I don't want to be a doctor! My dad is a doctor and he works long hours at the hospital. Doctors have really difficult jobs. When I was younger, I used to think I wanted to be a taxi driver, but now I want to be a pilot. It'll be great. I'll fly all over the world and visit lots of different countries.

Jenny Yes, but you'll have to study first. My cousin Peter is a pilot and he had to take lots of exams.

Kevin Oh, I know you have to study, but it doesn't matter. I'm sure I can do it. Does your cousin like his job?

Jenny Yes, I think so. He earns quite a lot of money and he has a lot of days off, so he's happy.

Kevin I'll be happy too. I don't want to do a boring job. I don't know how people can be chefs or work in a shop. They're horrible jobs!

Jenny Well, everyone's different, you know. We don't all want the same thing. My sister Anna is a manager in a supermarket. She likes her job. Anyway, maybe we should both go home and start studying!

Kevin Good idea. See you later.

Jenny Bye.

Key to Spin 2 Workbook

Introduction

1

I – me (given)	it – it
you – you	we – us
he – him	they – them
she – her	

2

1	it (given)	4	us
2	them	5	you
3	her	6	him

3

1	my (given)	4	your
2	our	5	its
3	their	6	her

4

1	Is there (given)	4	Are there
2	There is	5	there aren't
3	there isn't	6	There are

5

1c (given) **2b 3c 4b 5b 6c**

6

1 There is a clock behind the glass of milk. (given)
2 There aren't two eggs in front of the clock.
3 There is a cup of coffee between the bread and the cereal.
4 There is an egg next to the glass of milk.
5 There are two drinks in the picture.
6 There isn't an apple in the picture.

Unit 1

Lesson 1

1

1	aunt (given)	4	wife
2	only	5	cousin
3	nephews	6	grandchildren

2

1	cousins (given)	4	nieces
2	embarrassing	5	miss
3	relatives		

3

1d (given) **2a 3c 4e 5b**

4

1	work (given)	5	Do...like
2	doesn't rain	6	don't get up
3	wants	7	teaches
4	visits	8	goes

5

1a (given) **2c 3b 4b 5a 6c**

6

1 My family is always nice to me. (given)
2 The three o'clock train is never late.
3 Beth doesn't often visit her cousins.
4 Grandma usually helps me with my homework.
5 Mum is sometimes embarrassing.
6 Do Mikey and Kristie sometimes travel through time?

Lesson 2

1

1	safe (given)	4	looking for
2	diary	5	wings
3	distances		

2

1	PARENTS (given)	5	FEED
2	ALBATROSS	6	PAIR
3	WARM	7	SPEND
4	MOVE		

3

1	on (given)	4	at
2	for	5	after
3	for	6	of

4

1 'm/am not feeding (given)
2 're/are watching
3 isn't/is not visiting
4 's/is chasing
5 are flying
6 isn't/is not raining

5

1 Adam and Beth are playing a board game now. (given)
2 He isn't visiting his cousin today.
3 Is Tom watching the video diary this morning?
4 Are you looking after your brother today?
5 The globe isn't spinning at the moment.
6 The puffins are moving their wings now.

6

1 Are the albatrosses flying? No, they aren't. (given)
2 Are they watching TV? Yes, they are.
3 Is Ann feeding her dog? Yes, she is.
4 Is Sue looking for her mobile phone? No, she isn't.
5 Is the dog sleeping? Yes, it is.
6 Is the boy travelling by plane? No, he isn't.

Lesson 3

1

1	rude (given)	4	grow up
2	building	5	miss
3	fashion	6	mad

2

1c (given) **2b 3a 4b 5c 6b 7c 8c**

3

1d (given) **2c 3a 4e 5b**

4

1	usually (given)	4	always
2	on Saturdays	5	sometimes
3	this	6	every day

5

Students' own answers

Unit 2

Lesson 1

1

1	kitchen (given)	4	bedroom
2	stairs	5	sink
3	coffee table	6	palace

2

```
U H B J E H I D Q J X O
B T W I N D O W X W M Q
Y J A Q P T K S X O W V
D B R K E X A F T E P H
R N D P J S L R H G C Y
U A R M C H A I R D Z X
Z S O F A O K D D N I G
A V B N C W O G G V K S
O V E N Q E F E X M G C
J G U K T R C D U H S Z
```

1 window (given)   **5** sofa
2 armchair   **6** fridge
3 oven   **7** shower
4 wardrobe

3

1e (given) 2a 3d 4c 5b

4

1 moved (given)   **4** tidied
2 wanted   **5** helped
3 painted

5

1 We didn't arrive at the palace at 5 o'clock. (given)
2 They didn't look for new furniture yesterday.
3 She didn't want a huge swimming pool.
4 He didn't shout at his baby brother.
5 We didn't clean the kitchen this morning.
6 Mikey didn't open the fridge.
7 It didn't rain all last week.
8 You didn't stay with your aunt last summer.

6

1 Did Maria watch TV last night? No, she didn't. (given)
2 Did they paint the walls green? No, they didn't.
3 Did they climb up the stairs? Yes, they did.
4 Did I tidy my bedroom? No, you didn't.
5 Did Andreas stay at home? Yes, he did.
6 Did you cook dinner last night? No, I/we didn't.

Lesson 2

1

1 bucket (given)   **4** running
2 floor   **5** machine
3 temple

2

1 curtains (given)   **4** mirror
2 bookcase   **5** rug
3 roof

3

1 magical (given)
2 huge
3 wooden
4 mirrors
5 floor
6 balcony

4

1 put (given)   **4** ate
2 drank   **5** wrote
3 slept   **6** took

5

1 gave (given)   **5** grew up
2 went   **6** sold
3 bought   **7** came
4 became

6

1 Sally caught the ball. (given)
2 David bought a vacuum cleaner.
3 We spent a week in Italy.
4 Mum and Dad sat on the balcony.
5 I met my friends.
6 Grandpa read a story.

Lesson 3

1

1 sitting room (given)
2 houseboat
3 cottage
4 flat
5 hut
6 village

2

Students' own answers

3

Students' own answers

4

1 live (given)   **4** move
2 flat   **5** modern
3 village

5

1 so (given)   **4** but
2 and   **5** but
3 because   **6** and

6

Students' own answers

Review 1

2

1 It's in Bavaria, Germany. (given)
2 He lived there for 172 days.
3 You can see magnificent views of the mountains.
4 It had running water and a central heating system.
5 It looks like Sleeping Beauty's Castle in Disneyland Park, USA.

3

1a (given) 2c 3b 4c 5b 6a 7b 8b 9a 10a 11c 12c

4

1b (given) 2b 3b 4c 5c 6a 7c 8a 9c 10c 11a 12c

Unit 3

Lesson 1

1

1 competition (given)   **4** brilliant
2 practise   **5** fault
3 skater   **6** way

2

1 take (given)   **4** keep
2 give   **5** go
3 try

3

1e (given) 2c 3b 4d 5f 6a

4

1a (given) 2a 3b 4c 5c

5

1 Diana wasn't dancing with Adam last Saturday. (given)
2 We weren't skating all morning.
3 The boys weren't surfing at 6 o'clock yesterday morning.
4 I wasn't swimming at the pool yesterday afternoon.
5 He wasn't practising for the game till 3 o'clock.
6 You weren't sending emails last night.

6

1 Were the girls skating yesterday morning? Yes, they were. (given)

2 Was Paul swimming at this time yesterday? No, he wasn't.

3 Were the boys riding their bikes this morning? No, they weren't.

4 Was Ann listening to music yesterday afternoon? Yes, she was.

5 Was Josh playing tennis this morning? No, he wasn't.

6 Was Bob studying last night at nine o'clock? Yes, he was.

Lesson 2

1

1	bored (given)	4	scared
2	take up	5	entertaining
3	hill	6	activity

2

1	excited (given)	5	bored
2	exciting (given)	6	boring
3	tiring	7	interesting
4	tired	8	interested

3

1	make (given)	4	entertaining
2	throw	5	sliding
3	equipment	6	Put on

4

1	fell (given)	4	started
2	arrived	5	was walking
3	when		

5

1	saw (given)	4	was putting on
2	weren't playing	5	were you doing
3	heard	6	came

6

1 Did Mum make lunch while the baby was sleeping? (given)

2 Joan was sitting in the garden when the guests arrived.

3 Did Jessica fall down while she was skiing?

4 We fell asleep while we were watching TV.

5 They were playing chess when Dad came home.

6 Were you waiting for her when you saw the bus?/Were you waiting for the bus when you saw her?

Lesson 3

1

1	finish (given)	4	download
2	stand	5	make
3	exercise	6	become

2

1	used (given)	4	did
2	use	5	use
3	play	6	didn't

3

1 Tell me about your free time. (given)

2 I can't stand doing homework.

3 Do you like painting?

4 Well, I have more time at the weekends.

5 When did you start cycling?

4

1	and (given)	4	while
2	when	5	while
3	and		

5

Students' own answers

Unit 4
Lesson 1

1

1 shopping list (given)

2 chicken legs

3 marmalade

4 prawn

5 onion

6 kumquat

2

1	DELICIOUS	4	THIRSTY
2	EXOTIC (given)	5	FULL
3	STARVING	6	DISGUSTING

3

1	site (given)	4	dinner
2	recipe	5	noodles
3	juice	6	list

4

1	many (given)	5	How many
2	How many	6	many
3	How much	7	much
4	much	8	How much

5

1T (given) 2F 3F 4F 5T 6F

6

1e (given) 2a 3d 4b 5c 6f

Lesson 2

1

1d (given) 2f 3b 4c 5a 6e

2

1	Chop (given)	4	Fry
2	Add	5	Mix
3	Boil	6	Slice

3

1	calm (given)	4	luxury
2	cinnamon	5	Bitter
3	bar		

4

1	some (given)	5	every
2	Every	6	any
3	any	7	no
4	no	8	some

5

1 everywhere (given)

2 nothing

3 anywhere

4 something

5 somebody

6 Nobody

6

1	someone (given)	5	Everything
2	any	6	anything
3	some	7	no
4	nothing	8	Everybody

Lesson 3

1

1	webpage (given)	5	delicious
2	email	6	exotic
3	cooking	7	address
4	recipe		

2
1 for dinner (given)
2 I'd like
3 Would you
4 a good idea
5 What

3
Students' own answers

4
Students' own answers

5
1 Dear Kristen (given)
2 How are you?
3 First
4 Then
5 Last of all,
6 Bye for now!
7 Love from Monica

6
Students' own answers.

Review 2
2
1b (given) 2d 3a 4c

3
1b (given) 2c 3a 4a 5a 6a 7b 8b
9c 10b 11c 12c

4
1a (given) 2b 3b 4c 5b 6a 7c 8b
9a 10c 11a 12b

Unit 5
Lesson 1
1
1 canteen (given) 4 dinosaur
2 bell   5 cheat
3 rucksack   6 sharp teeth

2
1 died out (given) 4 flashed
2 gigantic   5 real
3 travelled   6 showed

3
1 break time (given) 4 head teacher
2 term   5 rucksack
3 uniform   6 canteen

4
1 have been (given)
2 have studied
3 has helped
4 has told
5 have already bought
6 have sent

5
1 for (given)   5 just
2 just   6 never
3 since   7 for
4 just   8 already

6
1 has ... opened (given)
2 has washed
3 has drawn
4 have bought
5 has broken
6 have ... made

Lesson 2
1
1 exam (given)   4 report
2 education   5 experience
3 library   6 marks

2
1 PE (given)   5 PE
2 PL   6 PE
3 S   7 PL
4 PL   8 S

3
1 medals (given)
2 successful
3 champion
4 cycling
5 gym
6 indoor
7 experience

4
1 yet (given)   4 yet
2 ever   5 ever
3 yet   6 ever

5
1c (given) 2b 3a 4b 5b 6c

6
1 Have they gone to the zoo? No, they haven't. (given)
2 Has Jennifer opened her present? Yes, she has.
3 Has Mark bought a new car? Yes, he has.
4 Has Ashley made biscuits? No, she hasn't.
5 Has Kevin finished the exam yet? No, he hasn't.
6 Have the boys won medals? Yes, they have.

Lesson 3
1
1 advert (given)   4 interviewed
2 given   5 staff
3 gets on

2
1 Where do you go to school? (given)
2 What is your favourite subject?
3 What are you good at?
4 What are you bad at?
5 Who is your favourite teacher?

3
1 How long has ... been (given)
2 How long has ... played
3 How long has ... worked
4 How long has ... taught
5 How long have ... lived
6 How long has ... had

4
1 I go to the Simple English Language School in Athens. (given)
2 The school has a staff of four teachers.
3 The thing I like best is writing.
4 There is only one thing I don't like about the language school.

5
Students' own answers

Unit 6
Lesson 1
1
1 documentary (given) 4 paint
2 tribe   5 bodies
3 colourful   6 abroad

2

```
U L I S S V H L U H T R
D I B B T H R O A T Y R
Y E L B O W S U K O B P
W T A G M Q E T D K G D
V K B H A N K L E N V K
D P X N C M U K H E Z O
G Z N S H O U L D E R I
H O Y S R Q O R Y U V Z
N A V F S J P F D A E H
Y J I I T A I L W O J G
```

1	stomach	**5**	knee
2	shoulder (given)	**6**	tall
3	ankle	**7**	throat
4	elbows	**8**	chest

3

1c (given) **2d 3e 4a 5b 6f**

4

1 has washed (given)
2 hasn't tidied
3 cut
4 have travelled
5 had
6 has landed
7 lived

5

1

1e (given) **2b 3d 4c 5f 6a**

6

Students' own answers

Lesson 2

1

1	pain (given)	**4**	make-up
2	luck	**5**	scare
3	hunt	**6**	war

2

1	skin (given)	**4**	toothache
2	headache	**5**	throat
3	temperature	**6**	burn

3

1	war (given)	**4**	actors
2	face painting	**5**	tribe
3	make-up	**6**	scare

4

1	hers (given)	**4**	ours
2	his	**5**	mine
3	yours	**6**	theirs

5

1b (given) **2c 3c 4a 5c 6b**

6

1	his (given)	**4**	hers
2	ours	**5**	mine
3	yours	**6**	theirs

Lesson 3

1

1d (given) **2f 3a 4e 5c 6b**

2

1 What's the matter? (given)
2 I've got a bad cough.
3 Open your mouth.
4 Is it serious?
5 Take this medicine.

3

1	cough (given)	**8**	advice
2	tribe	**9**	sore
3	toothache	**10**	headache
4	spots	**11**	throat
5	reason	**12**	sneeze
6	pain	**13**	skin
7	temperature	**14**	ankle

4

Students' own answers

5

Order of paragraphs: 2 4 1 (given) 3

6

Students' own answers

Review 3

2

1 oldest specialist school (given)
2 day
3 in countries around the world
4 2003
5 Daisy Chute

3

1a (given) **2b 3b 4a 5b 6c 7a 8a
9c 10a 11b 12c**

4

1b (given) **2a 3c 4c 5b 6b 7b 8b
9c 10b 11a 12c**

Unit 7
Lesson 1

1

1b (given) **2e 3a 4c 5d**

2

1	BRANCH (given)	**4**	LEAVES
2	NEST	**5**	FARM
3	SOIL	**6**	STONES

3

1	frilled (given)	**4**	environment
2	nest	**5**	natural
3	recorder	**6**	second

4

1 is going to be (given)
2 are going to wear
3 will work
4 Will ... feed
5 is not going to snow
6 won't forget

5

Students' own answers

6

1 will (given)
2 is going to
3 will
4 will
5 will
6 is going to

Lesson 2

1

1 display (given)
2 neck
3 hiss
4 spot
5 face

2

1	lake (given)	**4**	seeds
2	squirrel	**5**	trap
3	fence	**6**	beetle

3

1	beetles (given)	**4**	hiss
2	spot	**5**	wildlife
3	necks		

4

1 feeding (given)   4 Living
2 looking after   5 swimming
3 walking   6 taking

5

1T (given) **2F 3T 4T 5F 6F**

6

1 She can't stand working on the farm. (given)
2 Feeding wild animals is dangerous.
3 She misses spending time with her friends.
4 I'm not very good at looking after plants.
5 They hate helping in the garden.
6 Working in an office is boring.

Lesson 3

1

1 cruel (given)   4 accident
2 bring   5 seriously
3 pets   6 treat

2

1 cuddly (given)   4 fur
2 funny   5 hutch
3 sleep   6 rabbit

3

1a (given) **2c 3b 4c 5b 6c 7a 8c**

4

1 maggie – Maggie (line 1) (given)
2 we (2nd) – We (line 3)
3 together – together. (line 4)
4 She's fantastic? - She's fantastic! (line 5)
5 biscuits meat – biscuits, meat (line 6)
6 Chicken – chicken (line 8)
7 don't they! – don't they? (lines 8 & 9)
8 pet dog isn't it? – pet dog, isn't it? (line 12)

5

Students' own answers

Unit 8
Lesson 1

1

1 plant (given)
2 electronic
3 apart
4 separately
5 away
6 protect

2

1A BAG (given)
1D BOTTLE
2 CAN
3 NEWSPAPER
4 LITTER BIN
5 BATTERY
6 PROTECT

3

1PL (given) **2PL 3G 4PA 5G 6PA 7PL 8PA**

4

1 put litter in the bins (given)
2 don't use a lot of water
3 won't die out
4 will recycle them
5 use paper bags
6 will protect the environment

5

1 don't (given)   4 don't
2 will come   5 will save
3 will help   6 don't

6

1 don't look after (given)
2 will harm
3 will happen
4 do
5 don't protect
6 will die out
7 will be
8 Will it help
9 recycle
10 will save

Lesson 2

1

1 climate (given)   4 rubbish
2 pollution   5 panel
3 Solar   6 electricity

2

1 waste (given)   4 harm
2 cause   5 protect
3 turn off   6 pollute

3

1 fact (given)
2 climate
3 electricity
4 forecast
5 products

4

1 weren't, would start (given)
2 Would you use, helped
3 turned off, would save
4 wouldn't be, went
5 wouldn't harm, used
6 recycled, would we protect

5

1c (given) **2b 3a 4b 5c 6b**

6

1 If I told my parents to recycle more, they would listen to me. (given)
2 If I saw people polluting the beach, I would shout at them.
3 If I worked for an environmental group, I would write an article.
4 If we used things again and again, we wouldn't have so much rubbish.
5 If I had an old computer, I would find an electronics recycling plant.
6 If lions and tigers died out, I wouldn't be happy.

Lesson 3

1

1b (given) 2d 3e 4a 5c

2

1 never pollute the beach (given)
2 recycle plastic bottles
3 ride my bike to work
4 always turn off the lights
5 always throw away rubbish

3

Students' own answers

4

1 would help (given)
2 created
3 bought
4 would save
5 recycled
6 would save

5

Students' own answers

Review 4

2

1 In all the oceans except the Arctic. (given)
2 Female turtles make their nests on beaches.
3 Seven.
4 They hunt them for their meat and eggs.
5 Environmental groups.

3

1c (given) 2b 3b 4a 5c 6c 7a 8a 9b 10a 11a 12a

4

1a (given) 2b 3c 4b 5c 6b 7c 8a 9c 10b 11c 12a

Unit 9

Lesson 1

1

1	circle (given)	4	passport
2	dizzy	5	magnificent
3	book		

2

1	Turn (given)	4	ahead
2	Cross	5	round
3	right	6	Go

3

1	past (given)	4	dizzy
2	expect	5	out
3	round	6	straight

4

1 Do we have to cross (given)
2 have to book
3 have to wait
4 didn't have to ask
5 don't have to do
6 Did you have to go

5

1 must/have to (given)
2 don't have to
3 mustn't
4 must/have to
5 doesn't have to
6 mustn't

6

1b (given) 2b 3a 4a 5c 6b

Lesson 2

1

1	offer (given)	4	marine
2	international	5	tunnel
3	capital	6	hire

2

1 BANK (GIVEN)
2 SHOPPING CENTRE
3 MUSEUM
4 SKYSCRAPER
5 FOUNTAIN
6 SQUARE

3

1 mythology (given)
2 kite
3 sightseeing
4 pattern
5 bite

4

1	can (given)	4	can't
2	couldn't	5	could
3	can	6	could

5

1e (given) 2d 3c 4f 5b 6a

6

Students' own answers

Lesson 3

1

1 comfortable (given)
2 swimming costume
3 special
4 guide
5 right-hand
6 famous

2

1	might (given)	5	might
2	might not	6	should
3	shouldn't	7	might not
4	Should	8	should

3

1 How can I get to (given)
2 Go past
3 turn left
4 the left-hand side
5 How far
6 straight ahead

4

1 lovely Greek (given)
2 interesting little
3 beautiful clean
4 amazing ancient Greek
5 correct
6 fantastic small
7 correct

5

Students' own answers

Unit 10

Lesson 1

1

1	screen (given)	4	level
2	program	5	artist
3	grow up		

2

1 KEYBOARD
2 PRINTER
3 DESIGN (GIVEN)
4 LAPTOP
5 WEB CAMERA
6 MONITOR
7 MOUSE

3

1 testers (given) 4 program
2 complete 5 tests
3 designed 6 mouse

4

1 is used (given)
2 are given
3 played
4 taken
5 paid
6 are recycled
7 made
8 Are your friends' addresses

5

1 are tested (given)
2 Is this program used
3 is known
4 are not made
5 are given
6 Are you paid
7 are not designed
8 are read

6

1 The invitations are sent by email. (given)
2 This computer game isn't played by many people.
3 The characters aren't chosen by us.
4 Tickets are sold at the train station.
5 Are Bob and Jane invited to the party?
6 Is air pollution caused by cars?

Lesson 2
1

1 download (given) 4 visited
2 invent 5 communicate
3 send 6 invention

2

1 receive (given) 4 visit
2 download 5 upload
3 surf 6 invent

3

1 surf (given) 4 emails
2 blog 5 MP3 player
3 design 6 communicate

4

1c (given) 2f 3d 4e 5a 6b

5

1 was made (given)
2 was shown
3 was created
4 was interviewed
5 was given
6 was liked

6

1 were, invented (given)
2 was created
3 was given
4 Were, uploaded
5 were booked
6 wasn't shown
7 wasn't taken

Lesson 3
1

1 champion (given) 4 spaceship
2 crash 5 team
3 wheels 6 car race

2

Students' own answers

3

1c (given) 2e 3f 4b 5d 6a

4

1 caled – called (given) (para 1 line 3)
2 desined – designed (para 1 line 4)
3 fan – fun (para 1 line 6)
4 begining – beginning (para 2 line 1)
5 chouse – choose (para 2 line 2)
6 carefull – careful (para 2 line 7)
7 loose – lose (para 2 line 8)
8 enterteining – entertaining (para 3 line 2)

5

Students' own answers

Review 5
2

1 Kuala Lumpur (given)
2 Cesar Pelli, an Argentinean architect
3 You must get there early.
4 You can buy luxury goods.
5 You can learn about the history of science and technology.

3

1a (given) 2c 3a 4c 5b 6a 7a 8a 9c 10 b 11b 12b

4

1c (given) 2a 3b 4a 5c 6b 7c 8c 9a 10a 11b 12a

Unit 11
Lesson 1
1

1 wander (given) 4 travel
2 flight 5 passenger
3 comfortable 6 adventurous

2

1 check-in desk (given)
2 coach
3 passenger
4 seat belt
5 metro
6 motorbike

3

1 more adventurous (given)
2 more comfortable
3 more expensive
4 easier
5 more interesting

4

1c (given) 2a 3c 4b 5a 6b

5

1 worst (given) 4 as fast
2 better 5 more
3 the most 6 cheapest

6

1 safer than (given)
2 bad as
3 the most frightening
4 the cheapest
5 more interesting than
6 the most comfortable

Lesson 2
1

1 afford (given) 4 journey
2 bench 5 uncomfortable
3 coach 6 thief

2

1. ESCALATOR (GIVEN)
2. STREET SIGN
3. LUGGAGE
4. TIMETABLE
5. TICKET MACHINE
6. CARRIAGE
7. INSPECTOR

3

1T (given) **2**M **3**M **4**T **5**T **6**M **7**M **8**T **9**M **10**T

4

1T (given) **2**F **3**F **4**F **5**T **6**T

5

1a (given) **2**c **3**b **4**c **5**b **6**a

6

1. both (given)   4. neither
2. both/either   5. either
3. either   6. either

Lesson 3

1

1c (given) **2**d **3**e **4**b **5**a

2

1. enough (given)   4. too
2. too   5. enough
3. too many   6. too late

3

1. Excuse me, how can I get to Hope Street? (given)
2. Can I buy a single ticket to Duke Street, please?
3. Can I buy a travel pass, please?
4. Where do I get off for the Transport Museum?
5. Can I travel to the island by boat?

4

1. Tourists in the summer (given)
2. Timetable
3. Cost
4. What can we do?

5

Students' own answers

Unit 12
Lesson 1

1

1. slip (given)   4. Grab
2. rescue   5. admire
3. panic   6. follow

2

1. DETECTIVE
2. SAILOR
3. ARTIST (given)
6. PHOTOGRAPHER
4. MECHANIC
5. CHEF
7. RESCUER

3

1c (given) **2**d **3**a **4**b **5**f **6**e

4

1. quickly (given)   5. easily
2. well   6. angry
3. beautiful   7. dangerous
4. hungrily

5

1. well (given)   5. fast
2. healthily   6. carefully
3. quickly   7. happily
4. hard

6

Students' own answers

Lesson 2

1

1a (given) **2**a **3**b **4**a **5**b

2

1. explore (given)   4. conservationist
2. manager   5. prevent
3. experience

3

1. full-time (given)   4. part-time
2. dead   5. member
3. qualifications   6. population

4

1e (given) **2**b **3**d **4**f **5**c **6**a

5

1. who are (given)
2. which live
3. where we found
4. who works
5. where they spent
6. which has

6

1. Teachers are people who work in schools. (given)
2. That's the restaurant where John works.
3. Sheila has got a job which she really enjoys.
4. Spiders are creatures which have eight legs.
5. Restaurants are places where chefs work.
6. This is the rucksack which I take to school.

Lesson 3

1

1. university (given)   4. outdoors
2. skills   5. fixing
3. in   6. apply

2

1. explaining (given)
2. helping
3. qualifications
4. working
5. skills
6. fixing

3

Students' own answers

4

Tiring work (given)

work at weekends and holidays; enjoyed working with the people, learned a lot about cooking

5

Students' own answers

Review 6
2

1F (given) **2**T **3**F **4**T **5**F

3

1a (given) 2c 3c 4b 5b 6c 7a 8b
9a 10b 11c 12c

4

1b (given) 2c 3a 4a 5b 6c 7a 8b
9c 10b 11c 12c

Crossword puzzles

Units 1 – 2
1 WIFE
2 FURNITURE
3 SAFE
4 WARDROBE
5 VACUUM
6 DISTANCE
7 COUSIN
8 CENTURY
9 MISS

Units 3 – 4
1 THIRSTY
2 STARVING
3 COMPETITION
4 RECIPE
5 BRILLIANT
6 EMPEROR
7 FAULT
8 PRACTISE
9 HILL

Units 5 – 6
1 EDUCATION
2 TEMPERATURE
3 KNEE
4 TRIBE
5 SORE
6 GIGANTIC
7 ABROAD
8 WAR
9 LIBRARY

Units 7 – 8
1 SOLAR
2 SEPARATELY
3 ENVIRONMENT
4 LEAVES
5 BRUSH
6 RECYCLING
7 BRANCH
8 LITTER
9 SECOND

Units 9 – 10
1 MARINE
2 MAGNIFICENT
3 COMMUNICATE
4 HIRED
5 CAPITAL
6 PASSPORT
7 LEVELS
8 DOWNLOAD
9 DIZZY
10 STRAIGHT

Units 11 – 12
1 RESPECT
2 PREVENT
3 RESCUE
4 ESCALATOR
5 LUGGAGE
6 WANDER
7 MEANS
8 SEATBELT
9 AFFORD
10 POPULATION